Italian Cardinals, Reform, and the Church as Property

Published under the auspices of the

CENTER FOR MEDIEVAL AND RENAISSANCE STUDIES

University of California, Los Angeles

Publications of the
UCLA CENTER FOR MEDIEVAL AND RENAISSANCE STUDIES

1. Jeffrey Burton Russell, *Dissent and Reform in the Early Middle Ages* (1965)
2. C. D. O'Malley, ed., *Leonardo's Legacy: An International Symposium* (1968)
3. Richard H. Rouse, *Serial Bibliographies for Medieval Studies* (1969)
4. Speros Vryonis, Jr., *The Decline of Medieval Hellenism in Asia Minor and the Process of Islamization from the Eleventh through the Fifteenth Century* (1971)
5. Stanley Chodorow, *Christian Political Theory and Church Politics in the Mid-Twelfth Century: The Ecclesiology of Gratian's Decretum* (1972)
6. Joseph J. Duggan, *The Song of Roland: Formulaic Style and Poetic Craft* (1973)
7. Ernest A. Moody, *Studies in Medieval Philosophy, Science, and Logic: Collected Papers 1933–1969* (1975)
8. Marc Bloch, *Slavery and Serfdom in the Midddle Ages: Selected Essays* (1975)
9. Michael J. B. Allen, *Marsilio Ficino: The Philebus Commentary, A Critical Edition and Translation* (1975)
10. Richard C. Dales, *Marius: On the Elements, A Critical Edition and Translation* (1976)
11. Duane J. Osheim, *An Italian Lordship: The Bishopric of Lucca in the Late Middle Ages* (1977)
12. Robert Somerville, *Pope Alexander III and the Council of Tours (1163): A Study of Ecclesiastical Politics and Institutions in the Twelfth Century* (1977)
13. Lynn White, jr., *Medieval Religion and Technology: Collected Essays* (1978)
14. Michael J. B. Allen, *Marsilio Ficino and the Phaedran Charioteer: Introduction, Texts, Translations* (1981)
15. Barnabas Bernard Hughes, O.F.M., *Jordanus de Nemore: De numeris datis, A Critical Edition and Translation* (1981)
16. Caroline Walker Bynum, *Jesus as Mother: Studies in the Spirituality of the High Middle Ages* (1982)
17. Carlo M. Cipolla, *The Monetary Policy of Fourteenth-Century Florence* (1983)
18. John H. Van Engen, *Rupert of Deutz* (1983)
19. Thomas K. Keefe, *Feudal Assessments and the Political Communty under Henry II and His Sons* (1983)
20. John C. Shideler, *A Medieval Catalan Noble Family: The Montcadas, 1000–1230* (1984)
21. Michael J. B. Allen, *The Platonism of Marsilio Ficino: A Study of His Phaedrus Commentary, Its Sources and Genesis* (1984)
22. Barbara McClung Hallman, *Italian Cardinals, Reform, and the Church as Property: 1492–1563* (1985)

Italian Cardinals, Reform, and the Church as Property

Barbara McClung Hallman

UNIVERSITY OF CALIFORNIA PRESS
Berkeley   Los Angeles   London

University of California Press
Berkeley and Los Angeles, California

University of California Press, Ltd.
London, England

Library of Congress Cataloging in Publication Data

Hallman, Barbara McClung.
  Italian cardinals, reform, and the church as property.

  (Publications of the UCLA Center for Medieval and
Renaissance Studies ; 22)
  Bibliography: p.
  Includes index.
  1. Catholic Church. Curia Romana—History—
15th century. 2. Catholic Church. Curia Romana—
History—16th century. 3. Cardinals—Italy—History—
15th century. 4. Cardinals—Italy—History—16th
century. 5. Catholic Church—Finance—History—15th
century. 6. Catholic Church—Finance—History—16th
century. I. Title. II. Series.
BX1818.H3   1985   262'.135   84–8501

ISBN 0–520–04937–3

Printed in the United States of America

1 2 3 4 5 6 7 8 9

Contents

List of Illustrations

Tables

Acknowledgments

This work owes debts to many. From 1969 to 1971, a grant from the Foreign Area Fellowship Program supported my initial research in Italy, and a sabbatical leave for 1980–1981 from the California State University system helped me to complete it. The original dissertation, accepted at UCLA in 1974, profited from the support and guidance of its director, Professor Lauro Martines, in whose seminar I first became attracted to Italian studies. Professors Carlo Cipolla, Gene Brucker, and Elisabeth Gleason all read the revised manuscript and gave me valuable advice. The meticulous work of Professor John Monfasani and Carol D. Lanham, my editor, improved the manuscript significantly and saved me from many errors. I also wish to thank the entire Monfasani family—John, Adrianne, and their children, Alexander, Cristina, and now Mark—for their friendship and companionship during the long months away from home. My own children, Guy and Charlotte, grew up with the scholarship and have been patient and supportive over the years. Finally, my thanks to my husband, Ralph Jefferson Hallman, without whom nothing would have been possible and to whom I dedicate this book.

Abbreviations

AC	Archivio Segreto Vaticano, Acta Camerarii
AM	Archivio Segreto Vaticano, Acta Miscellanea
ANG	*Acta Nuntiaturae Gallicae: Correspondance des nonces en France* . . . (14 vols. to date, Rome 1961–)
Arm.	Archivio Segreto Vaticano, Armarium
ASRSP	*Archivio della R. Società Romana di Storia Patria*
AV	Archivio Segreto Vaticano, Acta Vicecancellarii
BR	*Bullarium Romanum* (25 vols. Turin 1857–1885)
Ciacconius	Alphonsus Ciacconius, *Vitae et res gestae Pontificum Romanorum et S. R. E. Cardinalium ab initio nascentis Ecclesiae usque ad Clementem IX* . . . (4 vols. Rome 1630–1677)
CT	*Concilium Tridentinum: Diariorum, actorum, epistularum, tractuum nova collectio* (13 vols. to date, Freiburg im Breisgau 1961–)
DBI	*Dizionario biografico degli Italiani* (15 vols. to date, Rome 1960–)
Delumeau	Jean Delumeau, *Vie économique et sociale de Rome dans la seconde moitié du XVIᵉ siècle* (2 vols. Paris 1957–1959)
Eubel	Conrad Eubel, *Hierarchia Catholica Medii et Recentioris Aevi* (6 vols. Regensburg 1913)
Ferraris	Lucius Ferraris, *Prompta biblioteca canonica, juridica, moralis, theologica, necnon ascetica, polemica, rubricitica, historica* (9 vols. Rome 1770–1784)
Hay	Denys Hay, *The Church in Italy in the Fifteenth Century* (Cambridge 1977)

Litta	Pompeo Litta, *Famiglie celebri italiane* (10 vols. Milan 1819–1883)
MC	Archivio di Stato, Rome, Archivio Camerale, Mandati Camerali
Olin	John C. Olin, ed., *The Catholic Reformation: Savonarola to Ignatius Loyola, Reform in the Church, 1495–1540* (New York 1969)
Partner, "Papal Financial Policy"	Peter Partner, "Papal Financial Policy in the Renaissance and Counter-Reformation," *Past and Present* 88 (1980) 17–62
QFIAB	*Quellen und Forschungen aus italienischen Archiven und Bibliotheken*
Reinhard, "Nepotismus"	Wolfgang Reinhard, "Nepotismus: der Funktionswandel einer papstgeschichtlichen Konstanten," *Zeitschrift für Kirchengeschichte* 86.2 (1975) 145–185
Reinhard, *Papstfinanz und Nepotismus*	Wolfgang Reinhard, *Papstfinanz und Nepotismus unter Paul V.* (1605–1621), vol. 6 of *Päpste und Papsttum* (2 vols. Stuttgart 1974)
RSCI	*Rivista di storia della Chiesa in Italia*
Sanuto	Marino Sanuto, *I diarii* (59 vols. Venice 1879–1903)
Vat lat	Biblioteca Apostolica Vaticana, Codices vaticani latini

1
Church Property, Abuse, and Cardinals

The Christian church has been beset with controversy, heresy, schism, and cries for reform ever since it became a legal institution in the Roman Empire. Indeed, it is possible to view the entire history of the church as a series of reform movements.[1] Through this history runs as a recurrent theme the demand to eradicate the three classical abuses that perennially plagued the church—simony, pluralism, and nepotism. The purchase of sacred office, the possession of more than one sacred office, and the use of sacred office for the aggrandizement of one's family are all venal abuses. They have nothing to do with theology, doctrine, or authority—they are solely concerned with money, or with money and property.

Reformers in the fifteenth and sixteenth centuries focused upon the venality of the church and particularly upon the fiscal practices of the Roman curia as targets for reform efforts. It is surely paradoxical that the very success of the church in the acquisition of wealth, combined with the emergence of the papacy as its undisputed head, led to the incidents that precipitated the Protestant revolt. The extension of papal control over church properties inevitably created an intricate and expanding system of church government, which had the twin duties of ministering to the spiritual needs of the faithful and attending to the temporal administration of property.[2] It was precisely this latter responsibility, for the material needs of the church and its servants, that brought about the pressures for change which culminated in reform movements within, and ultimately outside of, the church. It is no accident that the Roman practices Martin Luther attacked in his *Address to the Nobility of the German Nation* in 1520 were substantially the same as those identified by the members of Paul III's reform commission in the *Consilium de emendanda ecclesia* of 1537, or that the same practices were still being denounced by the fathers at the Council of Trent in 1546 and 1547.[3] These were largely fiscal devices, and they involved the accumulation, alienation, and distribution of moneys—incomes, rents, emoluments—that derived from the wealth of the church. To their critics, these abuses finally reduced to the old trilogy: simony, pluralism, and nepotism.

Echoing the voices of medieval Catholic reformers, the commission that wrote the *Consilium* of 1537, headed by the celebrated Venetian Gasparo Contarini, boldly cited the power of the pope himself as the first cause of the church's subsequent corruption:

Thence it came about, . . . that teachers at once appeared who taught that the pope is the lord of all benefices and that therefore, since a lord may sell by right what is his own, it necessarily follows that the pope cannot be guilty of simony. Thus the will of the pope, of whatever kind it may be, is the rule governing his activities and deeds: whence it may be shown without doubt that whatever is pleasing is also permitted.

From this source as from a Trojan horse so many abuses and such grave diseases have rushed in upon the Church of God that we now see her afflicted almost to the despair of salvation.[4]

The commission then listed the practices of the Roman curia which it found particularly heinous: the appointment of unfit clergy, the reservation of incomes from church benefices, the inheritance of church benefices, even by the sons of priests, the use of "expectative graces" or the reservation of benefices not yet vacant, pluralism in sacred office, non-residence of clergy, simony, and other scandals.[5] At the core of all was the management of church property. As the commission saw it, the church had come to be regarded by its leaders as a vehicle for private profit-making rather than as an institution primarily charged with the care of the souls of the faithful.[6] What was needed, they said, was not an innovation, but rather a simple adherence to the existing laws of the church.[7] Predictably, these judgments met with hostility at the court of Paul III and provoked spirited rebuttals. Resistance proved so strong that the attempts to reform the central departments of the Roman court were postponed after 1539.[8]

But what happened then? Almost at once, events tended to obfuscate the nature of the original protest, and quarrels increasingly revolved about questions of theology, doctrine, authority, and, as the polemic continued to degenerate, about the personal probity of the protagonists on all sides. The initial issues, thus beclouded, tended to disappear from historical writing, both contemporary and modern, Protestant and Catholic. One result has been a curious gap in accounts of the reform, renewal, and resurgence of the Roman Catholic Church. In virtually all of the standard studies, treatment of the Catholic Reformation follows the same pattern: it outlines the mundaneness of the Renaissance popes of the fifteenth and early sixteenth centuries; it elaborates upon the venality of the Roman court during the same period; it notes the initial delay in the Roman response to the Lutheran challenge; and it cites the beginnings of reform during the pontificate of Paul III (1534– 1549), the futile struggles of the reform commissions of the 1530s, and the several abortive attempts to convene an ecumenical church council. Then, almost universally, the argument shifts, and suddenly we are reading about St. Ignatius and the foundation of the Society of Jesus, the establishment of the Holy Office of the Inquisition, the convening of the Council of Trent, and the inauguration of the Index of Prohibited Books. The discussion focuses upon ideas, politics, education, missionary work, saints, and so forth, and it never returns to the material questions about the fiscal practices of the church, the very questions with which it began.[9] What happened to the reformers and their specific targets for reform during the ensuing years?

Denys Hay devoted the first chapter of his *Church in Italy* to the historiography of the Italian church, and noted that scholarship had made little progress from the seventeenth century to the twentieth.[10] Peter Partner remarked on the paucity of institutional studies of the papacy for the fifteenth and sixteenth centuries.[11] Perhaps the silence in the literature reflects a tacit assumption that reform in these mundane matters occurred almost automatically once the papacy in the person of Paul III launched a serious reform program. If so, we have neglected some astute advice proffered by a legate to the first sessions of the Council of Trent. Writing to one of his agents in 1545, Cardinal Marcello Cervini cautioned, "Watch more, if you can, the hands of men than their mouths."[12]

There does exist, of course, a broad literature on Rome and the papacy during these years; much of it touches upon our central question, none focuses upon it directly.[13] Several careful studies of some of the curial offices appeared before World War I, and, more recently, two works on the dataria, an office important to the development of papal finance in the sixteenth century, have been published.[14] Papal finance itself is a subject central to the history of fiscal abuse and reform, and here too, recent studies have added much to our understanding of that century.[15] Works on particular practices—the resignation of benefices, expectative graces, and testamentary laws— tend to trace them through theory, papal constitutions, and canon law, rather than through actual practice.[16] All of this scholarship contributes to the elucidation of church history, but none attempts to answer the question posed here: what happened to the fiscal abuses at the Roman curia during the sixteenth century?

What follows, then, undertakes to fill in some of the lacunae, to shed some light on the nature and extent of Catholic reform by taking Cardinal Cervini's advice and watching the hands of men rather than their mouths. The men who logically present themselves for scrutiny are those who were responsible for the leadership and direction of the church during the first half of the sixteenth century: the members of the Sacred College of cardinals.[17] I have singled out the cardinals from among the many curial officials working in Rome because of their importance at the centers of power. Chief advisers to the pontiffs, cardinals were the veritable "hinges" of the church. In theory, at least, popes issued every pronouncement, every decree, "with the advice and consent" (*cum consilio et consensu*) of the cardinals, and the consultation process was almost continuous: consistories were held every week or ten days. In addition, membership in the college increased steadily throughout the century despite repeated attempts to fix the number of cardinals, until the modifications of 1586 set the maximum number at seventy.[18] Through the cardinals and their families, my study investigates the

TABLE 1.1   ITALIANS IN CONCLAVES: 1471-1590

Election of	Cardinals Voting	Italians	Percentage Italian
Sixtus IV (1471)	19	14	74%
Innocent VIII (1484)	26	22	85
Alexander VI (1492)	23	21	91
Pius III (1503)	36	22	61
Julius II (1503)	37	23	62
Leo X (1513)	25	19	76
Adrian VI (1522)	39	36	92
Clement VII (1523)	36	32	89
Paul III (1534)	34	23	67
Julius III (1550)	49	31	63
Marcellus II (1555)	39	32	82
Paul IV (1555)	45	35	78
Pius IV (1559)	42	33	78
Pius V (1566)	49	46	94
Gregory XIII (1572)	52	46	88
Sixtus V (1585)	41	36	88
Urban VII (1590)	53	47	89

material aspects of church life from 1492 and the election of Alexander VI, under whom reform efforts at the curia were begun, through 1563 and the final sessions of the Council of Trent.[19]

I have limited the population to Italians in the college (table 1.1) for two reasons: (1) Italians were in the absolute and overwhelming majority throughout and beyond the period; and (2) with the exceptions of Alexander VI, a Spaniard, in 1492, and Adrian VI, a Fleming, in 1522, they have elected one of their own countrymen to occupy the throne of Peter until our own day and the election of John Paul II.[20] The subjects include all Italian cardinals who were active at the time of the Fifth Lateran Council in 1512, the final opportunity for church reform prior to the appearance of Luther, through the last creation of cardinals by Paul III in 1549, by which time the first sessions of the Council of Trent had already charted the course of Catholic reform. The overall chronological limits remain 1492–1563. In the interests of brevity, I have omitted prelates who were later elevated to the papacy, although members of each successive papal family appear on the list, with the exceptions of Marcellus II (1555) and Pius IV (1559–1565). Cardinals from border areas were also treated arbitrarily. I have excluded Savoyards from the list because they seem to have been regarded by their contemporaries as French rather than Italian, and because they did not reside in Rome.[21] What emerges is a group of 102 Italian cardinals—a number small enough to be manageable and large enough to be significant (table 1.2). For purposes of comparison, the men have been divided into three subgroups: (1) those active in 1512 and subsequent creations through 1519; (2) those created cardinal between 1520 and 1539; and (3) those created cardinal between 1540 and 1549.

The principal archival materials I used are found in the Archivio di Stato, Rome, and in the Biblioteca Apostolica Vaticana and the Archivio Segreto Vaticano in Vatican City. Fiscal records consist of the orders of the *camerarius (camerlengo)*, the official in charge of dispersing the funds of the camera apostolica, the central treasury of the church; they are found in the Archivio Camerale of the Archivio di Stato in Rome. These Mandati Camerali are in chronological sequence, and the dates of the many volumes sometimes overlap. In the same archive, the series Diversorum del Camerlengo contained only one volume, 369, which fell within the purview of this study. Other financial material, recording the incomes and expenditures of the dataria, the second important curial treasury, is preserved in the Biblioteca Apostolica Vaticana in the series Vaticani latini, volumes 10599 through 10605, which cover the years 1531–1534, 1535–1550, and 1554–1555.

TABLE 1.2   NAMES AND DATES OF THE CARDINALS

Cardinal	Red Hat	Death
1512-1519		
Raffaele Riario	1477	1521
Federico Sanseverino	1489	1516
Domenico Grimani	1493	1523
Ippolito I d'Este	1493	1520
Marco Cornaro	1500	1524
Francesco Soderini	1503	1524
Nicolò Fieschi	1503	1524
Adriano Castellesi	1503	1521
Marco Vigerio	1505	1516
Leonardo Grosso della Rovere	1505	1520
Sigismondo Gonzaga	1505	1525
Sesto Franciotto della Rovere	1507	1517
Antonio Maria del Monte	1511	1533
Pietro Accolti	1511	1532
Achille Grassi	1511	1523
Bandinello Sauli	1511	1518
Alfonso Petrucci	1511	1517
Lorenzo Pucci	1513	1531
Bernardo Dovizi	1513	1520
Innocenzo Cibo	1513	1550
Francesco Conti	1517	1521
Giovanni Piccolomini	1517	1537
Giandomenico de Cupis	1517	1553
Nicolò Pandolfini	1517	1518
Raffaele Petrucci	1517	1522
Andrea della Valle	1517	1534
Bonifacio Ferrerio	1517	1543
Giovanni Battista Pallavicino	1517	1524
Scaramuzza Trivulzio	1517	1527
Pompeo Colonna	1517	1532
Domenico Jacobazzi	1517	1528
Lorenzo Campeggio	1517	1539
Ferdinando Ponzetti	1517	1527
Luigi de' Rossi	1517	1519
Silvio Passerini	1517	1529
Francesco Armellini	1517	1528
Tommaso de Vio	1517	1534
Egidio da Viterbo	1517	1532
Cristoforo Numai	1517	1528
Franciotto Orsini	1517	1534
Paolo Emilio Cesi	1517	1537
Alessandro Cesarini	1517	1542
Giovanni Salviati	1517	1553
Nicolò Ridolfi	1517	1550
Ercole Rangone	1517	1527
Agostino Trivulzio	1517	1548
Francesco Pisani	1517	1570

Continued on next page

TABLE 1.2 CONTINUED

Cardinal	Red Hat	Death
1520-1539		
Benedetto Accolti	1527	1549
Agostino Spinola	1527	1537
Nicolò Gaddi	1527	1552
Ercole Gonzaga	1527	1563
Marino Grimani	1527	1546
Antonio Sanseverino	1527	1543
Gian Vincenzo Carafa	1527	1541
Andrea Matteo Palmieri	1527	1537
Girolamo Grimaldi	1527	1543
Pirro Gonzaga	1527	1529
Francesco Cornaro	1527	1543
Girolamo Doria	1529	1558
Ippolito de' Medici	1529	1535
Antonio Pucci	1531	1544
Alessandro Farnese	1534	1589
Guido Ascanio Sforza	1534	1564
Girolamo Ghinucci	1535	1541
Jacopo Simonetta	1535	1539
Gasparo Contarini	1535	1542
Marino Caracciolo	1535	1538
Ennio Filonardi	1536	1549
Jacopo Sadoleto	1536	1547
Cristoforo Jacobazzi	1536	1540
Rodolfo Pio	1536	1564
Girolamo Aleandro	1536	1542
Nicolò Caetani	1536	1585
Ippolito II d'Este	1538	1572
Pietro Bembo	1538	1547
Federico Fregoso	1539	1541
Uberto Gambara	1539	1549
Pier Paolo Parisio	1539	1545
Bartolomeo Guidiccioni	1539	1549
Ascanio Parisani	1539	1549
Dionisio Lorerio	1539	1542
Jacopo Savelli	1539	1587
1540-1549		
Giovanni Morone	1542	1580
Marcello Crescenzio	1542	1552
Gian Vincenzo Acquaviva	1542	1546
Pomponio Cecci	1542	1542
Roberto Pucci	1542	1547
Tommaso Badia	1542	1547
Gregorio Cortese	1542	1548
Cristoforo Madruzzo	1542	1578
Andrea Cornaro	1544	1551
Francesco Sfondrato	1544	1550

Continued on next page

TABLE 1.2 CONTINUED

Cardinal	Red Hat	Death
Federico Cesi	1544	1565
Durante Duranti	1544	1558
Nicolò Ardinghello	1544	1547
Girolamo Capodiferro	1544	1559
Tiberio Crispo	1544	1566
Ranuccio Farnese	1545	1565
Giulio della Rovere	1547	1578
Girolamo Verallo	1549	1555
Filiberto Ferrerio	1549	1549
Bernardino Maffei	1549	1553

The Archivio Segreto Vaticano has records of consistories in three series: the Acta Camerarii, kept under the aegis of the *camerarius;* the Acta Vicecancellarii, kept under the aegis of the *vicecancellarius;* and the Acta Miscellanea, which cover the earlier years of the period. There are some gaps for the initial years under study, but from volume 2 of the Acta Camerarii they are complete and increasingly clear and informative. The Acta Camerarii and the Acta Vicecancellarii record the same consistories with slightly different perceptions of the events.

Minutes of papal briefs are also in the Vatican Archives in the series Armarium 40 (57 volumes), Armarium 41 (72 volumes), and Armarium 42 (63 volumes). These are drafts—sometimes very rough drafts—of papal letters. They cover the period from 1478 to 1629 and proved to be of extraordinary value to this work.

Before embarking upon a program of watching hands rather than mouths, it will be useful to catalog briefly some background information about the principals—their places of origin, their social class, their educational training.

The great majority of the cardinals were from central or northern Italy: 76 percent of the first group, 66 percent of the second group, and 65 percent of the third group were from the cities and towns of the center or north (table 1.3). This is to say that the majority of cardinals derived from the most sophisticated cultural and intellectual ambience in all of Europe. Furthermore, if we include Rome, increasingly important as an urban center, in the calculations, these proportions increase dramatically: 90 percent of the first, 80 percent of the second, and 95 percent of the third group were city people.[22] Throughout the period, no single city or region—Venice, Genoa, Florence, Rome, Naples—ever enjoyed a numerical advantage sufficient to influence the policies and directions of the Sacred College.

Partly because of the diversity of Italian political and economic systems, an attempt to distinguish separate social classes entails not a little risk. In Genoa, for example, the old knightly class became leaders in trade and finance; in Florence, to claim membership in the old knightly class was politically dangerous; in Venice, no old knightly class existed; and in Rome, the old knightly class continued the military traditions of its ancestors. Still, each city clearly had an aristocracy, a ruling group. The attempt to place each prelate within the confines of a particular class creates even more problems. Pietro Accolti and his nephew Benedetto, for example, were members of an ancient, noble, Ghibelline family of Arezzo; there they ranked as nobles or at least patricians.[23] Arezzo, however, was part of the Florentine *contado* by the sixteenth century and subject to Florentine dominion. In addition, the family had but recently transferred from Arezzo to Florence in the person of Cardinal Pietro's father, Benedetto Accolti the elder, a noted jurist. Both cardinals Pietro and Benedetto Accolti were born in Florence and considered themselves Florentine, and, by the standards of that society, they were clearly new men.[24]

Acknowledging these difficulties, we can still discern four general classes to which the cardinals belonged: (1) nobility, (2) patriciate, (3) new families, and (4) humble families (table 1.4). The nobility comprises the old knightly class, the feudal nobility, whose families date at least from the twelfth century and earlier; cardinals of such lineage have been located in this category even though their families may also have produced merchants and civil servants. The patriciate includes prominent families from merchant republics such as Venice or Florence, conspicuous families from the smaller towns, such as the Numai of Forlì or the Cortesi of Modena, and civil-servant families notable in public life, such as the Simonetta and Moroni of Milan or the Palmieri of Naples. New families are those only a few generations in evidence by our period; I include in this category the prelates who founded the fortunes of their families and succeeded in establishing their heirs as part of the Italian ruling class. Humble families are those whose prominence began and ended with the achievements of the cardinal-members on our list.

The statistics are revealing. Almost 30 percent of the first group of cardinals were members of the nobility, another 31 percent were patrician, about 24 percent were new men, and almost 15 percent were humble. The first two categories, the existing ruling classes, account for some 61 percent of the whole, and, together with the new families, they comprise about 85 percent. Percentages for the 1520–1539 cardinals are similar: 40 percent nobility, 28 percent patrician, 17 percent new

TABLE 1.3   CARDINALS' PLACES OF ORIGIN

	1512-1519	1520-1539	1540-1549
Venice	M. Cornaro F. Pisani D. Grimani	G. Contarini F. Cornaro M. Grimani P. Bembo	A. Cornaro
Milan	S. Trivulzio A. Trivulzio	J. Simonetta	G. Morone
Genoa	I. Cibo G. B. Pallavicino N. Fieschi B. Sauli	G. Doria G. Grimaldi A. Spinola F. Fregoso	
Florence	P. Accolti N. Pandolfini L. Pucci N. Ridolfi G. Salviati F. Soderini L. de' Rossi	B. Accolti N. Gaddi I. de' Medici A. Pucci	R. Pucci N. Ardinghello
Rome	A. Cesarini P. Colonna F. Conti D. Jacobazzi F. Orsini A. della Valle G. de Cupis	N. Caetani A. Farnese G. A. Sforza C. Jacobazzi J. Savelli	G. Capodiferro P. Cecci M. Crescenzio T. Crispo R. Farnese G. Verallo
Naples	F. Ponzetti F. Sanseverino	M. Caracciolo G. V. Carafa A. M. Palmieri A. Sanseverino	G. Acquaviva
Gaeta	T. de Vio		
Lombardy Mantua	S. Gonzaga	E. Gonzaga P. Gonzaga	
Brescia Cremona		U. Gambara	D. Duranti F. Sfondrato
Piedmont Biella	B. Ferrerio		F. Ferrerio
Trentino Trent			C. Madurzzo
Veneto Verona			B. Maffei
Friuli Motta		G. Aleandro	

Continued on next page

TABLE 1.3 CONTINUED

	1512-1519	1520-1539	1540-1549
Liguria			
Savona	M. Vigerio		
	R. Riario		
	L. G. della Rovere		
	S. F. della Rovere		
Emilia-Romagna			
Forlì	C. Numai		
Carpi		R. Pio	
Ferrara	I. I d'Este	I. II d'Este	
Modena	E. Rangone	J. Sadoleto	G. Cortese
			T. Badia
Bologna	L. Campeggio		
	A. Grassi		
Urbino			G. della Rovere
Tuscany			
Bibbiena	B. Dovizi		
Monte Sansavino	A. del Monte		
Cortona	S. Passerini		
Siena	A. Petrucci	G. Ghinucci	
	R. Petrucci		
	G. Piccolomini		
Lucca		B. Guidiccioni	
Umbria			
Cesi	P. E. Cesi		F. Cesi
Perugia	F. Armellini		
Lazio			
Corneto	A. Castellesi		
Viterbo	E. da Viterbo		
Banco		E. Filonardi	
Marches			
Tolentino		A. Parisani	
Campagna			
Benevento		D. Lorerio	
Calabria			
Cosenza		P. Parisio	

men, and 14 percent humble. Again, the older ruling classes together with the new men amount to roughly 85 percent of the whole. The figures for the 1540–1549 group depict a different pattern: only 10 percent nobility, 35 percent patrician, 40 percent new men, and 15 percent humble. The increased proportion of new men may reflect a trend, an increasing accessibility to high church office for new families

TABLE 1.4   SOCIAL CLASS OF THE CARDINALS

	1512-1519	1520-1539	1540-1549
Nobility	S. Gonzaga	M. Caracciolo	G. Acquaviva
	F. Sanseverino	G. V. Carafa	M. Crescenzio
	B. Sauli	A. Sanseverino	
	G. B. Pallavicino	P. Gonzaga	
	N. Fieschi	E. Gonzaga	
	E. Rangone	R. Pio	
	A. Trivulzio	U. Gambara	
	S. Trivulzio	G. Doria	
	I. I d'Este	G. Grimaldi	
	G. Piccolomini	F. Fregoso	
	F. Conti	A. Spinola	
	A. della Valle	I. II d'Este	
	F. Orsini	N. Caetani	
	P. Colonna	J. Savelli	
Patriciate	D. Jacobazzi	F. Cornaro	F. Ferrerio
	N. Ridolfi	G. Contarini	N. Ardinghello
	G. Salviati	P. Bembo	G. Cortese
	F. Soderini	M. Grimani	A. Cornaro
	L. de' Rossi	B. Guidiccioni	G. Morone
	A. Petrucci	A. Parisani	G. Capodiferro
	R. Petrucci	G. Ghinucci	D. Duranti
	B. Ferrerio	J. Simonetta	
	C. Numai	A. M. Palmieri	
	A. Grassi	I. de' Medici	
	L. Campeggio	C. Jacobazzi	
	G. de Cupis		
	F. Pisani		
	M. Cornaro		
	D. Grimani		
	N. Pandolfini		
New Men	L. G. della Rovere	G. A. Sforza	R. Pucci
	S. F. della Rovere	A. Farnese	C. Madruzzo
	M. Vigerio	N. Gaddi	B. Maffei
	P. Accolti	A. Pucci	G. Verallo
	A. Cesarini	B. Accolti	G. della Rovere
	L. Pucci		F. Sfondrato
	A. del Monte		F. Cesi
	P. E. Cesi		R. Farnese
	I. Cibo		
	R. Riario		
Humble	B. Dovizi	D. Lorerio	T. Badia
	T. de Vio	J. Sadoleto	P. Cecci
	F. Armellini	G. Aleandro	T. Crispo
	F. Ponzetti	P. Parisio	
	A. Castellesi	E. Filonardi	
	E. da Viterbo		
	S. Passerini		

and an increasing opportunity for such families to enter the ranks of the established ruling classses.[25] As we shall see, service to the Holy See presented a variety of avenues to wealth and favor.[26] Be that as it may, it is still clear that the new families combined with the older ruling groups continued to represent 85 percent of the total number. Overall, then, the figures for the entire list of 102 cardinals show that a huge majority, 85 percent, were members of the old or emergent ruling classes of Italy.

The educational backgrounds of the cardinals also proved difficult to classify. What follows here, then, is even more tentative than the preceding paragraphs. Still, it seems useful to attempt to assess the educational environment of the college in order to gain some notion of its general intellectual orientation. The problems are several. First, we lack specific information for a significant number of cardinals. Second, even when the information is available, it is frequently not specific enough to distinguish between the traditional scholastic philosophy and the newer *studia humanitatis*. I have resorted to the expediency of lumping such programs together under the category of "letters," even though this does violence to the distinctions between them. Third, a number of cardinals seem to have pursued curricula which do not quite fit into the usual categories. Ippolito II d'Este, for example, studied Greek and Latin, but also military arts, music, and dance before going off to the University of Padua at age sixteen.[27] His education was designed to produce a Renaissance prince. This sort of program might be called a courtly education. We distinguish, then, however arbitrarily, four primary areas of educational focus: (1) letters, (2) court, (3) law, and (4) theology. And there was one physician, Ferdinando Ponzetti, who also held a degree in theology.[28] He qualifies in two categories.

There are further complications. Gregorio Cortese of Modena, for example, studied canon and civil law at Padua and began his career as a familiar of Cardinal Giovanni de' Medici, the future Leo X. He was unhappy in Rome, however, joined the Benedictine Order, and thereafter acquired a reputation as a theologian.[29] He accordingly appears among them, in spite of his legal training. Ercole Gonzaga of Mantua, on the other hand, enjoyed the customary education of a prince and then attended the University of Bologna, where he studied philosophy under the controversial Pietro Pomponazzi between 1522 and the latter's death in 1525.[30] I have located him in the "letters" category rather than "court" because he was far more than a Renaissance prince during the rest of his career.[31]

14   Church Property, Abuse, and Cardinals

TABLE 1.5   EDUCATIONAL BACKGROUNDS OF THE CARDINALS

	1512-1519	1520-1539	1540-1549
Law	P. Accolti	B. Accolti	N. Ardinghello
	F. Soderini	G. Ghinucci	R. Pucci
	L. Pucci	J. Simonetta	D. Duranti
	G. Salviati	P. Parisio	M. Crescenzio
	N. Ridolfi	C. Jacobazzi	F. Sfondrato
	N. Pandolfini	B. Guidiccioni	F. Cesi
	S. Trivulzio		B. Maffei
	A. Trivulzio		G. Morone
	R. Riario		G. Verallo
	A. Grassi		
	L. Campeggio		
	A. del Monte		
	G. de Cupis		
	P. E. Cesi		
	G. B. Pallavicino		
	D. Jacobazzi		
	A. Cesarini		
	N. Fieschi		
	F. Armellini		
	S. Passerini		
Letters	A. Castellesi	J. Sadoleto	P. Cecci
	P. Colonna	P. Bembo	A. Cornaro
	I. Cibo	M. Grimani	R. Farnese
	B. Dovizi	F. Cornaro	C. Madruzzo
	D. Grimani	A. Spinola	G. della Rovere
	M. Cornaro	F. Fregoso	
	B. Sauli	J. Savelli	
	G. Piccolomini	G. Grimaldi	
		R. Pio	
		A. Farnese	
		G. A. Sforza	
		E. Gonzaga	
		E. Filonardi	
		A. Parisani	
		I. de' Medici	
Court	I. I d'Este	G. V. Carafa	G. Capodiferro
	S. Gonzaga	M. Caracciolo	G. Acquaviva
	F. Orsini	I. II d'Este	
	F. Sanseverino	U. Gambara	
	R. Petrucci	P. Gonzaga	
	A. Petrucci		
	E. Rangone		
	L. de' Rossi		
Theology	C. Numai	G. Aleandro	T. Badia
	M. Vigerio	D. Lorerio	G. Cortese
	T. de Vio	G. Contarini	
	E. da Viterbo	A. Pucci	
Medicine	F. Ponzetti		
Unknown	F. Conti	G. Doria	T. Crispo
	B. Ferrerio	N. Gaddi	F. Ferrerio
	F. Pisani	A. M. Palmieri	
	L. G. della Rovere	A. Sanseverino	
	S. F. della Rovere	N. Caetani[1]	
	A. della Valle		

[1]Attended university; curriculum unknown.

With these warnings in mind, let us look at the figures (table 1.5). Although over 12 percent of the 1512–1519 cardinals remain unclassified, the findings for the remainder appear significant: almost 43 percent law, 17 percent letters, 17 percent court, 8 percent theology, and 2 percent medicine (Ponzetti). Letters predominated among the 1520–1539 cardinals: 14 percent unknown, 17 percent law, 42 percent letters, 14 percent court, and 11 percent theology. Lawyers were in the ascendancy again among the 1540–1549 cardinals: 10 percent unknown, 45 percent law, 25 percent letters, 10 percent court, and 10 percent theology. A comparison of tables 1.4 and 1.5 shows that nearly half of the cardinals trained in law were also either new men or of humble origin; clearly, a career in law brought opportunities for advancement in the church. The proportionate decline in the percentages for courtly education reflects the proportionate increase in the numbers of new men in the later years. Theologians were in short supply for the entire list, slightly less than a tenth of the whole. Most of them were either new men or of humble origin, and most were monks.

Thus the composite portrait of the typical Italian prelate depicts a man from an urban center, probably in central or northern Italy, a member of the existing or emerging ruling class, trained in letters or, more likely, the law.[32] Men such as these grappled with the crises besetting the church during the first half of the sixteenth century.

A final preliminary task remains. Because the following pages concentrate upon money and property, we need some estimate of costs of living and currency values. Although prices and values fluctuated from time to time and from city to city, and an inflationary trend continued throughout the century, we can at least extract an idea of the relative worth of money from a few examples.[33] Figures for curial officials in sixteenth-century Rome provide clues. The Dominican Tommaso Badia was named master of the Sacred Palace by Pope Clement VII in 1529. As such, he was the domestic theologian of the pontiff and the chief censor of the church for theological writings.[34] He had no income at all from ecclesiastical benefices as nearly as I can tell, and his total annual stipend was 120 ducats of gold.[35] During the 1530s, a certain Fra Roberto, *theologo* in the apostolic palace, received three *scuti* of gold per month, a *scuto* valuing about 7 percent less than a gold ducat.[36] And in the following decade, Egidio Zephyro, one of the more important persons at the curia because of his position as *depositario* of the dataria, had an annual salary of 100 *scuti* of gold.[37] Apparently, one could live at the curia on three to ten *scuti* of gold per month.

One gold ducat was thus worth a great deal. How many did a cardinal need in order to maintain himself according to his rank? A prince of the church was expected to display a certain degree of magnificence, to patronize artists and scholars, to found and finance charitable organizations, to underwrite the repair of religious edifices and the building of new ones, to be munificent with the poor. All of this required large sums of money, and the cardinals themselves have left us an estimate of a suitable amount. During the conclave that elected Julius II and again during the conclave that elected Leo X, the cardinals decided that any one of them who lacked an annual income of 6,000 ducats of gold or more was entitled to a pension from the church of 200 such ducats per month—an annual stipend of 2,400 gold ducats.[38] Ecclesiastical princes set themselves high standards of living.

Whence all this cash? Cardinals residing in Rome were entitled to portions of the "divisions" of their own *camera,* the treasury of the Sacred College, held three or four times each year, but these moneys never approached anything close to 6,000 ducats.[39] There were also the incomes from the various administrative positions such as the standing legations, which came to be numbered at six: Bologna, the Marches of Ancona, Romagna, Umbria, the *Patrimonio,* and the Campagna.[40] Pensions from the apostolic camera and the dataria were also ordered for "poor" cardinals.[41] The vast bulk of cardinals' incomes, however, came from ecclesiastical benefices.[42] This situation meant that any reform of the benefice system would directly impinge upon the personal finances of the very men to whom the labors of reform were entrusted. The system obviously made change difficult, but, even in the midst of reform efforts, the church was still obliged to see to the needs of its servants. As Girolamo Capodiferro wrote to Alessandro Farnese in 1542, "If man does not live by bread alone, it is even truer that he cannot live by words alone."[43] In the following pages we shall examine the ways in which cardinals accumulated, alienated, and distributed the wealth of the church.

for any reason or should its new occupant fail to pay moneys due from it.[23]

Records of the consistories held between the years 1492 and 1563 thus depict a kaleidoscopic succession of nominations, resignations, translations, exchanges, reservations, and other dispositions of ecclesiastical benefices. These records are almost solely concerned with "consistorial" benefices, those, that is, under the direct jurisdiction of the pope. By our period, all episcopal and archepiscopal sees and most important monasteries were consistorial, the papal will being circumscribed only by those of the secular rulers beyond the mountains.

BISHOPRICS

The proper discharge of a bishop's duties preoccupied reformers throughout the century.[24] A modern historian of the church, H. O. Evennett, even wrote that "all their efforts centred round the restoration of the episcopate, morally and administratively; and the strengthening of the episcopate in every respect, as the nodal point of every aspect of the reform, may be regarded as a cornerstone of the counter-reformation Church."[25] Episcopal duties clearly required residence and the care of souls, and therefore reformers particularly deplored the simultaneous possession of more than one episcopal see.[26] Pluralism in bishoprics was also a highly visible abuse—the bishop was either in residence or he was not—and an enduring scandal. Accordingly, the investigation of pluralism begins with bishoprics and the Italian cardinals who presided over them.

Two caveats are in order. First, the statistics presented here are necessarily incomplete. The figures that make up the following tables and graphs represent minimums and therefore indicate trends rather than absolutes. Second, the tables record the total number of bishoprics each cardinal possessed during his entire career, and most of these were held consecutively. Nevertheless, anyone who held two or more episcopal sees simultaneously at any time has been defined as a pluralist.

More than 65 percent of the cardinals in the first period (1512–1519) practiced pluralism in bishoprics. Furthermore, almost 43 percent of them dealt with as many as five or more cathedral churches during the course of their careers (table 2.1, fig. 2.1). Life-styles or reputations do not distinguish pluralists from nonpluralists, nor do reformers stand out from nonreformers in the matter of bishoprics.

Among the cardinals who apparently did not practice pluralism, for

TABLE 2.1 NUMBER OF BISHOPRICS HELD BY 1512-1519 CARDINALS

Number	Cardinal	Number	Cardinal
0	L. de' Rossi	5	D. Grimani
			S. F. della Rovere[2]
1	F. Conti		M. Cornaro
	N. Pandolfini		
	A. Petrucci	6	I. I d'Este
			P. Accolti
2	B. Dovizi[1]		L. Campeggio
	T. de Vio[1]		N. Fieschi
	D. Jacobazzi[1]		
	S. Gonzaga[1]	7	G. de Cupis
	F. Armellini[1]		A. Cesarini
	F. Ponzetti[1]		N. Ridolfi[3]
	B. Ferrerio[1]		L. Pucci
	A. Castellesi[1]		A. del Monte
	B. Sauli		P. E. Cesi
	L. G. della Rovere[1,2]		
	M. Vigerio[2]	8	F. Soderini
3	A. Grassi	9	A. della Valle
	R. Petrucci		G. Salviati[3]
	E. Rangone[1]		
	C. Numai	10	I. Cibo[3]
	E. da Viterbo		
	G. B. Pallavicino	11	P. Colonna
	G. Piccolomini		A. Trivulzio
			R. Riario[2]
4	S. Trivulzio[1]		
	F. Pisani		
	F. Orsini[1]		
	S. Passerini		
	F. Sanseverino		

[1]Bishoprics held consecutively.
[2]Nephew of Julius II.
[3]Nephew of Leo X.

example, appear two who were notorious in their day for irregular personal lives, Luigi de' Rossi and Francesco Conti.[27] Other non-pluralists include Ferdinando Ponzetti and Francesco Armellini, both of whom were considered unconscionably venal by their contemporaries.[28] Armellini's reputed avarice was so scandalous that it even brought him a stinging public insult from a fellow cardinal: "In a consistory where they were considering certain new taxes proposed by him [Armellini] to provide for some needs of the apostolic see, Cardinal Pompeo Colonna suggested that the most useful, honest, and expeditious

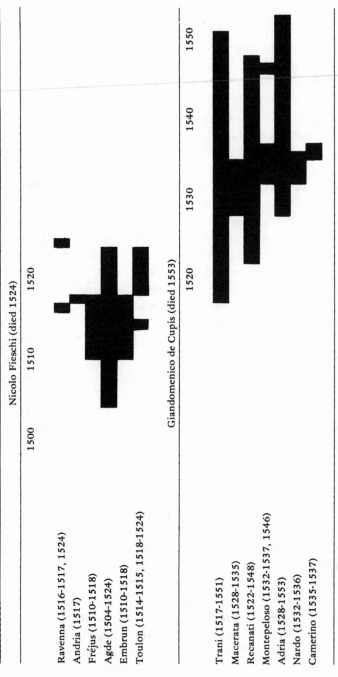

FIGURE 2.1   EXAMPLES OF PLURALISM IN BISHOPRICES: 1512-1519 CARDINALS

course of all would be to have Cardinal Armellini flayed, to send his pelt through the states of the church, and to make anyone wishing to look at it pay a *quattrino*."[29] Unsavory fame has followed Armellini to this day, perhaps undeservedly.[30] The harsh judgments of both Armellini and Ponzetti probably stemmed from their humble births and their pursuit of wealth through means deemed unsuitable for princes of the church. Cardinal Colonna took the more acceptable course, collecting eleven bishoprics during his lifetime. Men with unblemished records also avoided pluralism in bishoprics, among them the learned Nicolò Pandolfini, bishop of Pistoia for forty-four years, and the distinguished Dominican theologian and teacher Tommaso de Vio, called Cajetan.[31]

Pluralists represented the entire spectrum of the college of cardinals—papal nephews, political appointments, lawyers, courtiers, monks. That two of the most ardent reformers of the period appear here attests to the relaxed climate of the papal court. Cristoforo Numai, general of the Franciscans and the first Observant Friar to wear the purple, possessed three cathedral churches during his career: Alatri (1517–1528, death), Isernia (1523–1524), and Riez (1526–1527).[32] The general of the Augustinians, Egidio da Viterbo, left three bishoprics vacant when he died in 1532: Viterbo, Zara, and Lanciano.[33] At that time he was also collecting the income from the titular patriarchate of Constantinople, some 800 ducats per year, which he had kept when he traded the patriarchate for the archbishopric of Zara in 1530.[34]

We can begin to sort out contemporary practices by surveying the episcopal career of one of this group's more active cardinals. Antonio Maria del Monte, a successful lawyer and auditor of the Rota, presided over seven bishoprics from time to time. Bishop of Città di Castello in 1503, he left it to his fellow judge of the Rota, Achille Grassi, in 1506 and transferred to the archdiocese of Manfredonia.[35] Shortly after elevating del Monte to the cardinalate in 1511, Pope Julius II named him bishop of Pavia as well.[36] He kept both churches until 1513, when he resigned Manfredonia to his nephew, the future Julius III.[37] In 1516, still bishop of Pavia, he obtained Novara.[38] Then, in 1521, del Monte ceded Pavia in favor of the same nephew, reserving its income for himself, and in 1525 he also ceded Novara, reserving its income as well.[39] During the spring of 1529, del Monte presided briefly over two more bishoprics, Rimini and Cajazzo; he resigned both, keeping the income of Rimini.[40] Finally, from February to July of 1530, del Monte was bishop-elect of Alatri.[41] Thus the only bishopric del Monte held at the time of his death in 1533 was the one attached to his title as cardinal bishop of Porto, but he had provided for his nephew—destined for a brilliant career—and amassed incomes and pensions from several others. His fellow lawyers, Giandomenico de Cupis, Paolo Emilio Cesi, Pietro Accolti, and Lorenzo Campeggio all pursued similar careers. These were all new men, the founders of their families' fortunes.

Cardinals of the first group from established families, while no less nepotistic, did not bother with such manipulations. Marco Cornaro, a member of the Venetian patriciate, died in 1524 and left vacant the patriarchate of Constantinople, the bishoprics of Padua and Verona, and two monasteries.[42] Ippolito I d'Este, of the princely Ferrara family, resigned his archdiocese of Milan to his nephew in 1519, but when he died the following year he still held the bishoprics of Eger in Hungary, Ferrara, and Modena, and the archbishopric of Capua.[43] The far-flung properties that fell vacant in 1524 at the death of Giovanni Battista Pallavicino, a Genoese nobleman, included the bishopric of Cavaillon in France, the island bishopric of Hvar in the Adriatic Sea, a monastery in the diocese of Amiens, a monastery in the diocese of Turin, and a monastery in Dalmatia.[44] Clearly there was no question of residence.

Indeed, the number of non-Italian cathedral churches which the cardinals of this group held further underlines the acceptance of pluralism as the normal state of affairs during these years. Italian cardinals possessed twenty-four French, nine Spanish, three English, and two Hungarian bishoprics. Popes nominated Italians to bishoprics in Denmark, Germany, Switzerland, and Scotland as well, but, owing to the nature of the times after 1517, possession never materialized.

In the early decades of the century, the very language of consistorial records accentuated the abuse. When Cardinal Nicolò Fieschi resigned Ravenna to a nephew in 1517, the nephew was allowed to keep another diocese, "in such a way that he not cease to be bishop-elect of Fréjus."[45] Again, when Cardinal Lorenzo Campeggio was named bishop of Salisbury, England, in 1524, the record notes specifically that he would "not cease to be bishop of Bologna, with the retention of his benefices."[46] Apparently, however, the reform impulse altered at least the language of pluralism: I found no repetition of the clause *ita quod non desinat esse episcopus* after 1530.[47] Pluralism in bishoprics did not disappear after 1530, but the modified phraseology of the consistorial records suggests that it became less routine. Perhaps reform was beginning to take effect.

The traffic in bishoprics by the cardinals of the next period, 1520–1539, does indeed display a different pattern (table 2.2, fig. 2.2). The careers of these thirty-five cardinals are of particular interest because it

TABLE 2.2   NUMBER OF BISHOPRICS HELD BY 1520-1539 CARDINALS

Number	Cardinal	Number	Cardinal
1	M. Caracciolo	4	J. Simonetta
	D. Lorerio		J. Savelli[4]
	J. Sadoleto		I. de' Medici[2]
	G. Aleandro		E. Gonzaga
	P. Gonzaga		U. Gambara
	C. Jacobazzi		M. Grimani
	P. Parisio		
		5	G. Doria
2.	R. Pio		B. Accolti
	F. Cornaro[1]		G. Ghinucci
	G. Contarini		A. M. Palmieri[1]
	E. Filonardi[1]		G. Grimaldi
	P. Bembo[1]		G. V. Carafa
			N. Caetani[4]
3	B. Guidiccioni[1]		
	N. Gaddi	6	I. II d'Este
	F. Fregoso		
	A. Pucci	7	G. A. Sforza[3]
	A. Parisani		
	A. Spinola	13	A. Farnese[3]
	A. Sanseverino		

[1]Bishoprics held consecutively.
[2]Nephew of Clement VII.
[3]Grandson of Paul III.
[4]Relative of Paul III.

was in these years, scholars agree, that the true reform of the church under papal direction began.[48] The group includes four members of the reform commission of 1536–1537: Gasparo Contarini, Federigo Fregoso, Jacopo Sadoleto, and Girolamo Aleandro; and three who have been classified as conservative reformers: Ercole Gonzaga, Bartolomeo Guidiccioni, and Dionisio Lorerio.[49] The statistics reveal the alteration in the habits of cardinals in regard to bishoprics during these years. Although almost 66 percent of them still held plural bishoprics at some time, only 25 percent possessed five or more. Cardinals of this group are also more easily identifiable by the test one would expect: nonpluralist equals reformer; pluralist equals nonreformer.

Nonpluralists included political promotions such as Marino Caracciolo, Francesco Cornaro, and Pirro Gonzaga, and curial career men such as Pier Paolo Parisio and Ennio Filonardi, none of whom was renowned for reform programs or works.[50] There were several genuine reformers who avoided pluralism in bishoprics, however: Girolamo

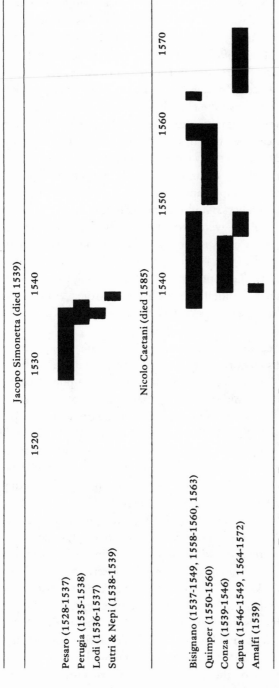

FIGURE 2.2   EXAMPLES OF PLURALISM IN BISHOPRICS: 1520-1539 CARDINALS

Aleandro, Jacopo Sadoleto, Dionisio Lorerio, and Bartolomeo Guidiccioni. Guidiccioni was the only Cardinal of this group to hold three
bishoprics consecutively: Teramo (1539–1542), Chiusi (1544– 1545),
and Lucca (1546–1549, death).[51] His resignation from Teramo illustrated his thoughts on reform and cited a cause rarely seen in the records.
He ceded the diocese "because, continually hindered by public occupa-
tions, he could not visit the church of Teramo, over which he presided,
nor provide the care that was clearly necessary to the same church."[52]

As was the case with their seniors, the pluralists among this group
of cardinals came from every category in the college, and papal relatives
were prominent among them. Clement VII favored his nephew Ippolito
de' Medici with the important office of vicechancellor, four bishoprics,
and other rich benefices. Guido Ascanio Sforza and Alessandro Farnese,
grandsons of Paul III, were probably the most highly rewarded of all
102 cardinals under investigation, at least in regard to the accumulation
of incomes derived from church property. Raised to the purple while
still in their teens, they both embarked upon long careers at the court,
working for their grandfather and his successors.[53] Other relatives of
Paul III who prospered were Jacopo Savelli and Nicolò Caetani of
Sermoneta.

Benedetto Accolti was the only cardinal of this group with a tainted
reputation. His major critic, however, was Paul III, and it was not
Accolti's well-known lechery which irritated the pope, but rather his
problems in the administration of the Marches of Ancona.[54] Accolti
possessed the bishoprics of Cadiz (1521–1523), Cremona (1523–1549,
death), Ravenna (1524–1549, death), Bovino (1530–1535), and Policas-
tro (1530–1534).[55] His career as bishop was not dissimilar to that of
his friend Ercole Gonzaga of Mantua. Gonzaga, regarded both then
and now as a sincere and conservative reformer, held Mantua (1521–
1563, death), Fano (1528–1530), Savona (1529–1532), Fano again
(1537), Tarazona in Spain (1537–1546), and Fano once more (1560).[56]

Other members of reform circles who practiced pluralism in bishoprics
were Federigo Fregoso and Gasparo Contarini. It is perhaps unfair to
number Contarini among the pluralists. International politics clearly
prevented his taking possession of the diocese of Salisbury to which
Paul III nominated him in 1539; he neither protested the promotion
nor resigned the bishopric, however, and, at least in theory, held Salisbury together with his diocese of Belluno until his death in 1542.[57]
Even Gian Pietro Carafa, the future Pope Paul IV and one of the most
zealous reformers of the century, held plural bishoprics early in his

career. Already bishop of Chieti, he was named archbishop of Brindisi
on 20 December 1518, "with the retention of his church of Chieti for
six months, and with a decree that unless he resign the other, it shall
be deemed vacant after the six months have passed."[58] The six months
turned into more than five and one-half years, but finally, on 29 July
1524, Egidio da Viterbo announced to the cardinals in consistory "the
causes which moved the bishop of Chieti to cede his churches, that is
to say, Chieti and Brindisi."[59] Ten days later, the pope and the college
accepted his cession of both sees.[60] Carafa, the pope told the emperor,
had resigned these bishoprics freely because "he had devoted himself
totally to pious works and contemplation."[61]

Not all churchmen imitated Carafa's dedication, but the performance
of these cardinals nevertheless constituted an improvement. And, although many continued to accept non-Italian bishoprics, the proportion
of Italians with foreign dioceses dropped from 45 percent to 33 percent,
and the total number of such sees also diminished.[62]

The careers of cardinals of the third group (1540–1549) contrasted
sharply with those of their seniors (table 2.3, fig. 2.3). Unlike his older
brother, for example, Ranuccio Farnese resigned his bishoprics upon
taking others, holding successively Naples (1544–1549), Ravenna
(1549–1564), and Bologna (1564–1565, death). He was also the titular
patriarch of Constantinople from 1546 to 1550.[63] Even for the grandson
of a pope, pluralism in bishoprics was no longer acceptable. The statistics

TABLE 2.3   NUMBER OF BISHOPRICS HELD BY 1540-1549 CARDINALS

Number	Cardinal	Number	Cardinal
0	T. Badia	3	T. Crispo
			D. Duranti
1	F. Ferrerio		B. Maffei
	G. Acquaviva		
	N. Ardinghello	4	G. Verallo
	R. Pucci		R. Farnese[1, 3]
	G. Cortese		G. della Rovere[1, 2]
			F. Sfondrato[1]
2	M. Crescenzio[1]		
	A. Cornaro	5	F. Cesi[1]
	P. Cecci[1]		
	C. Madruzzo		
	G. Morone[1]		
	G. Capodiferro[1]		

[1]Bishoprics held consecutively.
[2]Great-nephew of Julius II, grandson-in-law of Paul III.
[3]Grandson of Paul III.

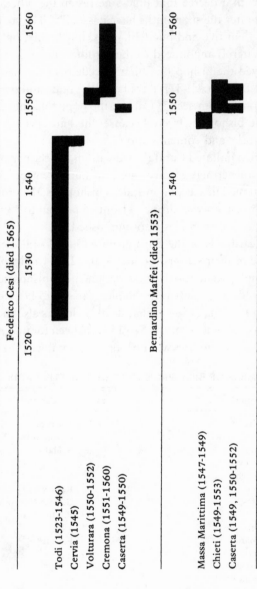

FIGURE 2.3 EXAMPLES OF PLURALISM IN BISHOPRICS: 1540-1549 CARDINALS

depict a dramatic reversal: a full 70 percent of these cardinals were *not* pluralists. Nonpluralists ranged from the austere Dominican Tommaso Badia, who had no bishopric at all, and Giovanni Morone, reformer, diplomat, and the last president of the Council of Trent, to Federico Cesi, an active curialist who held five bishoprics during his career.[64]

Furthermore, even the prelates here classified as pluralists were far less culpable than those of the earlier periods. Tiberio Crispo, for example, the half brother of Paul III's daughter, Costanza, had three bishoprics in succession from 1543 to his death in 1566. He was guilty of pluralism only in holding two of them for some months during the last year of his life.[65] Crispo's restraint strikingly illustrates the altered way of life at the Roman curia; he has not enjoyed a reputation for personal piety.[66] In fact, pluralists of this group seem to have displayed a reluctance to resign bishoprics rather than an eagerness to collect them. Bernardino Maffei had been archbishop of Chieti since November 1549 when the diocese of Caserta reverted to him in July 1550. Pope Julius III ruled that Maffei must resign Caserta within six months, "according to the tenor of the decree recently published about this."[67] But Maffei only ceded Caserta in February 1552, more than a year after the deadline.[68] Despite the delay, he *did* resign. And only one Italian cardinal of this last group held a bishopric "beyond the mountains."

These distinctly different patterns reflect modifications in personnel and attitudes in Rome. This is not to say that the twenty cardinals promoted by Paul III between 1540 and 1549 represented shining examples of reform. Only cardinals Morone, Badia, and Cortese fully qualified as reformers, and the creations of Tiberio Crispo at the instance of the pope's daughter in 1544, of the pope's grandson Ranuccio Farnese, at the age of fifteen in 1545, and of Giulio della Rovere, the fourteen-year-old brother of the pope's new grandson-in-law in 1547 all bore witness to an earlier morality. Nor were the 1540–1549 cardinals averse to their own enrichment; Girolamo Capodiferro built the sumptuous palace in Rome known today as the Palazzo della Spada, and the inheritance of Federico Cesi enabled his descendants to buy a *feudo* and enroll themselves among the Italian nobility.

What was changing in Rome was the notion that cardinals should secure adequate incomes by accumulating multiple bishoprics. From the moment early in his pontificate when Paul III announced his intention to call a reforming ecumenical council, servants of the curia had traveled as nuncios and legates to courts all over Europe, paving the way for its opening or announcing its opening to frequently skeptical rulers and non-Italian prelates. And pluralism in bishoprics was a public matter, a visible matter. While a Pompeo Colonna or a Raffaele Riario could consider holding eleven bishoprics a perfectly normal method of enhancing income, an Alessandro Farnese (as we shall see) expressed some embarrassment over his accumulation. Apparently reform had begun.

It took decades to eradicate pluralism in bishoprics. Throughout half a century of debate, tracts, memorials, and commissions on reform, nothing concrete happened. When the Council of Trent opened in December 1545, however, the pressure for curial reform increased markedly, and the papal legates to the council, cardinals Marcello Cervini and Gian Maria del Monte, repeatedly warned Rome about the intense indignation over certain curial practices that was being expressed by the assembling fathers.[69] Rome responded. Alessandro Farnese wrote Cervini on 22 January 1546 that because the matter of his own plural cathedral churches could be a topic of conversation at Trent, he wished Cervini to make it known that he, Farnese, would not fail to make a good example.[70] During January and February, Bernardino Maffei also reported from Rome to the legates that reform was well under way.[71] On 17 April, Maffei wrote Cervini that the reformation had actually begun in the consistory of the previous day, when the pope had refused to grant two French bishoprics to the cardinals of Bourbon and Ferrara.[72] The French ministers were much affronted by this, he added, "saying that the reformation ought not to begin with them."[73]

Pressures from Trent for something more tangible continued through the next months nonetheless, and Paul III acted decisively at last. On 18 February 1547, he issued an edict that forbade any prelate to hold more than one bishopric in addition to his cardinalate titular church. Any man in possession of more than one cathedral church must choose that which he wished to retain, and resign all others within six months if he was in Italy or within one year if he was elsewhere. Failure to comply would result in automatic deprivation.[74]

The first essential step had been taken, but the cardinals displayed no undue haste in following the papal mandate. A full year after its promulgation, on 24 February 1548, Paul III extended the time limit for an additional three months, "and, as soon as that three months should elapse, he conceded a further three-month period."[75] The matter came up again in the consistory of 16 May, where the college considered "what was to be done about the decree on the resignation of churches possessed by cardinals, and the business was remitted to another consistory."[76] Compliance finally began on 25 May, when cardinals Giandomenico de Cupis, Giovanni Salviati, Nicolò Ridolfi, Alessandro Farnese, and Ippolito II d'Este each selected the single bishopric he wished to keep.[77] The next move was obvious: the actual resignation of their other churches. Cardinal Ridolfi, who held five bishoprics in 1548, acted promptly. Having already ceded Orvieto on 16 May, he now resigned both Florence and Viterbo, naming Vicenza as his chosen church. He completed his obligations when he resigned Salerno on 19 December of the same year, after which he held only Vicenza to his death in 1550.[78] His cousin, Giovanni Salviati, ceded Saint-Papoul in 1549 and even Ferrara, his chosen church, in 1550, keeping no bishopric at all.[79] Most of the cardinals followed their example. Paul III had reason to congratulate himself. When he died in 1549, over 84 percent of the cardinals on our list who were still alive had complied with his reform decree.

There were exceptions, of course, and Julius III renewed and confirmed the Pauline order on 19 March 1550.[80] Ippolito II d'Este exchanged the archbishopric of Milan for Novara on the same day, but this action was apparently unrelated to the reform.[81] D'Este continued to keep the sees of Lyon and Autun, and he acquired Narbonne in June 1550. He resigned all four bishoprics during the following year and received another French church, Auch.[82] Although d'Este, cardinal of Ferrara, never fully grasped the spirit of the Catholic reform, he remained more or less within the limits of the law for the rest of his long career.[83] The resolve of Julius III seems to have prodded other reluctant cardinals to action, however. Giandomenico de Cupis, for example, had chosen Adria as his sole church in 1548, but he neglected to resign his other bishopric, Trani, until 1551.[84] Even Alessandro Farnese was not exempt. He had opted for Avignon in 1548 but had continued to hold Monreale in Sicily and the Portuguese church of Viseu: he resigned Avignon in 1551 and Viseu in 1552, keeping Monreale instead.[85] Cristoforo Madruzzo, cardinal of Trent, was allowed to keep both of his bishoprics, Trent and Brixen, in order to combat heretical tendencies in the latter area.[86] It took time, but by 1571 when Pope Pius V called for an assessment of the incomes of cardinals for a "donation" to support the war against the Turks, none listed more than one bishopric among his assets.[87] Apparently the reform was complete.

Still, many persons were unsatisfied with the results of the edicts of 1547 and 1550. A major impediment to the eradication of abuses attendant upon pluralism remained untouched. We mentioned earlier the options that were available to prelates when they resigned ecclesiastical benefices. The key to those options was a powerful device called the *regressus*. This was the right to take back a benefice one had resigned at any time it should happen to fall vacant. A similar device, the *accessus*, was in papal hands. Prelates regularly reserved the regress when they ceded benefices; popes could, as a special grace, grant a man the same right, the access, to a benefice he had not formerly held. Even in the face of the prohibition on plural bishoprics, then, cardinals could and did retain interest in and some control over their former properties. A prelate who held a regress could repossess a diocese, assign pensions from its income to himself or others, resign it again to a person of his choice, or keep it and resign another. The regress also made it possible for the traffic in bishoprics, so scandalous to reformers, to continue at least to some degree.

Two examples will illustrate the flexibility and importance of this tool. Girolamo Capodiferro, who is not classified here as a pluralist, reserved for himself the regress, the denomination, and an annual pension of 600 *scuti* from the diocese of Nice when he resigned it in 1544.[88] He then became bishop of St. Jean de Maurienne and remained such until his death in 1560. Meanwhile, Nice fell vacant in 1549, and Capodiferro used his regress, took the church back, resigned it almost at once, and reserved for himself a healthier pension of 1,300 *scuti* from its income which he continued to collect each year for the rest of his life.[89] For the sixteen years between his resignation and his death, the regress allowed Capodiferro to control the diocese of Nice, both in the person of its actual bishop and in its income. Giandomenico de Cupis used one of his regresses for a different purpose. On 14 November 1550, he repossessed the bishopric of Montepeloso and resigned it immediately. He reserved, however, a pension of 180 *scuti* of gold in gold for one of his illegitimate sons, Paolo de Cupis, bishop of Recanati.[90]

Thus cardinals carefully guarded rights of regress and ceded and exchanged them exactly as they dealt with the benefices themselves. For example, at the time of Ippolito II d'Este's nomination to Novara in 1550, Alessandro Farnese noted in the record that he held the regress to the bishopric and consented to its suspension for that instance only.[91] The history of the regress to a small diocese in southern Italy more clearly portrays the jealousy with which cardinals regarded these rights. Umbriatico, a bishopric with a modest annual income of about 200 ducats, had a bishop, a certain Desiderio Gilioni, from 1516 to 1520, but its regress was held by a cardinal, Nicolò Fieschi. Fieschi consented to the transfer of this right to another cardinal, Marco Cornaro, in

December 1520, and six months later both men ceded in favor of a third cardinal, Andrea della Valle, when he was nominated bishop of Umbriatico. Della Valle resigned in 1522 and reserved the regress to himself. When the bishopric fell vacant again in 1524, Clement VII gave it to Giovanni Piccolomini, a fourth cardinal, but with the following condition: that "if he [Piccolomini] should happen to cede the same church of Umbriatico, he cannot reserve the regress to himself, . . . because Cardinal della Valle holds the ancient regress to the same church."[92] The cardinal's diligence in protecting his rights in this matter underlines its significance. Andrea della Valle was not without other assets, after all; he presided over at least nine bishoprics from time to time.

Reformers in Rome and at the Council of Trent attacked the regress as weakening and circumventing the spirit of the reform edicts.[93] After 1548, to be sure, cardinals were bound to resign within six months any bishoprics acquired through the regress, but this restriction in no way diminished the utility of the instrument as a tool for patronage, nepotism, or the enhancement of personal income.[94] Pope Julius III complained about the practice in August 1550, when Federico Cesi asked for the nomination to the bishopric of Cremona. "Because of the quality of the times, that is to say [the problems of] both the reformation and the Council, and considering the degree to which accesses are hateful to all, . . . " the pope postponed his decision, and only named Cesi bishop of Cremona in March 1551.[95]

However "hateful to all" regresses were, their reform had to await the pontificate of Gian Pietro Carafa, Pope Paul IV. His initial decree was mild: on 4 May 1556 he declared that "from this very day, regresses and accesses will not be conceded [to any persons] except to the Most Reverend Cardinals, to whom all things, *etc.*, will be conceded."[96] The pope went further on 21 August of the same year by revoking all accesses to cathedral and metropolitan churches and to all lesser benefices, those of cardinals included. The same decree required the cardinals to prepare a list, signed by their own hands and sealed with their own seals, of all the regresses they possessed and to present it to the datary. Cardinals present in consistory had fifteen days in which to comply; those absent but in Italy had one month; all others had three months. Failure to complete the task would result in the annulment of the regresses.[97] Two weeks later, Paul IV extended the time limit for an additional fifteen days.[98]

Considering the length of the documents this order produced, it is not surprising that the pope found it necessary to allow additional time. Alessandro Farnese, leading the field as always, counted regresses to ten cathedrals, twenty-six monasteries, three preceptories, and 133 inferior benefices. "And, concerning the many others which we believe we have," he added, "we shall give a fuller account, having been granted the courtesy of an appropriate extension in order to examine our papers which are here in Rome."[99] His cousin, Guido Ascanio Sforza, had the next most extensive list: five cathedrals, twelve monasteries, and nineteen inferior benefices, of which ten were parish churches. In addition to regresses to numerous lesser benefices, several of the remaining cardinals also numbered regresses to plural bishoprics. Francesco Pisani had four, and cardinals Savelli, Ranuccio Farnese, Doria, Caetani, and della Rovere each had two. The others all had one cathedral church with the exception of Durante Duranti, who listed regresses to only one priorate and thirteen inferior benefices, eight of which were parish churches.[100]

There the matter rested for more than a year. Then, on 3 December 1557, Paul IV issued another reform edict. The pope noted that some cardinals, who in accordance with the decree of Paul III possessed only one bishopric in addition to the cardinalate title, still held regresses or accesses to many and the power to resign them to persons *grata* and *accepta,* "to the confusion of the ecclesiastical Order, enervation of the said decree, injury to the [cathedral] churches, which sometimes need persons of greater worth and fitness, and also not a little scandal to the faithful in Christ."[101] The pope therefore ordered that henceforth no more than one regress to a bishopric could be granted to any cardinal, and that any cardinal who held more than one regress must choose one and register it with the officials of the apostolic chancery within fifteen days, one month, or two months, depending on vicinity. All other regresses to bishoprics were forthwith canceled and annulled. Furthermore, if in the future a cardinal who already possessed a bishopric should take back another through his single regress, he had one month only in which to resign one or the other. Hesitancy would bring the loss of both churches "by the fact itself."[102]

This action should have been a severe blow to patronage and nepotism, even though the decree affected only regresses to bishoprics and not the multiplicities of regresses to lesser, "inferior" benefices. The subsequent behavior of the cardinals, however, suggests that they retained at least some room for manipulation. Nicolò Caetani, for example, was bishop of Quimper in Brittany at the time of the order, and he held regresses to both Capua and Bisignano in southern Italy. He took Bisignano back in December 1558 and resigned it the following month to his secretary, again reserving the regress. No doubt there was opposition from the strict Paul IV, because the transaction was re-recorded in February 1560 under the approval of the Carafa pope's successor.[103] Caetani then resigned Quimper in April of the same year, reserving to himself an annual pension of 800 *scuti*.[104] He repossessed Bisignano and resigned it again for the last time in early 1563, this time reserving only a pension of 800 ducats. The following year he acted on his regress to Capua and presided over it until 1572, when he resigned it in turn, reserving for himself the entire income of the archdiocese.[105] He held no bishoprics thereafter, but he continued to receive moneys from Quimper, Bisignano, and Capua each year until his death in 1585.

Indeed, the pressures in favor of patronage and nepotism apparently proved to be stronger at the court than the pressures for reform in this matter. The conclave that elected Pius IV in 1559 sought a relaxation of the Pauline decree.[106] During the consistory of 27 March 1560, the new pope brought up the matter of regresses, and the cardinals decided to remand the problem to those among them who had been appointed to deal with the reformation. Then the records are silent for more than two years until 4 May 1562, when the pope introduced a new decree stating that "more accesses and regresses are not to be conferred or granted even to the Most Reverend Lords Cardinals, . . . although the [single] regress now reserved to the same Cardinals remains valid."[107] Reform still seems doubtful, because the secretary added that "nothing, however, was concluded."[108] In any case, cardinals continued routinely to follow the old ways. Seven of the fourteen cardinals on our list who were still alive reserved regresses between 1560 and 1563.[109] In fact, a survey of the resignations of bishoprics by the cardinals of our population indicates that the habit of reserving regresses did not alter appreciably: 1512–1519 cardinals did so in almost 92 percent of their resignations, 1520–1539 cardinals did so in 81 percent, and 1540–1549 cardinals did so in more than 88 percent (fig. 2.4). Although the Council of Trent absolutely prohibited resignations with the reservation of the regress in 1563, these figures suggest that reform in this matter was more difficult to effect than in the matter of plural bishoprics and would have to await another generation.[110]

At any rate, the outright, public holding of plural bishoprics by Italian cardinals had ceased by 1571.[111] The Pauline decree of 1547 would probably have come sooner or later, but it is difficult to imagine that

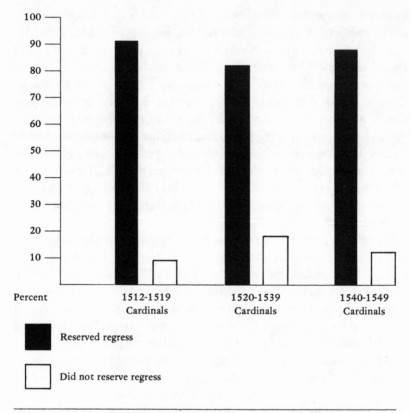

FIGURE 2.4   RESIGNATIONS IN WHICH CARDINALS
RESERVED THE REGRESS

the pope was not influenced by the alarming tone of the reports from
Trent during 1546, and particularly by the deep anger expressed by
Spanish prelates at Roman practices.[112] Italian cardinals would henceforth have to seek incomes elsewhere. One avenue still open was the
gathering of lesser benefices.

LESSER BENEFICES

Papal edicts restricted pluralism only in the possession of bishoprics
and regresses to bishoprics. Cardinals throughout the period collected
lesser benefices, including incompatible lesser benefices, in great numbers. The "tiny fortune" to which Pietro Bembo referred in 1527 consisted of at least twenty-eight separate benefices, twenty-six of them
received from the hands of Leo X during Bembo's years as papal secre-

tary. The annual revenue from these was not extraordinary by cardinalate standards—the total known income from nineteen of the benefices
was 1,593 ducats per year—but Bembo was still eleven years from his
promotion to the purple at the time.[113] His friend and colleague at the
court of Leo X, Jacopo Sadoleto, also held at least ten lesser benefices
in 1513, granted him by their mutual papal patron.[114] Both men were
regarded as "poor" by themselves and by their contemporaries.[115] As
one might anticipate, cardinals fared better. And, after the reform of
plural bishoprics, we find that the bulk of cardinalate wealth derived
from monasteries, other lesser benefices, and pensions from ecclesiastical
benefices.[116]

In fact, as sources of revenue the great monastic houses were fully as
attractive as bishoprics, frequently more so. Alessandro Farnese declared
an annual income of 5,000 *scuti* from the Cistercian monastery of Sts.
Vincenzo and Anastasia (*Tre Fontane*) outside Rome, and an additional
4,200 *scuti* representing half the "fruits" of another Cistercian monastery, Lucedio in Monferrato, in the assessment of 1571.[117] Other
wealthy foundations included Chiaravalle in Milan, San Leonardo in
Apulia, and Grottaferrato and Subiaco in the Patrimony of Peter.[118] All
of these went to cardinals, and some became the source of controversy
and dispute.[119] Occasionally, prelates even exchanged bishoprics for
monasteries. On 7 February 1533, for example, Federigo Fregoso traded
the archbishopric of Salerno to Nicolò Ridolfi for the priorate of Santa
Croce at Fonte Avellana near Gubbio.[120] According to the tax assessment of 1571, Avellana was worth 5,000 *scuti* of gold in gold per year,
Salerno worth only 5,000 Neapolitan ducats.[121] It was a particularly
advantageous transaction for the Genoese Fregoso, whose French sympathies had rendered him *persona non grata* to the emperor and made his
possession of a metropolitan see in the kingdom of Naples untenable.[122]

These rich foundations had become subject to papal promotion—they
were "consistorial"—but smaller, "inferior" benefices seldom appear
in the records of consistories.[123] Statistics for lesser benefices are therefore less complete than those for bishoprics (tables 2.4, 2.5, and 2.6).
Indeed, table 2.5 includes two "poor" cardinals—Sadoleto and Bembo—
among those holding the largest number of lesser benefices, suggesting
that what emerges from the records is only a suspicion of the reality.
Nevertheless, fragmentary as they are, the figures indicate that 76 percent
of the first group of cardinals, almost 83 percent of the second group,
and 60 percent of the third group held multiple lesser benefices. Or,
when bishoprics are taken into account, 91 percent of the first, 91

TABLE 2.4   MINIMUM NUMBER OF LESSER BENEFICES HELD
BY 1512-1519 CARDINALS

Number	Cardinal	Number	Cardinal
0	C. Numai	7	F. Soderini
	F. Ponzetti		I. Cibo
	F. Conti		
	A. Castellesi	8	P. E. Cesi
1	T. de Vio	9	L. G. della Rovere
	E. Rangone		D. Grimani
	E. da Viterbo		A. della Valle
	F. Armellini		
	L. de' Rossi	10	A. Trivulzio
	N. Pandolfini		A. del Monte
	M. Vigerio		N. Ridolfi
2.	S. Gonzaga	11	G. B. Pallavicino
	F. Sanseverino		
	S. F. della Rovere	12	A. Petrucci
	G. Piccolomini		
	S. Trivulzio	13	M. Cornaro
	G. de Cupis		F. Orsini
3	R. Petrucci	14	B. Ferrerio
4	L. Campeggio	16	G. Salviati
	A. Cesarini		
	B. Sauli	18	N. Fieschi
	F. Pisani		R. Riario
5	A. Grassi	20	P. Accolti
	I. I d'Este		P. Colonna
	B. Dovizi		
	D. Jacobazzi	21	L. Pucci
6	S. Passerini		

percent of the second, and 90 percent of the third group of cardinals
held *incompatibilia*. There is no evidence that papal dispensations to
do so diminished in number. On the contrary, popes frequently conferred
clusters of "inferior" benefices upon their servants—curial officials,
"familiars," and other members of the Roman court—as well as upon
cardinals. We can view papal provisions of multiple lesser benefices
most clearly in two sets of circumstances: when benefices were vacant
because of death, and when popes granted "expectancies."

TABLE 2.5   MINIMUM NUMBER OF LESSER BENEFICES HELD
BY 1520-1539 CARDINALS

Number	Cardinal	Number	Cardinal
0	G. Contarini	7	A. Pucci
	A. Sanseverino		
	J. Simonetta	9	A. Spinola
	B. Guidiccioni		U. Gambara
			G. Ghinucci
1	D. Lorerio		
	C. Jacobazzi	10	J. Sadoleto
			I. II d'Este
2	A. M. Palmieri		
	P. Parisio	11	I. de' Medici
	E. Filonardi		M. Grimani
	M. Caracciolo		
	F. Fregoso	12	R. Pio
3	G. Doria	15	A. Parisani
	F. Cornaro		
	E. Gonzaga	16	G. V. Carafa
	J. Savelli		
	B. Accolti	17	G. A. Sforza
4	G. Grimaldi	28	P. Bembo
	G. Aleandro		
	N. Gaddi	64	A. Farnese
5	N. Caetani		
	P. Gonzaga		

TABLE 2.6   MINIMUM NUMBER OF LESSER BENEFICES HELD
BY 1540-1549 CARDINALS

Number	Cardinal	Number	Cardinal
0	A. Cornaro	4	D. Duranti
	P. Cecci		F. Cesi
	T. Badia		G. Morone
			F. Ferrerio
1	F. Sfondrato		
	B. Maffei	5	T. Crispo
	R. Pucci		N. Ardinghello
	M. Crescenzio		G. Verallo
	G. Acquaviva		R. Farnese
2	G. Capodiferro	8	G. Cortese
			C. Madruzzo
3	G. della Rovere		

When a prelate with extensive church property died, his possessions became the subject of immediate concern at the curia. Upon the unexpected death of Ippolito de' Medici, for example, a host of rich benefices, including Avignon, Monreale, and four abbeys, together with a great number of smaller ones, fell vacant. Papal secretary Ambrogio Ricalcati wrote about this to Rodolfo Pio, nuncio to France, on 12 August 1535:

> Our *Signore* will be able to dispose of very few of his vacancies, even though they are enormous, because Monreale remains at the nomination of the Emperor, the two abbeys in France remain at the nomination of the Most Christian King, and no one has ever had possession of the abbey at Monferrato, nor even the hope of it. I shall not write more particulars about it [now] because those little pieces which Our *Signore* is able to grant have still not been distributed. Tomorrow there will be a consistory in order to do something for many of these new cardinals who are so poor, and . . . to write to ask the Most Christian King to confer the two vacant monasteries which are in France upon the Very Reverend and Illustrious Farnese.[124]

As it turned out, Alessandro Farnese obtained only one of the French monasteries, Caen in Normandy, worth an estimated 7,000 francs per year.[125] Of the other properties left vacant through Cardinal Medici's death, Farnese acquired Monreale and Avignon with the consent of the emperor and the Most Christian King, while his grandfather, Paul III, granted him the abbey of Sts. Vincenzo and Anastasia (*Tre Fontane*), outside Rome, the abbey of Lucedio in Monferrato, and the curial office of vicechancellor.[126]

The disposition of the "little pieces" left vacant by the Medici cardinal has disappeared from the record, but other grants of plural benefices left vacant by the death of their possessor were clearly made for the purpose of enlarging revenues, "so that you can support yourself more decently."[127] Clement VII, for example, gave the benefices left by a Jacopo Cardello to Cardinal Agostino Spinola on 4 December 1530, properties which brought 200 ducats of gold annually. The papal brief spelled out the indulgence for *incompatibilia*. Spinola could keep these benefices,

> together with St. Cyriaci in Termis, his cardinalate title, and also [the bishoprics of] Perugia and Savona over which he presides through apostolic disposition, and also whatever other churches, monasteries, priorates, preceptories, canonicates, prebends, dignities, and other ecclesiastical benefices with or without care [of souls], secular or regular of whatever order, which he possesses in title or *in commendam* or in any other manner or which he shall possess in the future, and also annual pensions which he collects [now] and shall collect in the future, to be held, ruled, and governed.[128]

With a similar indulgence, in January 1535, Paul III gave Ascanio Parisani eleven benefices in the dioceses of Pisa and Volterra with a total annual income of 400 ducats of gold *della camera*, benefices which were vacant because of the deaths of the two men.[129]

More frequently, these grants fail to specify a sum and simply name the properties in question. Thus, the four benefices bestowed upon Lorenzo Pucci in July 1527 may or may not have represented a substantial increase in his income; they were certainly pluralistic.[130] During the following year, Clement VII grouped together eleven benefices in the Spanish dioceses of Osma, Badajoz, Toledo, Cuenca, and Oviedo, vacancies left by four defunct Spaniards, and gave them to his relative, Giovanni Salviati.[131] Similarly, Nicolò Ridolfi in effect inherited the church properties of his late brother Cosimo in 1529—three parish churches and a monastery located in the dioceses of Tropea, Rome, and Brescia (that is, in southern, central, and northern Italy).[132] Not surprisingly, Alessandro Farnese seems to have acquired the largest clusters of inferior benefices: twenty-one parish churches and other benefices in the dioceses of Pisa and Lucca in 1536 and no fewer than thirty in the kingdom of Portugal in 1547.[133]

The years of reform did nothing to alter the practice of gathering together packages of benefices and conferring them as a whole. The last brief concerning this was dated 31 March 1560, and it involved two abbeys and three parish churches in the Spanish dioceses of Toledo, La Mancha, and Cartagena.[134] If anything, this practice probably increased with the years. And when vacancies were in short supply, the popes resorted to "expectative graces."

"Expectancies" or "expectative graces" were papal grants of benefices that were already occupied. Expectancies had long been condemned, at least since the Third Lateran Council in 1179.[135] The authors of the *Consilium* of 1537 also deplored the practice, and for reasons identical to those of the fathers in 1179: "The occasion is given to desire another's death and to hear of it with pleasure."[136] One can indeed detect a note of anticipation, at least, in comments about health. Rodolfo Pio reported from France in 1536 that the king had promised Ippolito II d'Este "a good abbey and the bishopric of Lyon, which would amount to 15,000 francs a year, if he who possesses them, who is very ill, dies."[137]

Despite the prohibitions and criticisms, despite regarding them with dislike, each pope from the time of Leo X at least through the pontificate of Julius III granted expectancies for large sums of money. Paul III decreed against the reservation of future vacancies in a bull entitled *De non acceptandis beneficiis generaliter reservatis,* and both Clement VII and Julius III revoked such graces.[138] We can safely assume that the strict reformer Adrian VI was likewise opposed. Nevertheless, each pope continued to use them.

These indulgences, whether granted for a single benefice or several, were confined to a particular geographical area, and they always cite a specific sum of money. Grants for smaller amounts usually restricted the bearer to possession of inferior benefices in one or more dioceses, but indulgences for large sums applied only to benefices worth at least 200 ducats per year. This latter provision served to set aside the small properties—those bringing less than 200 ducats—for purposes of patronage.[139] Occasionally a time limit was attached, and any benefices already reserved to popes, living cardinals, or their familiars were specifically excluded.

The brief written in favor of Pier Paolo Parisio in February 1538 contains the standard formula. Parisio, doctor of both laws and auditor of the camera apostolica, was still two years from the cardinalate dignity at the time, and the indulgence was therefore among the more modest of this type.[140] Paul III therewith reserved for Parisio "one, two, three, four, or however many ecclesiastical benefices with and without care, secular and regular of whatever order, even Cistercian or *Humiliati,* of which the fruits, rents, and produce together do not exceed 300 ducats of gold *della camera,* according to the common estimate of the annual value, existing in the cities and dioceses of Ravenna, Reggio, and Modena."[141] In 1541 the same pope reserved future vacancies for Agostino Trivulzio for the same amount of 300 ducats.[142] Most of the grants, however, stipulate much larger sums, varying from 1,000 to 10,000 ducats in gold.

The realization of any profit from this generosity was uncertain, for, as critics contended, it depended upon the health of the beneficiaries of the territory in question. There was also the danger of granting conflicting or overlapping rights. Two cardinals from Genoa provide an example. Girolamo Grimaldi had an expectancy from the duchy of Milan to the sum of 2,500 ducats and another reserving lesser benefices in the duchy of Savoy and the county of Geneva in the amount of 2,000 ducats. Clement VII, who had revoked these indulgences, was persuaded to revalidate them in March 1533, because "as we understand, you have not yet been able to collect any of the fruits."[143] Then, in June of the same year, the pope granted Grimaldi's compatriot Girolamo Doria an expectancy for 1,500 ducats in lesser benefices, also in Savoy and

Geneva.[144] The succeeding pope, Paul III, broadened Doria's indulgence in January 1535 with an expectancy of 2,000 ducats from the territory of Genoa.[145] More complications arose when Cardinal Grimaldi, upon being named legate *de latere* to the dominion of Genoa on 21 May 1535, received the right to confer vacant benefices in his legation, a right which the pope extended four days later to include even benefices that might be reserved to others, "as long as they are not reserved by reason of familiarity of His Holiness or of living cardinals."[146] This meant that the two men simultaneously had indulgences allowing them to take possession of vacancies in large numbers in Savoy and Geneva, while at the same time Doria had the right to 2,000 ducats of vacancies in Genoa and Grimaldi had the right to confer the same properties upon persons of his choice. The records do not reveal whether or not the two encountered differences in regard to Savoy and Geneva, but the potential for confusion was certainly there. As for the Genoese properties, there was no necessary cause for friction because Doria was a living cardinal. A possible conflict was nevertheless perceived, apparently, because Paul III reconfirmed Doria's indulgence on 6 June. "He told the Most Reverend Lord Cardinal Grimaldi that he did not wish to prejudice the favor he had given to the Most Reverend Doria," noted the secretary.[147]

Other evidence strengthens the suspicion that these indulgences carried more promise than substance. We do not know what profit the Venetian cardinals Marino Grimani and Francesco Cornaro derived from their 5,000-ducat expectancy in 1530, but other Venetian grants indicate small return.[148] In March 1547, for example, Paul III gave Durante Duranti an expectancy for benefices worth 1,000 ducats in the Veneto. More than three years later, however, Julius III reconfirmed the same indulgence, a fact that suggests the money had not been obtained.[149] Similarly, Julius III reconfirmed an earlier 1,000-ducat grant from Venice to Bernardino Maffei and Daniele Barbaro in 1553, because they had realized "little, if any, fruit from the graces and letters."[150] Gian Vincenzo Carafa was even less successful in the kingdom of Naples. Leo X gave him future vacancies there to the sum of 10,000 ducats in return for a loan to the apostolic camera. Clement VII confirmed the grant, and Paul III wrote to Naples on Carafa's behalf in 1535 and again in 1537. By the latter date, at least sixteen years after the original indulgence, Carafa had received benefices worth only 1,000 ducats.[151] Perhaps the license to take possession of a number of inferior benefices in the Neapolitan dioceses of Teramo, Cava, Santa Agata, and Caserta, dated 20 February 1540, was a partial fulfillment of Carafa's claim.[152]

Indeed, the reservation of future vacancies was a clumsy and uncertain method of enhancing incomes. The Council of Trent restricted expectancies in 1563, and modern canon law abolished them altogether.[153]

The fathers at Trent also forbade pluralism of any benefices with the care of souls in 1563, but, as we shall see, cardinals and their servants were granted special privileges. Throughout our period, cardinals continued to gather lesser benefices in large numbers.

PENSIONS

The annual pension provided another means for tapping the wealth of the church. Cardinals drew pensions from a number of sources, among them the central treasuries of the church—the camera apostolica and, in increasing numbers as the years passed, the dataria.[154] Ecclesiastical benefices, however, remained the primary sources of monetary pensions. Further, because the pensioner had no responsibility whatever for the administration of the sacred office from which his money derived, pensions were true sinecures.

But was there a question of pluralism, and the consequent danger of mortal sin, in accepting multiple pensions? Did a pension in fact constitute an ecclesiastical benefice? The church treated them as such in the sixteenth century, and multiple pensions were a target of the *Consilium* of 1537:

Another abuse, when benefices are bestowed or turned over to others, has crept in in connection with the arrangement of payments from the incomes of these benefices. Indeed, the person resigning the benefice often reserves all the income for himself. In such cases care must be taken that payments can be reserved for no other reason and with no other justification than for alms which ought to be given for pious uses and for the needy. For income is joined to the benefice as the body to the soul. By its very nature then it belongs to him who holds the benefice so that he can live from it respectably according to his station and can at the same time support the expenses for divine worship and for the upkeep of the church and other religious buildings, and so that he may expend what remains for pious uses. For this is the nature of the income of these benefices.[155]

Some of the reformers at the curia, then, regarded the reservation of pensions as an abusive practice, and papal briefs indicate that the popes of the sixteenth century concurred. Indulgences for pluralism thus included pensions among the properties prelates were allowed to hold simultaneously. The language of one of Girolamo Doria's dispensations, granted in 1533, is typical:

together with St. Thomas in Parione, your cardinalate denomination, and also all other cathedrals and monasteries and other ecclesiastical benefices, with or without care, secular or regular of whatever order, which you hold or shall hold in the future in title, or *in commendam,* or in any other manner, through whatever apostolic concessions and dispensations, *and also any ecclesiastical fruits and annual pensions from similar fruits which have been reserved and assigned to you or shall be reserved and assigned to you which you receive and shall receive in the future, whatever, however many, and of whatever quality they be, to be held, ruled, and governed.*[156]

In addition, as with other ecclesiastical benefices, pensioners required dispensations for illegitimacy. Giulio Grimani, for example, needed an indulgence for defect of birth before he was eligible to collect the pension assigned to him at the death of his father, Marco Grimani, the patriarch of Aquileia.[157] Even as recently as the late eighteenth century, pensions were viewed as true ecclesiastical benefices: "Another is sometimes called a *Pension,* which is the right to take part of the fruits of an alien [i.e. one to which the pensioner did not hold title] Benefice; and if it is conferred to anyone in perpetual title, it is a true Ecclesiastical Benefice."[158] Pensions in the sixteenth century were not only "perpetual" or granted for life; most of them were transferable to the heirs of the pensioner. Reformers had a right to be concerned. Income, by nature, may have been "joined to the benefice as the body to the soul," but it was diverted from it with increasing ease.

We have seen that a prelate had several options available when he ceded a benefice. In regard to its income, he could (1) keep all or a percentage, usually half, of the fruits, (2) assign himself a fixed annual pension from the fruits, or (3) assign a fixed annual pension to his successor and keep the remainder of the fruits for himself. He could also, of course, assign pensions to his relatives and retainers.[159]

Resigning cardinals reserved all or part of the incomes of their benefices with some regularity between 1492 and 1563 (fig. 2.5). The sudden rise in the numbers of such reservations between 1520 and 1529 probably resulted from the "Great Promotion" of cardinals on 1 July 1517. Pope Leo X, angered at an alleged plot against his life which he attributed to Cardinal Alfonso Petrucci, packed the Sacred College by creating an unprecedented thirty-one cardinals, twenty-seven of them Italians. However politically advisable this action may have been, it caused a fiscal crisis in the curia. Individual shares of the common and petty service taxes declined precipitously. Nicolò Fieschi, for example, collected 1,489 ducats from the camera of the college in 1517, but only

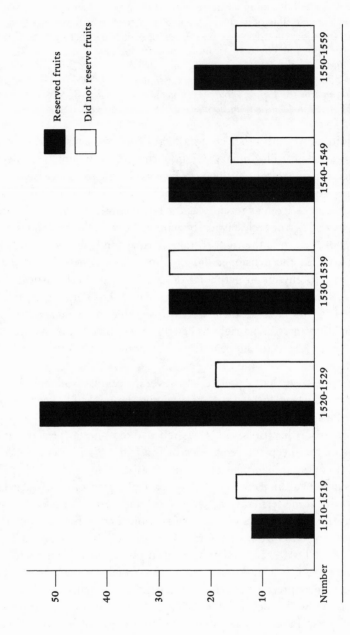

FIGURE 2.5   RESIGNATIONS IN WHICH CARDINALS RESERVED THE FRUITS, BY DECADES

Incomes from church benefices were used, then, as a matter of course, to support courtiers, both lay and ecclesiastical. Even when we confine the investigation here to the revenues of Italian cardinals, the number of such pensions is significant, and so are the amounts of money involved.

The decade from 1520 to 1529 saw a multiplicity of pensions from "alien" benefices in Italy to unrelated cardinals (fig. 2.9). Again, the "Great Promotion" of 1517 was responsible. Popes were hard pressed to find sufficient revenue to support the new cardinals as befitted their rank. Titles to benefices were not divisible, of course; one diocese, for example, could not have two bishops. Incomes, on the other hand, were clearly divisible by means of pensions, and popes tried to distribute

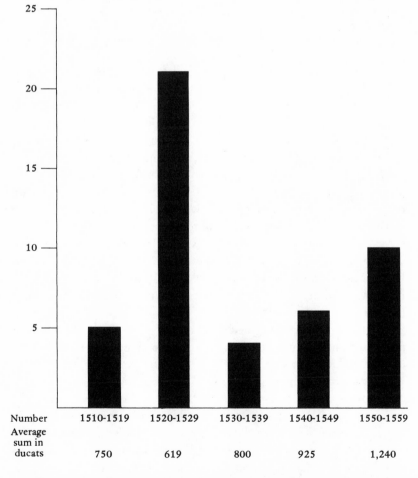

| Number | 1510-1519 | 1520-1529 | 1530-1539 | 1540-1549 | 1550-1559 |
| Average sum in ducats | 750 | 619 | 800 | 925 | 1,240 |

FIGURE 2.9   PENSIONS FROM ALIEN BENEFICES: ITALIAN BENEFICES

TABLE 2.7   CARDINALS OF THE GREAT PROMOTION AND
PENSIONS FROM ALIEN ITALIAN BENEFICES: 1517-1529

Cardinal	Amount of Annual Pension (ducats)
D. Jacobazzi	1,200
	1,300
G. de Cupis	500
L. Campeggio	500
F. Orsini	1,000
	500
	1,000
G. Piccolomini	800
E. da Viterbo	400
E. Rangone	1,500
F. Pisani	500 and ½ the fruits of Hvar
C. Numai	1,500
A. Trivulzio	400

available properties equitably. They therefore conferred the title of a vacant benefice to one new cardinal and a pension from the same property to another. So Adrian VI disposed of the benefices left vacant by the death of the bishop of Mondovi, Urbano de Maiolano, in May 1523. He commended a monastery in the diocese of Lyon to a veteran cardinal, Antonio Maria del Monte, and named the duke of Savoy's candidate to the episcopal church of Mondovi. The remainder of the property, however, he divided among some cardinals of the promotion of 1517. A monastery near Vercelli went to Bonifacio Ferrerio with a pension of 1,200 ducats from its fruits for Domenico Jacobazzi; a monastery in Turin went to Giovanni Battista Pallavicino with a pension of 500 ducats from its fruits for Giandomenico de Cupis; and Lorenzo Campeggio received a pension of 500 ducats from the fruits of the bishopric of Mondovi.[175] Examples of such conferrals can be multiplied (table 2.7).

Instances of this practice declined between 1530 and 1547, but then pensions from Italian benefices for unrelated cardinals increased in both number and average sum. Indeed, after 1550, the average pension was worth twice the average pension for 1520-1529. Alessandro Farnese's consistorial activities suggest a growing dependence upon monetary pensions. On 9 November 1549, the day before Pope Paul III died, Ranuccio Farnese resigned the archdiocese of Naples in favor of Gian Pietro Carafa, and the pope "reserved to me [Alessandro Farnese] an annual pension of 1,000 ducats of gold *della camera* from the fruits of the archepiscopal table of Naples, free and exempt, which, together with the other annual pensions perhaps assigned to them . . . do not exceed half the fruits."[176] The pope then conferred the bishopric of Cremona and the monastery of San Bartolomeo near Ferrara, properties of the late Benedetto Accolti, and reserved pensions of 1,500 ducats from Cremona and half the fruits of the abbey for Cardinal Farnese. The monastery was worth some 12,000 ducats per year, so Farnese's revenue had increased by about 8,500 ducats during a single consistory. In addition, Farnese had the right to transfer these pensions to persons of his choice—a powerful weapon on the eve of a conclave.[177]

Pensions from alien benefices "beyond the mountains" also attest to the increasing importance of these subventions for Italian cardinals. We saw earlier that the Italians on our list held fewer and fewer non-Italian bishoprics as the century progressed. What they substituted, apparently, were pensions from non-Italian benefices (fig. 2.10). The Florentine cardinals Soderini, Salviati, and Ridolfi received substantial subsidies from French benefices between 1520 and 1529, the largest being 2,000

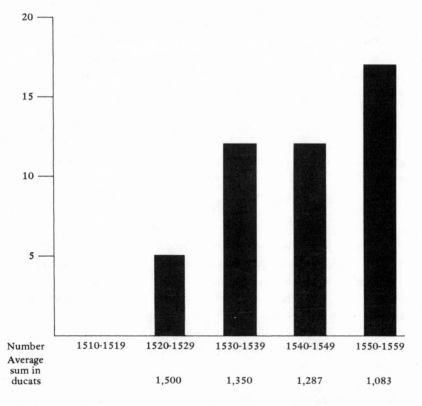

Number	1510-1519	1520-1529	1530-1539	1540-1549	1550-1559
Average sum in ducats		1,500	1,350	1,287	1,083

FIGURE 2.10 PENSIONS FROM ALIEN BENEFICES: NON-ITALIAN BENEFICES

ducats to Ridolfi from the diocese of Vaison.[178] These were probably connected to the pro-French policy of their relative, Clement VII, during the same decade. Later, in 1541, Gian Pietro Carafa obtained a pension of 250 ducats from two French monasteries. The last French grants were much larger: 1,500 ducats to Giandomenico de Cupis in 1550, 1,200 to Tiberio Crispo in 1551, and 500 to Alessandro Farnese in 1557.[179]

The remainder of pensions to our cardinals from non-Italian alien benefices came from the Iberian peninsula—two from Portugal, all others from Spain. With the exception of the three French pensions just mentioned, in fact, all non-Italian pensions were Spanish after 1550. These graces may have been a response to the strong aversion with which the Spanish episcopate regarded the nomination of non-Spaniards to Spanish benefices. The Spanish delegation at Trent demanded a halt to this practice in 1551, and in 1554 the first of the Spanish *gravamina* submitted to Rome asked "that the benefices of Spain not be given in title or *in commendam* or in any other way, even in confidence, to *foreigners*."[180] The emperor and the popes apparently deferred to these sentiments. After Ercole Gonzaga resigned Tarazona in 1546, only one Italian cardinal on our list, Girolamo Doria, continued to possess a bishopric in Spain.[181] The assigning of pensions from Spanish benefices was perhaps a less public way of supporting Italian cardinals.

Charles V used pensions to reward his courtiers in Spain; he also used them to favor his clients at the Roman curia. Thus, on 27 December 1520 he rewarded two cardinals of the 1517 promotion by nominating Alessandro Cesarini to the bishopric of Pamplona and reserving a pension of 2,500 ducats from the same diocese for Pompeo Colonna, both of whose families were strong imperial advocates in Rome.[182] After the imperialist victory in Genoa in 1528, the emperor favored cardinal members of families supporting his cause in that city, granting pensions of 2,000 ducats to Girolamo Doria, nephew of the celebrated admiral, and 3,500 ducats to Girolamo Grimaldi.[183] The impulse behind the 1,000 ducats in pensions awarded to Alessandro Cesarini in 1530, however, was of a different, nonpolitical nature. On 1 September 1530, Clement VII gave Cesarini the regress to the Augustinian abbey of Monte Aragona in the diocese of Huesca, Spain.[184] On the next day, Cesarini received two pensions from Spanish benefices. The cardinal recipro-cated:

The same Cardinal Cesarini *referente*, whereas His Imperial Majesty has nomi-nated the Most Reverend Cesarini to one pension of 500 ducats from the fruits of the episcopal table of the church of Segorbe, and another, also of 500 ducats, from the fruits of the episcopal table of Huesca, because of this, and also because he wishes to please His Imperial Majesty, the Most Reverend Cardinal ceded into the hands of His Holiness the lawsuit and contentions and also all of the rights he possesses in the rule and administration of the monastery of Monte Aragona in the diocese of Huesca.[185]

The pensions, then, constituted an out-of-court settlement of a property dispute. This incident provides a clue to the nature of patron-client relationships between the emperor and his Italian supporters. Neither Cesarini nor the pope behaved in an obsequious manner in this affair; here there was money involved.

The list of Italian cardinals who collected annual pensions from Spanish benefices in the years following 1537 contains surprises. First, most of the men were less clearly partisans of the emperor. The family of Uberto Gambara of Brescia was certainly connected with the imperial forces; his brother Brunoro was a *condottiere* for Charles V, and he himself had started his career as a soldier.[186] Other pensioners seem more cosmopolitan, however, and include papal relatives, jurists, diplomats, curial careerists, and one monk, Dionisio Lorerio, general of the Servites. Although all were in the emperor's favor, it is doubtful that they considered themselves his clients. The second surprising element is the sum of money these men drew from Spain. Cristoforo Jacobazzi's pension was a modest 400 ducats, but others, including Francesco Cornaro, Gasparo Contarini, Uberto Gambara, Pier Paolo Parisio, Dionisio Lorerio, Francesco Sfondrato, Rodolfo Pio, and Durante Duranti, each received between 700 and 1,000 ducats annually.[187] Jacopo Savelli and Giovanni Morone did even better, being awarded several pensions between 1542 and 1555 that amounted to 2,000 ducats each.[188] And, aside from Gambara, none of these pensioners was necessarily an adherent of imperial, or, in the latter years, of Spanish interests.

The most highly rewarded among Italian cardinals was an avowed imperialist. Ercole Gonzaga of Mantua had been French in sympathy early in his career, but he altered his allegiance in 1532 at the insistence of his brother Duke Federico of Mantua, who desired imperial investiture of his father-in-law's state of Monferrato.[189] Profit from Spanish benefices came slowly at first. When Charles V named him bishop of Tarazona in 1537, he even limited Gonzaga's income from the diocese to 500 ducats per year.[190] By January 1545, however, Gonzaga was "Protector of the kingdoms of Castile and Leon," and by April 1546 he was "Protector of Spain."[191] Pensions followed: 3,000 ducats from Badajoz in 1545, 2,000 from Seville in 1546, 2,000 from Siguenza in 1546, and 2,000 from Burgos in 1550. Moreover, the cardinal had the right to transfer half of the 1546 pensions to a son of his brother Ferrante. Gonzaga retained the favor of the emperor's son: Philip II of Spain confirmed the pension from Siguenza in 1560.[192] The cardinal of Mantua thus collected at least 9,000 ducats every year from Spanish bishoprics alone.

How much political control in Rome did these favors bring to lay rulers? While it is beyond the scope of this study to evaluate the political forces in motion during the period, a few words may be appropriate here. Italian cardinals, no matter what their allegiances to crowned heads beyond the mountains, continued to act and react as Italians, and as Italian princes at that. A firm imperialist such as Alessandro Cesarini did not hesitate to challenge the emperor when a question of personal income was involved. Still less were Italians ready to permit interference in family matters. Ercole Gonzaga himself provides an example, in spite of his annual 9,000 ducats from Spain, of personal independence from his imperial patron. When Charles V demanded that Ercole's nephew Lodovico Gonzaga leave the court and service of the French king, Henry II, in the spring of 1550, he had clearly overstepped propriety. The cardinal wrote immediately to his brother Ferrante and instructed him to tell the emperor to tend to his own business: "Although I am a good servant to the emperor, as everyone knows and as I have demonstrated whenever it has been necessary, nevertheless, I do not want His Majesty to be able to command me in matters which are improper, . . . especially when the affair involves the future income of a ward, as this boy is, who is my nephew and under my guardianship."[193] Lodovico Gonzaga remained at the French court; Ercole Gonzaga continued to collect his Spanish pensions.

Political implications aside, the statistics show that Italian cardinals became ever more dependent upon moneys from "alien" benefices. These practices did not cease in 1563 (fig. 2.11). In fact, in the decades following the last sessions of the Council of Trent, popes fell into the habit of reserving large sums in pensions, mostly from bishoprics and monasteries in Spain and Portugal, for "persons to be named."[194] Pope Pius IV himself, the promulgator of the Tridentine decrees, made such a reservation from his deathbed. On 8 December 1565, the pope assigned pensions of 10,000 ducats—5,000 from the archdiocese of Ravenna and 5,000 from the diocese of Bologna—for persons to be named by his cardinal nephews, Mark Sittich d'Altemps and Carlo Borromeo.[195]

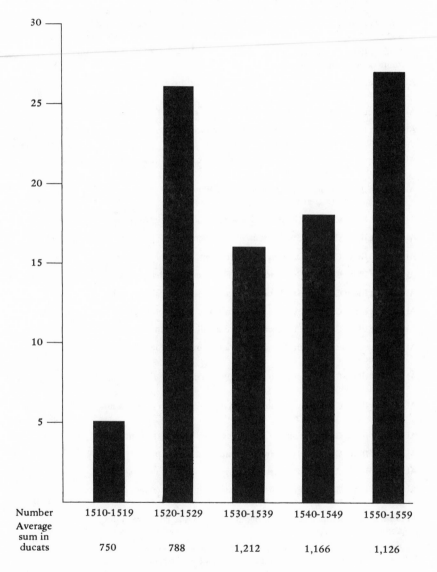

FIGURE 2.11   PENSIONS FROM ALIEN BENEFICES: ITALIAN AND
                          NON-ITALIAN BENEFICES COMBINED

TABLE 2.8   EXPENDITURES OF THE DATARY FOR ORDINARY
PROVISIONS OF CARDINALS: MARCH 1554
(from Vat lat 10605, fols. 26r-28v)

Al Rmo et Illmo Cardinal di Carpi scudi ottanta d'oro in oro et ottanta de moneta cioe di Giulii X per scudo per la sua provisione del presente mese—	152.80
Al Rmo el Illmo Cardinal Sta Croce scudi cento doro et cento di moneta per detto conto—	190.100
Al Rmo et Illmo Cardinal Morone scudi cinquanta doro et cinquanta di moneta per detto conto—	95.50
Al detto scudi cinquanta d'oro per la ricompensa sopra la Thes[a] di Camerino—	50
Al Rmo et Illmo Cardinal Verallo ducati cento d'oro in oro di Camera per la provisione della Sig[ra] di Justitia per el presente mese—	109
Al detto scudi cinquanta d'oro et cinquanta di moneta per la sua solita provisione del presente mese—	95.50
Al Rmo et Illmo Cardinal de Medici scudi cinquanta d'oro et cinquanta di moneta per detto conto—	95.50
Al Rmo et Illmo Cardinal Crispo scudi dugento d'oro per detto conto—	200
Al Rmo et Illmo Cardinal Sta Prasseda scudi dugento simili per detto conto—	200
Al Rmo et Illmo Cardinal di Perugia scudi trecento simili per detto conto—	300
Al Rmo et Illmo Cardinal Saracino scudi cento simili per detto conto—	100
Al Rmo et Illmo Cardinal San Vitale scudi cento simili per detto conto—	100
Al Rmo et Illmo Cardinal Messina scudi cento simili per detto conto—	100
Al Rmo et Illmo Cardinal Puteo scudi cento simili per detto conto—	100
Al detto scudi cinquanta simili et cinquanta di moneta per la revisione de brevi secreti di N. S.—	95.50
Al Rmo et Illmo Cardinal di Fano scudi Dugento d'oro per la sua provisione del presente mese—	200
Al Rmo et Illmo Cardinal Mignanello scudi cento d'oro in oro per la sua provisione del presente mese—	100
Al Rmo et Illmo Cardinal Pighino scudi cento simili per detto conto—	100
Al Rmo et Illmo Cardinal San Clemente scudi cento simili per detto conto—	100
Al Rmo et Illmo Cardinal d'Imola scudi dugento simili per detto conto—	200
Al Rmo et Illmo Cardinal Poli scudi cinquanta simili et cinquanta di moneta per detto conto—	95.50
Al detto scudi sessanta d'oro per la ricompensa sopra la Thesaureria di Camerino—	60
Al detto scudi cinquecento simili per sua provisione come Legato de latere ultra montes per un mese commiciando alli VI del presente—	500
Al Rmo et Illmo Cardinal Savello scudi cento di moneta per la ricompensa della pensione Napolitana per il presente mese—	90.100
Al Rmo et Illmo Cardinal Sermoneta scudi cinquanta d'oro et cinquanta di moneta per la sua provisione del presente mese—	95.50
Al Rmo et Illmo Cardinal Simoncello scudi dugento d'oro per detto conto—	200
Al Rmo et Illmo Cardinal de Nobili scudi dugento simili per detto conto—	200

Cardinals tended not to distinguish between pensions that derived from ecclesiastical benefices and those from other sources. Early in the period, for example, Pompeo Colonna owed Nicolò Ridolfi an annual pension of 1,000 ducats from his office of the vicechancery, an administrative position. Ridolfi, in turn, owed 1,000 ducats per year to Cristoforo Numai from his archbishopric of Florence. On 4 September 1524, the pope confirmed an agreement among the three cardinals which eliminated the middleman: Ridolfi and Numai both consented to the extinction of their pensions, and Colonna promised to pay the 1,000 ducats from the office of the vicechancellor directly to Numai. They had simplified matters, and the source of the funds was less important than the amount.[196] Similarly, when Jacopo Savelli agreed to the cancellation of his pension of 1,000 ducats from Naples in 1552, he was assigned a fresh one in the same amount to be paid from the dataria, "so that he should not suffer too much loss from the cancellation."[197] Jacopo Sadoleto likewise failed to distinguish differences between the two kinds of properties. Writing to Alessandro Farnese on 21 January 1543, Sadoleto asked for a pension from the legation of Bologna. "For it certainly seems to me," he said, "that I cannot maintain my status with dignity with less. I cannot have at Rome an income of more than 1,700 *scudi* in all, because even the pension from [the bishopric of] Verona . . . I have resigned to two of my nephews, upright and well-bred."[198] Moneys from the sacred property of the church appear to have been interchangeable with those from its secular offices.

To be sure, funds from the dataria were used to supplement the incomes of increasing numbers of cardinals during our period. Monthly stipends of 100 to 200 *scuti* of gold were paid by the datary to two cardinals on a regular basis under Clement VII, to twelve cardinals in the later years of Paul III, and to twenty-two cardinals by the pontificate of Julius III (table 2.8).[199] Pensions from the dataria or other offices were additions to and not substitutes for pensions from ecclesiastical benefices, however.

Indeed, the utility of pensions was manifest. Unlike actual title to benefices, pensions were largely a private matter, conferred in secret consistories with no ceremonial attached. If they were free and exempt, they were not subject to tax; if they were transferable to others, they were instruments of patronage; if they were transferable to successors, they became part of the pensioner's family inheritance. Thus pensions tended to separate from their origins in sacred office, with attendant priestly duties, and to disppear within the personal estates of the cardinals.

Pius V's assessment for the *donativo* for the war against the Turk in 1571 provides evidence of this development. Giovanni Morone collected at least 4,500 ducats in pensions from church benefices, but he declared none as taxable income and only 4,000 *scuti* of revenue not subject to tax. Giulio della Rovere, with at least 4,900 ducats in pensions, declared only his 1,000 ducats from Cremona as taxable, along with 13,000 *scuti* not subject to tax.[200] The financial declaration of Jacopo Savelli exemplifies this trend even more vividly. With at least 7,300 ducats in pensions, he listed only one—200 *scuti di moneta* from the bishopric of Catanzaro—as taxable. He also declared only 4,000 *scuti* of nontaxable income. Sixteen years later, however, when he wrote his last will and testament, Cardinal Savelli included as part of his personal property pensions from the bishoprics and archbishoprics of Canea, Coria, Naples, Capua, Benevento, Gubbio, and seven abbeys in addition to the Catanzaro pension. His estate was estimated at his death as bringing in some 40,000 *scuti* of annual revenue.[201]

Finally, Alessandro Farnese listed no taxable pensions in 1571, but declared 60,000 *scuti* not subject to tax, and a total income of 76,750 *scuti*.[202] Then in 1587, two years before his death, Farnese grew concerned over the state of his immortal soul and invited a Jesuit priest to his villa at Caprarola to discuss his money. At that time, Farnese estimated his total annual income at 120,000 ducats of gold. He and the Jesuit agreed at once that 50,000 ducats of this belonged to his personal patrimony, even though it included money from church offices and pensions from ecclesiastical benefices. The next question was how much of the remaining 70,000 ducats Farnese could keep without incurring the sin of pluralism. The Jesuit returned to Rome and consulted expert authorities on the matter. At length, considering the cardinal's lofty position as a grandson of Pope Paul III, the priest determined that 40,000 ducats should suffice for his annual needs. Farnese must donate the other 30,000 to pious works "under the penalty of being declared in mortal sin."[203]

In the matter of pensions, the major concern of the reform commission in 1537 had been the plight of the benefice itself, deprived of its income. The records of the period validate this concern. When Paolo Emilio Cesi acquired the affluent abbey of Chiaravalle in Milan in 1524, he found that he owed a total of eight annual "portions" of 1,000 ducats each in addition to "the remaining ancient pensions" from its reputed annual income of 12,000 ducats.[204] A monastery in Geneva suffered "many pensions which can take away everything" in 1529.[205] Lorenzo

Pucci, having reserved to himself all the fruits of the bishopric of Capaccio in 1523, discovered to his consternation that the diocese bore "so many annual pensions . . . that they absorb all the fruits of the same church."[206] In 1530, he therefore persuaded Pope Clement VII to force the pensioners to pay him, Cardinal Pucci, delinquent papal taxes on the property "because of the [fiscal] damage he has experienced in recent years."[207] Even as late as 1550, pensions were assigned that could legally exhaust the entire revenue of a benefice. When Julius III disposed of the bishopric of Vicenza in that year, he granted a pension from it of 1,000 ducats to Giovanni Morone and another of 1,800 ducats to Giulio della Rovere, "even if other pensions exist which are assigned to others from them [the fruits of Vicenza] and exceed half and absorb and include them all."[208]

The conferral of multiple pensions continued to be a problem throughout the century, although the later reformers focused on the pensioner himself and not the benefice. Alessandro Farnese's qualms about his wealth testify to this concern, and two papal bulls from late in the century underline the sacred origin of the money. Pius V, in 1571, ruled that all pensioners must recite a divine office of the Holy Virgin daily, and Sixtus V, in his bull *Cum sacrosanctum* of 1585, required pensioners to wear habits and be tonsured.[209] Eventually, however, the problem of pensions proved to be insoluble. According to the revised canon law, personal pensions are *not* ecclesiastical benefices.[210]

Qui altari servit de altari vivat, wrote Cardinal Sadoleto in 1543—"he who serves the altar should live by the altar."[211] The evidence shows that cardinals continued to do just that. Costs of living in Rome rose during the century, to be sure, and so did the number of cardinals. As Jean Delumeau has shown, however, the high clergy's standards of living did not decline, but rather, if anything, rose with the years.[212] As early as March 1546, the legates at Trent had cautioned Rome about this. "It seems," they wrote, "that two things about the court at Rome rob it of credit and scandalize the world: first, its avarice, and second, its pomp and luxury."[213] Pomp and luxury were central to life at the Roman court by 1546, however, and the social needs of cardinalate families were ever more pressing. Both Delumeau and Pecchiai remark on the inflation in dowries, for example, from 1,500 to 3,500 ducats at the beginning of the century to an astonishing 40,000 to 50,000 by 1576.[214] Roman families were constrained to build huge palaces and maintain luxurious coaches in which to proceed through the city on the newly constructed broad avenues.[215] The tone of life in the eternal city may have been more somber during the second half of the century, but conspicuous consumption and display were on the rise.[216]

The incomes of individual cardinals from benefices also rose, from a total of about 305,000 ducats of gold in 1523 to the million *scuti* of gold that appear on the tax assessment of 1571—and the tax list, as we have seen, represented only part of the actual incomes of the cardinals.[217] Princes of the church were expected to live like princes. Indulgences and dispensations continued to flow, "so that you may keep your state more decently according to the cardinalate sublimity, and more easily bear the burden of the expenses which you must, of necessity, continually undergo."[218] Even though the reformers of 1537 had advised the pope that cardinals should "be a law for others" and not be allowed to transgress the law, cardinals, along with their families and servants, did have special graces and continued to enjoy them.[219]

We saw at the beginning of this chapter that the servants of the church regarded ecclesiastical benefices as sources of income rather than sacred trusts, and that this attitude contributed to the problem of pluralism in office and the trafficking in benefices, a habit Denys Hay called one of the "oddities" of the church in Italy.[220] The years of reform did nothing to change this attitude. The public and visible scandal of cardinals holding plural bishoprics was successfully halted, but the need for incomes, ever larger incomes, endured. Thus the popes and cardinals resorted to less visible, less public methods of gathering moneys from sacred offices. Lesser benefices, many of which did not require residence, to be sure, continued to be collected in large numbers. A Tridentine decree forbade the holding of incompatible benefices in 1563, but papal dispensations easily robbed the order of its strength.[221] Pensions in increasing sums supplemented cardinals' incomes to make up for the losses that must have resulted from the restriction in bishoprics after 1547, pensions derived from resigned properties or from "alien" benefices. Regresses continued to be reserved.

Reform in the area of pluralism in the sixteenth century thus remained largely cosmetic. Indeed, the situation of the benefices from which pensions were drawn may even have worsened with the decades, for the cardinals collecting the moneys from them had no obligations whatever toward them. The wholesale reservation of pensions for "persons to be named by the pope"—particularly from archbishoprics, bishoprics, and monasteries in Spain and Portugal—took place *after* the closing of the Council of Trent, and rendered the conferral of such moneys even less visible. The rulings of the strict popes Pius V and Sixtus V on pensioners attest to a change in reform thought through the years. Whereas the authors of the *Consilium* of 1537 had concentrated upon the needs of the benefice and deplored the practice of separating its income from the title-holder by means of reservations of fruits, the later popes felt that all that was necessary was pious behavior on the pensioner's part. The clash between the monetary needs of the prelates and the ideals of the reformers had forced an alteration in those ideals. Practices that had seemed scandalous in the early years had become accepted as normal by the last years of the century. Revised canon law faced the matter squarely—and simply changed the rules: personal pensions are not defined as ecclesiastical benefices and neither are properties held *in commendam*. Churchmen are still enjoined from keeping income in excess of need, but cardinals of the Holy Roman Church are exempt from this law.

3
The Alienation of Incomes and Wealth

The management of the church's wealth and the incomes from church property both fell into the hands of laymen at a steady rate during these years. The habit of viewing ecclesiastical benefices as sources of private income fostered this alienation. Two principal methods were used: rentals and last wills. Both required special dispensation by the pope in the sixteenth century, and neither was new. In the first type of alienation, popes granted licenses to prelates that enabled them to rent out ecclesiastical benefices for a fixed period of time at a fixed sum of money. In the second type, popes granted licenses that allowed prelates to include incomes from church property in their last wills and testaments. Both kinds of alienation came under attack by reformers during our period, but neither was substantially altered.

BENEFICE-FARMING

"At present," wrote the Venetian Marino Sanuto in 1497, "the Church of God is sold for money to the highest bidder."[1] The blatant simony that characterized the pontificate of Alexander VI and provoked Sanuto's comment seems largely to have disappeared in succeeding years. The atmosphere of venality at the Roman court remained, however, and, if the church of God ceased to be for sale between 1497 and 1563, it was certainly for rent. All sorts of church property—tax revenues, the alum mines, the salt factories, the "venal offices" of the curia, and any other income-bearing institution in the possession of the church— were rented out, mortgaged, pawned to merchants.[2] During the conclaves of 1521 and 1555, the cardinals even mortgaged the pontifical miter and the papal tiara in return for loans from bankers.[3] It is not surprising, then, to find individual prelates renting out their benefices to laymen in return for cash payments.

The practice was time-honored. Indeed, Philip Jones considers it a major characteristic of the medieval agrarian scene in Italy. Long-term leases—the *emphyteusis* or *libellus,* usually for twenty-nine years—were of Byzantine origin; short-term contracts were a late Roman device. From at least the late ninth century, according to Professor Jones, the church acted to prohibit the long-term alienation of property. The renting out of church goods actually increased during the later Middle Ages nevertheless, by then in the form of commercial leases to businessmen.[4] Carlo Cipolla, studying Lombardy and the north, found the alienations widespread. "By the middle of the fifteenth century, . . . " he wrote, "the ruin of religious establishments in all of northern Italy was complete."[5] Evidence from the sixteenth century indicates that the ruin was probably more spiritual than financial.

Sixteenth-century records do, however, point to the same years, the middle decades of the fifteenth century, as the time in which serious efforts to curb the trend toward benefice-farming began. Individual religious houses, such as the abbey of Settino near Florence which Philip Jones examined, underwent reform efforts designed to recover alienated possessions during these years.[6] And in Rome, Pope Paul II voiced concern in May 1465, when he admonished all auditors hearing cases that involved alienation of benefices to keep only God before their eyes when rendering judgments. "Let no favor, no fear, nor expectation of reward subvert justice and conscience," warned the pope.[7] Then, in March 1467, the same pope issued the bull *Ambitiosae cupiditati,* which prohibited the renting, mortgaging, or other alienation of church properties for more than three years. There were exceptions: those alienations "permitted by law, or which concern things and goods which it has long been customary to concede *in emphyteusim,* and then in the apparent utility of the churches, or those which concern fruits and goods that cannot be kept because of the exigencies of the times" were still permitted.[8] As the Pauline bull was interpreted, moreover, alienations were lawful if occasioned by one or more of the following causes: (1) the necessity of the church, (2) the utility of the church, (3) piety, or (4) inconvenience.[9] These conditions were easily met in the sixteenth century.

Two kinds of papal briefs show how the system worked: (1) licenses to rent, sell, or exchange church property, and (2) confirmations of previously negotiated rental contracts. Almost all of them cite the 1467 bull of Paul II as the central prohibition of rentals beyond three years; they also state that it is *not to obstruct* the present license or confirmation. During the last years of our period, papal letters mention edicts of Boniface VIII and Paul IV restricting alienation which are also not

TABLE 3.1   CARDINALS RENTING OUT BENEFICES: 1514-1561
(from minutes of papal briefs)

Cardinal	Benefice*	Date	Time (years)
A. del Monte	Pavia, part	1514	?
U. Gambara	Mon in Cremona	1524	?
F. Orsini	Fréjus	1524	3
A. della Valle	Mon + Mileto	1527	?
P. Gonzaga	2 Mons in Cremona	1528	2
M. Grimani	Aquileia	1529	2
A. Cesarini	Pamplona	1530	3
P. E. Cesi	Mon in Milan	1531	9
A. della Valle	Mileto	1532	2
A. M. Palmieri	Sarni, part	1533	sale or exchange
I. de' Medici	Monreale	1533	5
A. Trivulzio	Bayeux	1533	8
G. Grimaldi	Bari & Venafro	1534	2
G. Doria	Noli, part Barcelona	1535	3
N. Gaddi	Cosenza	1535	3
E. Gonzaga	Mon, diocese illegible	1535	3
B. Accolti	Mon in Ferrara	1536	3
N. Gaddi	Cosenza	1536	2
B. Accolti	Mon in Salerno	1536	3
M. Caracciolo	Catania	1536	3
G. V. Carafa	Anglona	1537	3
A. Pucci	Vannes	1537	3
J. Sadoleto	Carpentras + Mon	1537	3
M. Grimani	Lesser Bens in Aquileia	1537	3
G. Salviati	Ferrara, part	1537	3
G. Doria	Noli, part	1538	sale or exchange
A. Pucci	Priorate in Geneva	1540	3
B. Accolti	Mon in Salerno	1540	3
F. Cornaro, E. Gonzaga	Mon in Taranto	1540	3
G. A. Sforza	2 Mons in Piacenza	1540	29
J. Savelli	Nicastro	1541	3
A. Parisani	Mon in Conza	1541	3
U. Gambara	Mon in Verona	1541	3
A. Farnese	Avignon	1542	3
I. Cibo	Turin	1542	16 ?
B. Accolti	Ravenna, mon in Ferrara	1542	3
N. Ridolfi	Mon in Gubbio	1542	3
G. Salviati	Ferrara	1542	3
N. Gaddi	Mon in Lyon, part	1543	sale or exchange
A. Trivulzio	3 mons in Milan	1545	3
G. A. Sforza	Corneto, Montefiascone	1546	5
G. de Cupis	Mon in Bologna	1547	9
G. A. Sforza	Mon in Milan	1547	9
G. A. Sforza	Parma	1547	9
F. Cesi	Mon in Milan	1550	9
I. Cibo	Mon in Milan	1550	?
G. A. Sforza	3 Villas in Parma	1553	9 each
G. A. Sforza	Villa in Parma	1553	7
G. Salviati	Ferrara, part	1553	6
F. Cesi	Lesser Bens in Cremona	1555	9
G. A. Sforza	Mon in Piacenza	1558	9
A. Farnese	Monreale	1561	6

*Mon = Monastery; Lesser Ben = Lesser Benefice

to obstruct the present transactions.[10] The terms used in the briefs are *arrendare* or *locare*, to lease or to rent. It should be noted that these arrangements were not loans secured by the income from church benefices, but rather genuine rental agreements—actual leases. Ecclesiastics remanded sometimes part, in most cases all, of the property of a benefice to the administration and management of laymen for a specific period of time in return for a specific amount of money. Instances of such rentals by the cardinals on our list increased in number over the years and involved about one-third of the men (table 3.1). Here again, our figures represent minimums; the language of the documents suggests that the renting out of church benefices was a widespread phenomenon.

Popes cited both general and explicit justifications for indulgences allowing the alienation of property, and they always mentioned the need for money. One recurring formula states that the pope gave the favor "so that you may sustain yourself more comfortably as befits your rank."[11] A common formula combined the needs of the lessor with those of the benefices in question:

Wishing to provide for your necessities and comforts as much as we can, . . . we grant and indulge you with the faculty to rent out all the fruits, rents, produce, rights, obventions, and emoluments of the patriarchal table of Aquileia, . . . and also those of all monasteries and other benefices whatsoever, secular as well as regular of any order, which in title or *in commendam* or in any other manner you possess, to any persons whatsoever, even laymen, with whom you will be able to effect a betterment equally of your own condition and that of the same table and those of the aforesaid benefices.[12]

Confirmations of earlier contracts usually cite only the desire to "provide for certain of your necessities."[13]

Sometimes the business of reform itself prompted these rentals—a curious fact when viewed from the twentieth century, but perfectly reasonable to contemporaries. Indeed, benefice-farming was so hallowed by time and custom that its potential for abuse was largely ignored by reformers in the sixteenth century. It is one of the few practices with which we are concerned here that was not singled out for correction by the authors of the *Consilium* of 1537. Two of those authors in fact found it expedient to rent out their benefices while they were engaged in reform work in Rome. Jacopo Sadoleto rented out a monastery and his bishopric of Carpentras for three years in June 1537, and Gian Pietro Carafa did the same with his recently repossessed archdiocese of Chieti in March 1538.[14] Both men had experienced unusual expenses while working on the reform commissions, and the papal letters make it clear that the indulgences were granted for purposes of personal financial relief. Paul III wrote to Carafa that he wished to help him "because, as you revealed to us a short time ago, you are in need of a certain quantity of money in order to pay some of your debts," and "to satisfy your many creditors as you in no way expect to be able [to do]."[15] The costs of reform caused Carafa to rent out Chieti and a monastery once again in May 1542. He was currently engaged in gathering, at his own expense, the furnishing and equipment for the Holy Office of the Inquisition, inaugurated on July 21 of the same year with the bull *Licet ab initio.*[16] Even the personal expenses caused by attendance at the Council of Trent were covered by benefice-farming.[17]

Alienation was also a convenient fiscal solution for extraordinary exigencies suffered by cardinals. After the sack of Rome in 1527, for example, Cardinal Francesco Pisani was one of the hostages conducted to Naples by the imperialists and incarcerated for some eighteen months in the Castel Nuovo. In this precarious situation, Clement VII expressed deep concern over Pisani's family and the need to protect his ecclesiastical properties and incomes. To ensure against loss, the pope first commended Pisani's bishopric of Padua and all his other benefices in that diocese to Luigi Pisani, a child at the time and a son of the cardinal's brother Giovanni. Then, on 30 June 1528, the pope licensed the same Giovanni, Luigi being too young, to rent out all the benefices held *in commendam* by his son.[18]

Under Paul III, Benedetto Accolti used benefice-farming to ease an equally unusual but very different financial crisis. From April to the end of October 1535, Accolti was imprisoned in the Castel Sant'Angelo on a variety of charges, principally complaints about his administration of the city of Ancona. He ultimately confessed, and, aided by the pleas of his friends at the curia, managed to persuade Paul III to release him upon the payment of a colossal fine, some 59,000 ducats.[19] The incomes from his dioceses of Ravenna and Cremona were pledged to underwrite the loans he was obliged to float, but these were apparently insufficient to service his debts. In April 1536, therefore, the pope granted Accolti the faculty to rent out his rich monastery of San Bartolomeo—worth about 12,000 *scuti* per year—for three years.[20] He also rented out his monastery of San Benedetto in Salerno, a contract renewed in 1540, and the entire archbishopric of Ravenna in 1542.[21] The price of Accolti's freedom thus made him one of the more active lessors of all the cardinals. The interesting fact here is that Paul III, who had but reluctantly agreed to allow Accolti to escape from the Castel Sant'Angelo with his life, still found it proper to let him retain all his benefices and even rent them out to bankers.

Other licenses seem closer in spirit to the thrust of the Pauline bull of 1467, stressing the needs of the benefice rather than those of the beneficiary. In December 1537, for example, Giovanni Salviati received the faculty to rent out 500 ducats from the income of the diocese of Ferrara so that he could pay for the repair of its cathedral, other church buildings, and the episcopal palace.[22] Similarly, Paul III granted Nicolò Gaddi the license to rent out the holdings of a monastery in the diocese of Lyon to the sum of 1,000 pounds of Tours (about 500 ducats of gold), for the express purpose of restoring its buildings.[23] Such motives are still today considered legitimate cause for alienation.[24] The problem in the sixteenth century was that rental contracts tended to endure far beyond the initial time limits.

Papal licenses imposed strict time limits upon most rental contracts. Those under consideration ranged from two to twenty-nine years. Almost half were three-year leases; another one-fifth were two-year leases. Taken together, two- and three-year contracts account for fully two-thirds of the total number.[25] The great majority, then, did not violate Paul II's *De rebus ecclesiae non alienandi* of 1467, which only prohibited rentals for more than three years. Almost all of the licenses cite the Pauline decree nevertheless: the parties did not wish to chance a challenge to the validity of the agreements.[26]

The next most common contract, about one-sixth of the total number, was a nine-year lease; all of these pertained to lands in the northern part of the peninsula—Bologna, Parma, Piacenza, Cremona, Milan, and Mantua. This duration had the sanction of long habit, "according to the usage of Lombardy which it has been customary to observe up to now."[27] So the abbey of Chiaravalle in Milan, already heavily burdened with pensions as we have seen, had "certain and perhaps all" of its property rented out by its owner, Paolo Emilio Cesi, for a period of nine years in 1531.[28] His brother and successor to the abbey, Federico Cesi, rented it out again in 1547 for another nine years at an annual return of 3,000 ducats of gold, and then renegotiated the contract in 1550 to increase the yearly payment by an additional 200 ducats.[29] Nor was this unusual. Guido Ascanio Sforza alone arranged at least seven nine-year leases of northern church properties between 1547 and 1558, including the bishopric of Parma.[30] Guido Ascanio was also responsible for the single transaction involving a twenty-nine-year rental. In 1540 and again in 1541, the pope wrote to the cathedral chapters of Piacenza about the negotiation of such a lease for two of Sforza's monasteries in that diocese. We do not know whether the matter was brought to successful conclusion, but it involved long-term alienations (*emphyteusis*) or permanent tenancy (*livellus perpetuus*), "from twenty-nine years to twenty-nine years, . . . according to the custom of those regions."[31]

Contracts for shorter durations covered not only most areas of the Italian peninsula, but also church properties outside of Italy. The single eight-year lease was for Agostino Trivulzio's bishopric of Bayeux, rented out in the fall of 1533.[32] Other alienated benefices beyond the mountains included the bishoprics of Fréjus, Vannes, and Carpentras in France, an abbey in France, an abbey in the diocese of Geneva, and the bishoprics of Barcelona and Pamplona in Spain, all rented out by Italian cardinals.[33]

Even with short-term contracts, Paul II's three-year rule could easily be circumvented: (1) contracts could be renewed, (2) benefices held in reserve could be alienated, and (3) successors to the benefice were bound to the agreements. We have already noted that cardinals Benedetto Accolti, Gian Pietro Carafa, and Federico Cesi renewed rental contracts; Ercole Gonzaga did the same with one of his abbeys under both Clement VII and Paul III.[34] The license that Julius III granted Giovanni Salviati in 1553 provides an even clearer instance of circumventing the three-year limitation. Salviati, who as we saw had obtained the right to rent out part of the income of Ferrara for the purpose of building repair in 1537, still had the property alienated sixteen years later. This time, the pope renewed the contracts, not for an additional three years, but for *two* additional three-year periods (*ad duo alia triennii*).[35]

Correspondence between Alessandro Farnese and Rodolfo Pio supports the suspicion that rental agreements tended to perpetuate themselves. When Farnese directed Pio, nuncio in France in 1535, to take possession of his recently acquired abbey of Caen in Normandy, neither man seemed surprised that the person responsible for administering the property was Mariotto Rucellai, a Florentine banker, or that the firm holding the rental contract on the abbey was Bindo Altoviti and Company, Roman merchants.[36] Indeed, Farnese's predecessor, the late Ippolito de' Medici, had merely consented to a contract earlier negotiated by his predecessor to the abbey, François, the cardinal of Tournon.[37]

The renting out of church properties held in reserve was also apparently commonplace. Cardinals resigned benefices, reserved the fruits, and then rented them out for cash sums, usually payable in Rome. These transactions required the consent of the present beneficiary, but, since almost all of them involved nepotism, consent was not difficult to obtain. Thus Agostino Trivulzio renewed a three-year lease of the fruits, rents, produce, houses, lands, and other goods of two monasteries and one *preceptoria* in the diocese of Milan in 1545 with the consent of his successors, Giovanni Battista Trivulzio and Antonio Trivulzio.[38] Similarly, Giandomenico de Cupis, having previously resigned a monastery in Bologna in favor of his son Bernardino, rented out all of its assets in 1547 for nine years.[39] Guido Ascanio Sforza rented out a monastery in Piacenza for nine years in 1558 with the consent of its present abbot, his brother Alessandro Sforza.[49] Further instances of the rental of reserved incomes include Ascanio Parisani in 1541, Guido Ascanio Sforza in 1546 and Federico Cesi in 1555.[41]

Two other cases illuminate this practice more fully. Franciotto Orsini became bishop of Fréjus in June 1524, and resigned in December of the same year in favor of his twelve-year-old grandson Leone Orsini, reserving for himself the fruits, administration, regress, and collation of benefices. Then, nine days after his resignation, he obtained a license to rent out the diocese for three years.[42] Gian Vincenzo Carafa did the same sort of thing. Bishop of Anglona since 1528, he resigned in 1536 in favor of his nephew Oliviero Carafa, reserving everything. Seven months later, Paul III confirmed a rental agreement through which the cardinal had alienated the bishopric for three years.[43] Both men had protected their own incomes, insured the transfer of church property to members of their families, and unburdened themselves of responsibility for the bishoprics.

These documents universally contain explicit clauses binding successors to the terms of the contracts. Typical phraseology states:

And also directing that if, perhaps, you should happen to cede or die within the aforesaid three years, the fruits, rents, produce, buildings, towns, taxes, possessions, goods, rights, obventions, and emoluments nevertheless are and remain pledged to the same Sebastiano actually and effectively for the said three years and not beyond, and that your successors in the diocese of Nicastro be held to observe each and every clause in the said document, including the one concerning payments in advance, for the duration of the three years, . . . as if they had obligated themselves to it personally.[44]

As in all papal briefs, this formula varied, but the essential binding clause always appears. Raffaele Riario even inserted a passage in his will protecting the men to whom he had rented out his benefices for six years.[45]

The men who leased ecclesiastical property from the cardinals received broad authority for the duration of the contract. Each lessee was granted the right "freely and lawfully to receive and keep and convert to his own use and utility the same fruits, rents, and produce" of the property.[46] At the same time, lessees had to be people with access to large amounts of ready cash. As we have seen, rich benefices tended increasingly to be burdened with multiple annual pensions for otherwise unrelated prelates, and the lessee was responsible for these payments in addition to the annual rent (*affictu*) that he owed the cardinal-renter.[47] And the rents were high. Although one contract called for the payment of only 140 *scuti* of gold per year, most were for much more substantial annual sums: 1,000 *scuti* to Benedetto Accolti for his Salerno abbey, 1,000 *scuti* to Jacopo Savelli for his bishopric of Nicastro, 2,000 *scuti* to Guido Ascanio Sforza for some property in the dioceses of Montefiascone and Corneto, 3,000 *scuti* to Federico Cesi for the monastery of Chiaravalle, each of these paid in gold.[48] Sforza also rented out the bishopric of Parma in 1547 for an annual return of 18,000 imperial pounds, and his series of contracts over other possessions in the same diocese, confirmed in 1553, called for total annual payments of 12,440 imperial pounds and 1,100 *scuti* of gold, or, reducing all sums to gold *scuti*, about 6,170 per year.[49] The largest rents of all were attached to the archdiocese of Monreale in Sicily. In 1533, Ippolito de' Medici concluded an agreement with the firm of Bindo Altoviti and Company which brought him 12,000 ducats of gold *della camera* each year for five years, with two years' rent payable in advance.[50] Alessandro Farnese had an even more lucrative contract over Monreale in 1561—19,000 *scuti* of gold in gold annually for six years.[51]

Payments in advance were not uncommon. The following phrase frequently appears in licenses to rent out church property: "and you may also receive and keep the payment in advance in a single sum and in hard cash."[52] Advance payments seem to have been less desirable to the lessees than to the cardinals, however: although twelve licenses to make contracts authorize the acceptance of the total rent in advance, only two briefs of confirmation of contracts already agreed upon include prepayment of the total sum.[53] The most common arrangement was a three-year lease with two years' rent payable in advance, and these advances, as we shall see, came under fire during the Tridentine period.

The lessees, then, had to be men of property, real or liquid. They are not always fully identified in the records, but they seem to be divisible into two general categories—*conductores*, or contractors, and *mercatores*, or merchant-bankers. The primary distinction between the two groups seems to have been the kind of ecclesiastical property they leased.

Only two of the lessees fit into neither category, being described simply as "clerks."[54] All others were laymen.

The designation *conductor* appears frequently in contemporary records. One could contract to do all sorts of business, of course, and the term was widely used. To students of Renaissance Italy the most familiar contractor is probably the *condottiere*, the contractor-at-arms. In rental agreements concerning church property, all but one document in which the lessee is called a contractor involve territories to which no sacred office was attached—properties, that is, that were not ecclesiastical benefices.[55] All but one of these agreements also bear a distinct flavor of overlordship rather than simple commerce. A Count Giorgio Bebbio, for example, leased a *villa* in the diocese of Parma from Guido Ascanio Sforza in 1553, and thereby gained the right not to its fruits, rents, and produce, but rather to its "goods, possessions, rights, tenants, and jurisdictions."[56] The other contractors did the same, leasing towns of assorted sizes, *terrae, villae, castri, castelli,* all for the relatively long periods of five, seven, or nine years, and all in the central and northern parts of Italy—Corneto, Montefiascone, and Parma.[57] Alienations such as these thus seem to have been made in the interests of the local country gentry, more in the nature of subinfeudations than commercial contracts, more concerned with landlordship than profit.

The rest of the lessees seem to have been merchants, and the properties they leased consisted exclusively of ecclesiastical benefices. Although several are described simply as "citizens," or "laymen," the tone of the documents is unmistakably commercial. Antonio Maria Busso, for example, "Milanese layman," leased Accolti's abbey in Salerno; geography suggests that he had extensive merchantile dealings.[58] The "laymen of the town of Caletri in the diocese of Conza" who leased Ascanio Parisani's abbey there were almost certainly merchants—"Antonio Angelo Marcuzio and Bernardino Bianco *and company*."[59] The others are clearly designated as *mercatores.*

Some of them may have been engaged in limited operations—the merchants of Rouen who leased Trivulzio's bishopric of Bayeux, for example, or the Veronese who leased Gambara's abbey in Verona—local people, perhaps, although local people with a good deal of ready cash.[60] Parochialism cannot characterize the rest of the men, however. Cornelio Malvezzi, the "Bolognese citizen" who leased Parma in 1547, belonged to a prominent family. The Malvezzi were regularly listed among the ruling group in Bologna from the years of Julius II, and later, allied by marriage to the Campeggii, they attained the status of nobility.[61] Besides farming the diocese of Parma, Malvezzi had other close business relations with Rome. From at least March to July 1550, he was the *depositario generale* for the apostolic camera, in charge of the reception and disposition of cameral funds, and he continued to work for the Holy See thereafter.[62] Other lessees headed banking firms having widespread financial dealings with the church. These "merchants following the Roman curia" included Sebastiano Monteauto, Luigi Rucellai, and Bindo Altoviti, all Florentines. Monteauto, who leased Avignon from Alessandro Farnese in 1542, headed a firm that had been working for the curia since the pontificate of Julius II.[63] Together with another Florentine merchant, Benvenuto Olivieri, he was *dohanerius* of the three *dogane* of Rome in 1543 and 1546; that is, the two bankers were in charge of collecting all the customs duties for the eternal city.[64] During 1545, he was treasurer of the state of Camerino.[65] His heirs kept the firm together and were still working for the church in 1557.[66] Luigi Rucellai, who leased abbeys in Milan from Agostino Trivulzio, belonged to the old Florentine merchant family that had acted as bankers for the Roman curia at least from 1494 in the pontificate of Alexander VI;[67] Luigi's successors continued the business at least through the reign of Paul IV.[68] Bindo Altoviti, who held the rental contracts on both the abbey at Caen in Normandy and the archdiocese of Monreale in Sicily, was probably one of the most active and successful bankers of the half-century.[69] The Altoviti were another old merchant family of Florence, and Bindo's father, Antonio Altoviti, having married a niece or granddaughter of Pope Innocent VIII, had moved the family banking operations to Rome during that pontiff's reign. Bindo took over the direction of the Altoviti bank, and, particularly after the Chigi bank closed in 1528, he played an increasingly active part in papal finances in a host of official positions, including *dohanerius* of the three *dogane*, *depositario generale*, *depositario* of the funds derived from the sale of the offices of the Knights of Loreto, and treasurer of the Marches.[70]

The principal lessees of ecclesiastical benefices, then, were Italian bankers, and those who farmed the largest properties numbered among the major figures in the financial world of Rome. They were in business to make money. Were these benefices financially healthy? Real estate in Italy, secular as well as ecclesiastical, had, after all, been subjected to serious depredation in the early years of our period, and one would expect diminished returns on landed wealth following the Italian wars. If we look at the rental transactions involving only two Italian benefices, however, we gain an impression of enduring prosperity.

The abbey of Chiaravalle is located just south of Milan, directly in the path of each successive invading army during the wars. Still, Marino Sanuto estimated its annual income in 1509 at an enormous 12,000 ducats of gold, from which a host of pensions were drawn; and Federico Cesi was able to arrange a lease bringing him 3,200 *scuti* of gold each year from the property in 1550.[71] Even though the more than 8,000 ducats in pensions had been significantly reduced by then, the income from Chiaravalle must have remained immense if the lessee was to realize any meaningful profit.[72] The same conclusion must be drawn about the archbishopric of Monreale in Sicily. In 1492, Pope Alexander VI ordered a monthly stipend for its archbishop, his nephew Cardinal Juan Borgia, to counteract the great expenses caused by the Turks.[73] It too was heavily encumbered with pensions, at least 3,000 ducats' worth in 1533, and yet in that same year, Bindo Altoviti pledged to pay Ippolito de' Medici 24,000 cameral ducats of gold as a down payment, and a total of 60,000 such ducats over five years.[74] Twenty-eight years later, Alessandro Farnese stood to receive 114,000 *scuti* of gold from Monreale over a six-year contract.[75]

It is possible, of course, that bankers used the commercial leasing of church benefices to gain access to additional and more lucrative business with the Holy See. The rental agreement entered into by Cornelio Malvezzi seems to have preceded his more extensive dealings with the apostolic camera. This was not the case with Monteauto, Rucellai, or Altoviti, however, and it is difficult to imagine that their sympathies for the fiscal needs of the cardinals ran deep enough to induce them to lose money. We must therefore assume, I think, that the bankers expected substantial profits from their investments. This suggests that the economic condition of many Italian benefices was better than we have imagined.[76] But what about the *spiritual* health of the benefices in question?

We have seen that even reformers in the curia engaged in benefice-farming. Nevertheless, however convenient and profitable rental agreements may have been for prelates and bankers, they must have been detrimental to the alienated parish churches, priorates, monasteries, bishoprics, and archbishoprics. In most of the instances cited here, benefices probably exchanged an absentee ecclesiastical landlord for an absentee secular landlord, but, while the former had been responsible for the spiritual health of the charge, the latter was in no way so restricted. Bankers sought profits, and, in the interests of their partners, must have been obliged to work the property for every *quattrino* it was worth. What happened to the spiritual life of the benefice under such circumstances? Rodolfo Pio offered a hint when he reported to Cardinal Farnese about the condition of the abbey at Caen. The monks there, he had heard, seemed to be good men, "which is not a small matter, considering how disordered the religious of these *commende* ordinarily are."[77] Sooner or later, one would expect the reform movement to address its efforts to the modification or elimination of benefice-farming.

A note of the consistory of 9 March 1517 does not promise a great deal. Three minutes of papal bulls were read to the cardinals on that day, including one "about the *moderation* of the Pauline bull prohibiting the alienation of church property or the renting out of it beyond three years."[78] There is no subsequent mention of what, if any, moderations were adopted by the pope and the college, but benefice-farming diminished not at all during the ensuing years. At the time of the Council of Trent's first sessions, however, some concern over contemporary habits began to appear in the documents. The briefs of 26 May 1546, for example, which approved some of Cardinal Sforza's leases, noted that Marcello Crescenzio authorized them only because there was no payment in advance.[79] And, although the license to rent out the monastery of Avellana at Gubbio which Filippo Ridolfi obtained in March 1550 reverted to the earlier *etiam unico contextu et anticipata solutione in pecunia numerata* formula, all of the subsequent briefs until the election of Pope Pius IV expressly forbade payments in advance.[80] It is not clear why payments in advance should have been considered particularly reprehensible during the Tridentine years; perhaps they suggested bribery or simony. Other language in papal briefs on rentals, however, also displayed a new and increasing uneasiness about the practice. All such documents dated between 1550 and 1558, for example, mention a "just price," and inserted between lines and in the margins of these briefs appear such phrases as "and also honest," "and in clear utility," and "lawful, however, and honest, and also not contrary to the holy canons."[81]

Still, it remained to the uncompromising Gian Pietro Carafa as Paul IV to launch a head-on attack on benefice-farming, and even this stern figure shrank from an attempt at complete eradication. On 14 July 1555, the pope issued a bull citing that of his predecessor, Paul II, and cataloging the circumventions and abuses of that edict. He then declared that all rentals of church property for a period of more than three years were null and void and that all parties to such contracts were to suffer the penalty of excommunication.[82] The bull left three-year contracts untouched, but even so it proved to be too much. On 11 September 1560, Pius IV, successor to the Carafa pope, published another bull on alienations in which he noted the annulment made by his predecessor: "Since, however, as we understand, diverse lawsuits, inquiries, and controversies have arisen because of the said letter and *motus proprius,* and also diverse burdens, damages, perturbations, and misfortunes have been generated and visited upon diverse persons, . . . in not a little vexation to the souls of the same persons," these victims had vehemently protested the execution of the Pauline bull and had appealed to the present pope. Pius IV, therefore, declaring that earlier canons fully provided for matters of alienation of church property, revoked, annulled, and canceled the 1555 edict of Paul IV. All sentences handed down in accordance with the bull were vacated and guilty parties absolved, and lawsuits then in progress were to be reviewed "according to the disposition of the common law."[83]

Apparently other rental practices also reverted to the pre-Carafa era under Pius IV. In September 1561, the pope granted his secretary Tolomeo Gallio a license to rent out his recently acquired bishopric of Martorano in southern Italy, a priorate in the diocese of Como, and a parish church in the diocese of Verona, with the rent to be paid in advance.[84] Later that year, the same pope granted the same right to the bishop-elect of Parma, Alessandro Sforza, for one of his prepositures.[85] Long-standing custom over the duration of rental agreements also prevailed. In September 1563, Pius IV gave the new cardinal of Mantua, Federico Gonzaga, the license to rent out the diocese of Mantua, the prepositure of its cathedral, and the opulent abbey of Lucedio in Monferrato for nine years.[86]

The Council of Trent decreed against long rentals and ordered provincial councils to see to their revision. Paolo Prodi's account of the attempts by the bishop of Bologna to implement reforms of rentals during the years 1569–1571, however, shows that the bishop was impeded by a special envoy from Rome.[87] Apparently other efforts to modify rental practices also met impediments. In 1616, at least, twenty-four of the thirty abbeys belonging to Cardinal Scipione Borghese were rented out.[88] And by the end of the seventeenth century, long rentals had become a commonplace. The lease on an abbey dated 22 August 1682 states that the terms are for "three three-year rentals, from three years to three years, and that when one is finished the other is understood to begin, according to ecclesiastical custom, and in everything conforming to the forms of the Sacred Council of Trent and the holy canons."[89] Again the fiscal needs of the cardinals had altered perceptions in Italy, and practices that had seemed abusive to the fathers at Trent had become "ecclesiastical custom." Revised canon law still allows the rental, sale, donation, or exchange of church property for reasons very similar to those outlined in the fifteenth century by Paul II: *urgens necessitas, utilitas ecclesiae,* or *pietas.*[90]

LAST WILLS AND TESTAMENTS

The inheritance of church moneys by lay heirs resulted in a different sort of alienation from that of benefice-farming. Even though rental contracts tended to be renewed and extended, they could run out or be annulled. The diversion of ecclesiastical wealth to laymen by means of a last will, on the other hand, was permanent. Benefices themselves could not be part of a prelate's personal estate, of course; they belonged to the church.[91] As we have seen in the preceding chapter, however, the incomes from ecclesiastical benefices, in the form of pensions and reservations, came to be incorporated among the belongings of cardinals. These, along with other properties accumulated during the course of a curial career, could, with papal license, legitimately be bequeathed to laymen. Indeed, even in the event of a prelate's dying intestate, the prevailing attitude at the papal court tended to honor the claims and rights of his heirs, clerical or lay.[92] The authors of the *Consilium* of 1537 clearly viewed will-making as abusive: "The license for bequeathing the goods of the church ought not to be given to clerics except for an urgent reason, lest the goods of the poor be converted into private delights and the amplification of houses," they wrote with some acrimony.[93] Their colleagues in the Roman curia did not necessarily agree.

A controversy between the republic of Venice and Pope Alexander VI which lasted for nearly a year can illustrate some aspects of the question of last wills and church property. Cardinal Giovanni Battista Zeno, a Venetian, died on 8 May 1501. The cardinal was exceedingly rich by reputation, and it was common knowledge that he had kept the bulk of his wealth in cash and other liquid assets close to him, hidden about in strongboxes. Venice, ever jealous of its jurisdictional rights and equally alert to the possibility of revenue, had shown a sharp interest in Zeno's last illness. Agents of the Council of Ten took custody of his house in Padua, and denied entrance or exit to all persons, including members of the Zeno family. Immediately following the cardinal's death, the same agents conducted a thorough search of the premises, seized all the treasure they found, and sent it to the Venetian *Signoria.* In behaving thus, Venice disregarded, indeed was serenely indifferent to, the claims of the Holy See. "And a messenger came to Padua from the legate with a brief from the pope, who excommunicated, *etc.*, because the pope wants the money for himself," wrote Marino Sanuto.[94] During the next weeks, the Venetians discovered additional cash and precious objects sequestered by the late cardinal at various of his churches and abbeys. In July, Sanuto recorded the distribution of his estate. Following payments of specific legacies, a total of 26,123 gold ducats remained in the hands of the republic.[95] Alexander VI continued to object, complaining to the Venetian ambassador at Rome that Zeno had not had the right to make a will, and that he, the pope, would lament to Emperor Maximilian I and to the kings of France and Spain and all the monarchs of the world that the Venetian *Signoria* had seen fit to lay hands on the moneys of the church. The pope threatened the interdict and other maledictions, but Venice remained adamant. This was one of the few quarrels in which the Borgia pope capitulated, apparently, though not before April 1502. Thus a major portion of the goods gathered by Cardinal Zeno, who had "hoped to use it to make himself pope," according to Sanuto, went instead to outfit galleys for the war against the Turks. Another substantial sum, 15,000 ducats of gold, was left to the relatives of the cardinal, all of them laymen.[96]

The episode demonstrates the following facts: (1) papal license was a necessary or at least advisable prerequisite for bequeathing church moneys, (2) prelates could and did bequeath church moneys to laymen, and (3) litigation and complications could and did arise over the disposition of such bequests.

Licenses to make wills appear frequently in the minutes of papal briefs. Sigismondo Pappagoda, bishop of Tropea, was a stark exception to the rule for prelates when he refused to make a will before he died in 1536. According to Ercole Gonzaga, Pappagoda had declared that all his possessions came from the mother church and that she should be his sole heir; nevertheless, Gonzaga reported, the emperor had surrounded the house of the dying bishop to protect those possessions.[97] Although lesser dignitaries in the hierarchy as well as cardinals obtained faculties to make wills, the grace seemed particularly appropriate for princes of the church. "This is our last will and our last testament," wrote Cardinal Jacopo Savelli in 1587, validated "through the authority of the faculties conceded in general by High Pontiffs to the Most Reverend Cardinals, and in particular . . . conceded to our person by Gregory XIII of holy memory."[98] Faculties granted to cardinals to make wills usually began thus: "Proceeding from the benignity of the apostolic see, it is a worthy thing that the prelates of the church, especially cardinals of the Holy Roman Church, who do not cease assiduously to labor for the healthy and prosperous state of the same church, should be free to dispose of the goods which they possess while living . . . by means of a last will."[99]

The most sweeping of these faculties then empowered the prelate to bequeath all his possessions, movable and immovable, including sums of money and any goods "of whatever quality, sum, value, price, or condition they be and of whatever kinds of property they consist, even if they or part of them derive from the ecclesiastical income of any cathedral church, even metropolitan, or from the titular cardinalate churches, or from monasteries, or from any other ecclesiastical benefice, secular or regular, which in title, *in commendam*, administration, or otherwise" the cardinal had possessed, continued to possess, or should possess in the future, "and also whatever fruits of similar churches, monasteries, and ecclesiastical benefices reserved to you or to be reserved, and whatever annual pensions from any ecclesiastical fruits, rents, and produce assigned to you or to be assigned in the future, and also by reason of the cardinalate honor."[100] The only exceptions in these blanket indulgences were vestments and other things pertaining to divine worship, and especially the cardinalate ring, which reverted to the pontiff in every case.[101]

Pope Alexander VI had ordered that one-third of the estate of any prelate who received the faculty to make a will must devolve to the apostolic camera and to the pope, or "ought to be converted to pious or other uses, even, perhaps, against the infidels [Turks] or for the construction of the Basilica of the Prince of Apostles in the City."[102] As happened with other decrees, however, this restriction was easily bypassed, and popes freely awarded the one-third to the estates of cardinals "in return for the work, or as compensation for the labors which, up to now, you have expended for the said Roman Church."[103] All licenses to make wills concluded with severe injunctions to all curial officials, auditors of the Rota, collectors, subcollectors, and any other persons against attempts to alter or subvert the terms of the indulgence.

Such carte blanche licenses were relatively rare. Examples of unrestricted faculties to bequeath church moneys include briefs to six cardinals of our group: Antonio Maria del Monte in 1533, Agostino Trivulzio in 1540, Ennio Filonardi in 1541, Antonio Sanseverino in 1543, Ascanio Parisani in 1545, and Durante Duranti in 1545.[104] Paul III bestowed the same favor upon his major domo, Bernardino Sylverio Piccolomini, archbishop of Sorrento, in 1547. Piccolomini never achieved cardinalate rank, but received this reward "because of the fidelity and continual service you have shown, up to now, to us and to the apostolic see, and which you do not cease constantly to exhibit."[105]

Some otherwise identical licenses to make wills specified a maximum value of the church moneys that could be alienated. For example, the indulgence granted to Girolamo Ghinucci on 1 July 1541, five days before his death, limited his estate to the sum of 2,500 ducats of gold in ecclesiastical incomes.[106] Most cardinals had more generous allotments for their heirs, however, ranging from Federigo Fregoso's limit of 4,000 ducats to Uberto Gambara's and Girolamo Aleandro's 10,000 ducats of gold.[107] Aleandro received an additional and unusual dispensation. He was authorized to bequeath his estate to any persons, be they relatives "or sons, even illegitimate and procreated by whatever sort of unlawful intercourse . . . or to any other persons, even to those in any way prohibited or by law incapable of receiving it."[108]

Briefs from the pontificate of Pius IV indicate that the granting of licenses to make wills had become even more common by 1563. During the consistories of 10 February and 10 March alone, no fewer than ten such licenses were issued, and they were issued to men who were not at the top levels of the church hierarchy. Ten bishops and archbishops thereby received the right to bequeath some 42,500 ducats in church moneys to their lay heirs.[109]

It is not the purpose of this chapter to examine the problem of nepotism in its broader aspects. We necessarily touch upon the topic in discussing the alienation of church incomes into the hands of laymen, however, because the principal lay inheritors of cardinals were, in fact, members of their families. Licenses directed that beneficiaries could be "any persons, even secular persons, whether they be relatives, servants, or others," and the inheritance could be diverted to "causes both pious and nonpious, and also to any other sorts of uses, even nonpious, as long as they be lawful."[110] In practice, the major heir, the *herede universale,* was almost always a close blood relation—uncle, brother, cousin, nephew, son. Bequests to friends, servants, and holy foundations were also abundant. Whether the estate was large or small, wills tended to follow the same general pattern.

Writing on the day before his death in 1520, Cardinal Bernardo Dovizi of Bibbiena, humanist factotum of the house of Medici, named his brother-cousins Guglielmo and Lorenzo Dovizi as his principal heirs. Other legacies went to the cardinal's sister Tita, to Cardinal Innocenzo

Cibo, to papal secretary Pietro Bembo, and to the shrine of the House
of the Blessed Virgin at Loreto.[111] Uberto Gambara named his brother
Brunoro as his universal heir; he also left property to the pontifical
court.[112] Dominican theologian Tommaso de Vio left all of his possessions to the poor, according to his biographer. In 1530, however, four
years before his death, he had turned over all of his material goods,
"which could not have been many" to his nephew, *il nobile signore*
Sebastiano de Vio, in order to free himself from mundane cares.[113]

Cardinalate families, then, took a lively interest in the disposition of
the goods possessed by their ecclesiastical relatives. If, as we have as-
serted, the churchmen themselves came to regard their benefices and
the incomes they yielded as personal property, so it happened that their
relatives assumed that they had some sorts of "rights" over these estates.
This frame of mind, which we describe below as the "dead hand of
nepotism," permeates the records.

Girolamo Aleandro's concern for the family of his secretary, Domenico Musso, is illustrative. Aleandro wrote to his son Claudio and
nephew Francesco on 2 April 1540, "We think that by now you will
have heard of the death of that poor man Messer Domenico, who died
of aepodipsia in less than three days, God keep his soul; we have written
to his brother to come here, and we shall see what to do with whatever
we shall find."[114] The situation quickly became murky. A large sum of
money, "which through common knowledge Messer Domenico was
known to have had," was nowhere to be found.[115] By 24 April the
brother had arrived, and he and the cardinal had searched diligently
without success. Aleandro lamented the hardship and loss to Musso's
parents and brothers. His solicitude for the family of his late secretary
is the more striking because he himself stood to sustain fiscal damage
from the disappearance of the funds. "Not finding his money would
put us under great strain, since he has not settled the accounts of the
management of our churches for five years," wrote the cardinal. It is
superfluous to add that the money in Musso's care derived from church
property.[116]

The paternal vicissitudes of Pietro Bembo depict the same assumption
more starkly. During the summer of 1542, the cardinal was greatly
disgruntled at the lack of progress his son, Torquato, had made in the
study of letters. At the same time, he was anxious about providing a
large enough dowry to ensure a suitable marriage for his daughter,
Elena. In June he wrote to his agent in Venice that the marriage negotiations might proceed more smoothly if it were mentioned that Elena
would inherit Torquato's portion of his, Cardinal Bembo's, estate should

the young man die. "Besides," he added, "I have made up my mind that if Torquato should not please me with that one delight which I have wanted so much from him, I say to make himself learned (to which he appears to me to be very little inclined), I shall not leave him the value of a single *picciolo* beyond those benefices which I have already given him, and I shall leave everything to my Elena."[117] By 13 July, Bembo's patience with his seventeen-year-old son had reached its limits. He wrote the boy an ultimatum, warning him that since he was already in his eighteenth year and could not even write a decent letter in the vulgar tongue, let alone a Latin epistle, he was to apply himself closely to his studies.

> About which I tell you, that if you do not make good and honorable progress and profit in letters within two years, you may be certain that you will not have any part of my inheritance; not the house at Padua, nor my studio, nor anything in it nor in the said house; not the things I have here, which are of the value of some thousands of ducats, and finally, not one boot-lace or one pot. And even if I did not have Elena, nor the children of Messer Giovan Matteo Bembo, nor those of Messer Bernardin Belegno, my nephews, yet I should rather leave all my goods to one of my friends or servants who loves me and obeys me than to you, who do not obey me and therefore also do not love me. . . . And perhaps I shall think to make better profit even of Villa Nova and Coniolo than to leave them to you; it will be enough for me to let you be the archpriest of Cortarolo with the pension from Bressana, and, indeed, these two would make greater support for your life than that which you have merited from me.[118]

The cardinal was speaking of an estate that consisted totally of church property or of goods collected with money from church property, and he was speaking of leaving it to his daughter, his nieces and nephews, his friends and servants. Furthermore, the specific properties he mentioned—the abbey of Villanova in the diocese of Verona, the priorate of Coniolo in the diocese of Brescia, the position at Cortarolo, and the pension from Bressana—were all bona fide ecclesiastical benefices.

As it happened, Torquato remained the universal heir in Bembo's last will. The house in Padua, however, was mortgaged to the sum of 2,500 ducats to Piero Gradenigo, Elena's husband, and the will stipulated that Torquato must pay his brother-in-law 800 ducats per year from Villanova and Coniolo until the debt was paid.[119] A few months after the cardinal's death, one of his old friends, Jacopo Sadoleto, intervened with the Holy See on behalf of the younger Bembo. On 8 July 1547, Paul III granted Torquato the right to rent out either Villanova or Coniolo for three years so that he might redeem his father's house in Padua.[120]

The minutes of papal briefs provide most of the evidence of action based upon the assumption that laymen had rightful claims to the estates of clerical relatives. Properties disposed of by means of a last will and testament did not require papal sanction beyond the original license. Papal intervention in these matters was therefore usually limited to situations in which a prelate died intestate or to those in which justice seemed to be in jeopardy. When a man died without having made a will, the goods he left were called, simply, "spoils."[121] These properties reverted to the pope, and he often gave them to the nearest clerical kinsman of the deceased. Should none be available, however, popes favored the nearest lay relative. Spoils comprised single, one-time-only grants of incomes from benefices, debts owed to the deceased, cash, jewels, and other assets held by the cardinal at the time of his death. The lay inheritor had no claim to future incomes in these cases. For example, on 16 October 1540, nine days after the death of Cardinal Cristoforo Jacobazzi, Paul III bestowed a legacy upon the brother of the defunct, Jacopo Jacobazzi, a layman and citizen of Rome.[122]

Moved by the singular merits of your brother, Cristoforo, Cardinal Jacobazzi of blessed memory, and by our paternal benevolence toward you and your respect toward us, we graciously give and liberally bestow upon you by this [letter] all the spoils, things, and goods owing to the said Cristoforo, Cardinal, at the time of his death by reason of the bishopric of Cassano which he possessed while living, wheresoever they be found, of whatever value they be, and in whatever things they consist, . . . devolving to us and to the apostolic camera.[123]

In the same manner, Paul IV gave his *affinis,* Giovanni Battista Carafa, a citizen of Naples, all the property devolving to the Holy See which had belonged to Giovanni Antonio Carafa "of blessed memory, once bishop or bishop-elect of Venafro, your paternal uncle, as we understand."[124]

The relatives of Silvio Passerini, cardinal of Cortona, seem to have been overly enthusiastic in collecting a similar grant. The cardinal had died intestate on 20 April 1529, and his brother Cosmo and nephews Leo and Nicolò Passerini, laymen of Cortona, petitioned the pope for some of his belongings. Clement VII obliged on 13 May, granting them the spoils owed to the cardinal at the time of his death by reason of the bishopric of Cortona and a monastery in the same diocese—one half to Cosmo, the other half to the two nephews—along with the faculty to dispose of the property "freely and lawfully according to your wishes."[125] The heirs apparently interpreted their indulgence broadly.

Twenty months later, in January 1531, the pope informed the new bishop of Cortona, Leonardo Bonafidei, that he had commanded the three Passerini under penalty of excommunication to restore within ten days the household goods, beds, furniture, utensils, books, and other things they had removed from the episcopal palace.[126] They soon returned to favor, however, for on 28 July 1531 Clement VII granted them title to half of some real estate left by their late kinsman in Città di Castello, and on 17 May 1533 the same pope intervened on their behalf in a dispute with the community of Chiusi over more of the cardinal's legacy.[127]

Monetary pensions from church benefices differed from spoils in that they continued to be collected annually by the heirs. As we saw earlier, pensions that were transferable to successors became part of the personal estates of cardinals and could be bequeathed through a last will. Legatees, clerical and lay, then received these moneys each year for life, at least in theory.

The unusual circumstances surrounding the disposition of the estate of the late Aldobrandino Orsini in 1528 required considerable papal intervention, intervention that can shed some light on the practice. Orsini, the archbishop of Nicosia, had resigned in 1524 and had reserved for himself the denomination and annual pensions of 1,800 ducats— 1,000 from the archdiocese and 800 from two monasteries in Aquileia and Ceneta—both of which were transferable.[128] After his death four years later, Clement VII acted to protect the rights of the principal heirs, the illegitimate young sons of the late archbishop. In December 1528 the pope named Lodovico Orsini, count of Pitigliano and paternal uncle of the children, as their tutor and guardian, but attempted to safeguard their inheritance by removing its administration from his hands. The incomes of the Orsini boys, and particularly "the ecclesiastical pensions owed to them by the present archbishop of Nicosia, . . . and all other goods and rights," were entrusted to Ansaldo Grimaldi and Company, Genoese merchants following the Roman curia, for the duration of their minority.[129] Again church income was in the hands of bankers, this time in the interests of young children, at the specific direction of the pope himself.

Papal interference also took the form of direct appeal to executors on behalf of claimants who felt unjustly treated. During the spring of 1563, for example, Pius IV wrote several such letters to the dowager duchess of Mantua and her sons Cardinal Federico and Duke Guglielmo Gonzaga, the executors of the estate of the late Cardinal Ercole Gonzaga.

Among the petitioners for whom the pope asked subvention were a Corrado Gonzaga, servant of the decedent, and Anna Gonzaga, "nun, daughter of the late Cardinal of Mantua."[130]

Popes were not always inclined to generosity toward lay claimants, however. At times, families and creditors of dead prelates felt compelled to bring suit against the apostolic camera for moneys the pope had claimed for the church. When Cardinal Pompeo Colonna died in Naples in 1532, his old enemy Pope Clement VII declared that he had died intestate and ordered that all his goods be seized and sequestered and held for the Holy See.[131] The cardinal, however, had earlier pronounced himself, by means of a public document, the true debtor of some merchants from Lucca "in notable quantity, exceeding the sum of 17,000 ducats," and had assigned to them certain of his goods, *mobilia et immobilia*. The merchants therefore brought suit against the apostolic camera which dragged on for many months. Apparently, a decision by the cameral court had to await the death of Clement VII. Favorable judgment was finally handed down in November 1534, and the new pope, Paul III, confirmed it in the following January and remanded the still-sequestered property to the Lucchesi.[132] It had taken them two and one-half years to recover their loan.

A longer-lasting lawsuit ultimately bypassed the courts. Imperiale Doria, bishop of Sagona on the island of Corsica, designated as universal heir in his last will his uncle, the famous admiral and prince of Melfi, Andrea Doria. After the bishop's death in early 1544, a controversy arose between the prince and the apostolic camera over the inheritance, a controversy that lasted for almost six years. Among the disputed property, most of which was situated in the kingdom of Naples, was the substantial sum of "twenty thousand ducats or thereabouts, coin of those parts." On 13 March 1550, at the instance of another of the admiral's nephews, Cardinal Girolamo Doria, Pope Julius III intervened, recalled the lawsuit to himself, vacated all litigation, imposed silence upon the judges, and awarded the prince all that he had claimed.[133]

The perpetual danger of a post mortem challenge to a last will made it prudent for cardinals to name powerful persons at court as executors. Gregorio Cortese named three: cardinals Reginald Pole and Uberto Gambara and Paul III's major domo, Bernardino Sylverio Piccolomini.[134] Some cardinals chose to name a universal heir reinforced by an authoritative prelate as executors. Bernardo Dovizi did so in designating two executors, his cousin Guglielmo Dovizi and Cardinal Lorenzo Pucci.[135] Raffaele Riario's executors were his nephew and universal heir Cesare Riario, together with Cardinal Giulio de' Medici, vicechancellor of the church and later Pope Clement VII.[136] Giovanni Battista Pallavicino had four executors: his brother Balbilano Pallavicino, cardinals Andrea della Valle and Lorenzo Pucci, and Pope Clement VII.[137] Girolamo Ghinucci similarly named his brother Paolo Ghinucci, and also Cardinal Alessandro Farnese.[138] Probably the most impressive group was that chosen by Rodolfo Pio of Carpi, who had two future saints and two future popes as executors of his will: Carlo Borromeo, later saint; Michele Ghislieri, later Pope Pius V and saint; and Ugo Boncompagni, later Pope Gregory XIII.[139] Prelates were profoundly concerned to safeguard the proper disposal of their estates after death.

Most last testaments were probably relatively simple documents. The instrument through which Ippolito I d'Este left his fortune to his brother at his death in 1520 consists of two sheets of parchment. After citing the license to make a will granted him by Leo X, leaving instructions for the embellishment of the cathedral of Milan and for the disposition of his cadaver, and designating 2,000 ducats to be distributed among the members of his household, Ippolito simply left everything to his brother, Duke Alfonso I of Ferrara: "To all other goods movable and immovable, lands and rights wherever they may be, . . . and also to his fruits and rents of any kind, also ecclesiastical, the said Lord Testator instituted, elected, named, and desired his universal heir to be the Most Illustrious and Excellent Prince and our Lord, Lord Alfonso d'Este, Duke of Ferrara, his brother."[140]

Some fifty-two years later, his nephew Ippolito II d'Este, "by the grace of God sound in mind, sense, and intellect, although infirm and lying in bed," signed his own last testament. On 1 December 1572, the day before his death, Ippolito named two universal heirs: his nephews Alfonso II, duke of Ferrara, and Cardinal Luigi d'Este. This document too is very general. It does specify that the famous Villa d'Este at Tivoli and the palace of Montecavallo on the Quirinale Hill in Rome, both of which properties, strictly speaking, belonged to the church, should go to Luigi, on condition that Luigi leave them in turn to the next Estensi cardinal, or, should there be none, to the dean of the college of cardinals.[141] For the rest, it simply lumps together the old cardinal's goods and bequeaths them to the universal heirs.[142] The will itself does not tell us what the inheritance contained.

The testament written in 1587 by Jacopo Savelli, cardinal bishop of Porto, vicar of Rome, and High Inquisitor of the Holy Office, is far more complex, almost fifty manuscript pages long. By describing in detail the future disposition of his goods, Cardinal Savelli has left us a much clearer picture of how church income was alienated through last wills than do the succinct instruments of the Estensi. Savelli's meticulousness was perhaps atypical, but he had good reason for prolixity. His will disinherited his two brothers, Bernardino Savelli and Mariano Savelli, the bishop of Gubbio, and the moribund cardinal was anxious to forestall their almost certain attempts to contest it. He deprived them because he believed them to be the source of a malicious rumor, which, he imagined, had cost him the triple crown in the conclave that elected Sixtus V in 1585.[143]

> And because the aforesaid Mariano, bishop, and Bernardino . . . more than thirty years ago gave out the lie, knowing certainly the contrary, that we had sons who were studying at Padua, and that we wanted our income for them, thinking that they could force us to spend our money according to their wishes so that we could free ourselves of this evil rumor we declare as we have always done that we never had, nor do we have now, any children, neither male nor female, and that this has been a complete calumny given out by our aforesaid brothers.[144]

The controversy caused by this deprivation probably accounts for the existence of a copy of the will in the Vatican library. The disinherited brothers were apparently successful in their challenge, because Bernardino was allowed to float a loan in 1589 based upon revenues of properties specifically denied him by the cardinal's will.[145] We also find Bernardino Savelli having to pay a "composition for the testament of Cardinal Savelli of blessed memory" of 25,000 *scuti* of gold in gold in 1592.[146] These circumstances make Savelli's will one of great interest, a testament that provides revealing insights into the mind of the cardinal and his thoughts on church property and rights.

The cardinal began the document by recommending his soul to God and many saints and giving directions for his funeral, a particularly sumptuous one. He then turned to the disposition of his property. He entrusted the task of carrying out his wishes to four executors, none of them, significantly, members of his family: his major domo, Count Prospero della Gengha, and his brother, Count Nicolò della Gengha, or, should they be impeded, Giovanni Bentivoglio, secretary to the Holy Office of the Inquisition and his brother, Giulio Bentivoglio. These agents were directed to make an inventory of all the cardinal's movable goods, and to sell at auction in Rome all the gold, silver, and furnishings found at the time of his death and not otherwise bequeathed.[147] Next, Savelli ordered them to sell all the grain, crops, and wines of Poggio

Natio, Poggio Mogiano, Rocca Priora, Frascati, Castelgandolfo, Quarto d'Albano, and the abbey of San Paolo d'Albano. Then they must collect all the incomes of the bishopric of Porto, Savelli's cardinalate church, and of the *commenda* of San Filippo nella Marca, the reservations of the fruits of the bishopric of Gubbio and the abbey at Gubbio, the reservations of the fruits of the priorate of Piacenza and the archdiocese of Benevento, the incomes of the prepositure of Canossa, of the abbey of Aragona, of the abbey of San Lorenzo in Cremona, "and of whatever other place where fruits shall be found at our death." Should any of the above properties be found to have been rented out, the executors must collect the payments from the lessees. They also must collect "all the moneys that we have from the [episcopal] churches of Canea, Coria, Naples, Capua, and Catanzaro," as well as the profits from the silk tax (*gabella della seta*) of the prince of Bisignano, and, finally, "all the incomes located in whatever place and in whatever manner and for whatever cause, and all the money and credit in whatever place and in whatever manner and for whatever cause they be owed to us."[148]

What was to be done with all this cash?

> We also wish that with all the money that shall have been derived from the gold, silver, and furnishings, and from the grain, crops, and wine, as above, and also with all the money collected from the incomes, rentals, and credits, . . . which has not been disposed of by us through the will, codicils, legacies, or gifts, . . . [the executors] shall buy as many *censi* or *monti non vacabili* as possible.[149]

Censi were interest-bearing bonds on mortgaged property; *monti non vacabili* were interest-bearing shares in the papal debt which were transferable to heirs. What Savelli was requesting, in effect, was the conversion of his assets into a portfolio of relatively safe, interest-bearing bonds.[150] Further, the executors must take any profits from these investments as well as fruits from other landed properties and continue to buy *censi* and *monti non vacabili*.[151] The process was to continue: "We wish [the executors] always to be careful to reinvest the aforesaid cash in as many other *censi* or *monti non vacabili* as possible, . . . for the augmentation of the inheritance."[152]

Having thus dealt with his liquid assets, Savelli turned to a lengthy discussion of his landed property. Although anxious to keep the inheritance out of the reach of his brothers, the cardinal was not abandoning his family: the universal heir to this vast estate was to be the eldest son of brother Bernardino. Except for that part inherited from his paternal grandparents, however, he was barred from possession until he reached the age of twenty-five. In the meantime, the executors were to be the heirs *usufruttuarii;* that is, they had full rights to the real and corporeal possession of the estate and to its control and management.[153]

Savelli continued with a long series of admonitions, accompanied by increasingly severe pecuniary penalties that ended with total deprivation for any heirs who should attempt to contravene the terms of his last testament. Furthermore, if the executors should die or fail in any other way, the entire congregation of the Holy Office of the Inquisition became executor of the will and heir of the usufruct. The cardinal concluded his last testament with a series of individual bequests.[154]

The document shows that Savelli perceived his private property as indistinguishable in kind from his ecclesiastical property. Although the cash from the fruits of church benefices differed from his other property in that it (apparently) ceased to come in with his death, he lumped it together with his personal treasure and secular lands indiscriminately. This money was not to be converted to "pious uses," but rather into income-bearing bonds. He then bequeathed the bulk of this estate, much of it derived from the wealth of the church, to laymen—the Savelli universal heir and his descendants, and servants and their descendants, including "the three dwarfs." Although the cardinal clearly anticipated that trouble, litigation, perhaps even violence would result from his last will, it was not the reformed Catholic hierarchy he feared. He saw his antagonists as "the universal heir, or his descendants, or other sons or descendants of Bernardino, or Bernardino himself, or Mariano, bishop of Gubbio."[155] In order to combat them and ensure the execution of his wishes, he invoked the help and protection of the most powerful forces in Italy—princes, cardinals, and the congregation of the Holy Office.[156]

The men who witnessed Savelli's will were equally orthodox: Brother Tommaso Zolio, Order of Preachers, master of the Sacred Palace; Brother Agostino of Corneto, procurator general of the Order of St. Augustine; Brother Riccardo Baronio, procurator of the Order of St. Jerome; Stefano Tucio of Messina, priest of the Society of Jesus; Giovanni Francesco Bordino of Florence, doctor of civil and canon law; Otto Narcia of Liège, priest of the Society of Jesus; and Francesco Chicchio, a priest from Lucca.[157] One must assume that none of the witnesses, who included the chief theologian of the church and members of religious orders at the forefront of the Catholic reform, held any objections to an instrument that alienated the revenues of three archbishoprics, five bishoprics, six monasteries, and one prepositure.

The Holy Roman Church thus believed, at the end of our period as at the beginning, that it was a worthy thing for prelates of the church, and especially cardinals, to be allowed to dispose of their possessions in life by means of a last will and testament as they approached the final days of their journey. Although the reformers of 1537 singled out the practice of granting licenses to make wills as deplorable, it never became a target of reform projects. Licenses to bequeath ecclesiastical incomes contained ever-larger maximum sums under Pius IV, from 10,000 ducats to 20,000, 25,000, and even 40,000 ducats.[158] Inflation in both incomes and costs is reflected here in *licentiae testandi*. Revised canon law, as it did with pensions, *commendae*, and rentals, made church custom legal. Among the privileges accorded to cardinals today is the right to "dispose of the fruits (income) that they receive from the various benefices that they have been permitted to retain after their promotion to the cardinalate, as well as from any pensions or *commendae* they have been granted after their assumption to the cardinalate. This disposition they may make to anyone they wish, even by bequests in their last wills and testaments."[159]

The extent to which church wealth was alienated by means of commercial contracts or last wills during the sixteenth century remains uncertain. It is clear that both practices continued and even became more common, at least in Italy. We have outlined both practices in detail, almost to the point of tedium, to demonstrate the manner in which they became customary.

Rentals of church property offered another method, besides pensions, for prelates to collect moneys in the eternal city itself and enhance their incomes without being burdened with the care of their charges. When the property in question had already been resigned, the convenience for the prelate was even greater. The fact that the curial records reveal a certain uneasiness about rental agreements between 1550 and 1558—with remarks about a "just price," "in clear utility," and "no payments in advance"—indicates that Rome did regard the practice as open to abuse. The response to Paul IV's edict of 1555, however, shows that rentals were so deeply entrenched that it was impossible to restrict them even to the canonical three years. Pius IV not only revoked his predecessor's bull but even resumed granting licenses to collect moneys in advance. The Tridentine decree ordered provincial synods to review such transactions, but the spirit of the law was easily circumvented by the linguistic device of the "triennium." Leases of multiple benefices became church custom, and church custom became canon law. We can only speculate upon what this meant to the inhabitants of the properties in question. For the cardinals and other prelates, it was more than convenience. They were turning into *rentiers,* living in Rome or on country estates, collecting pensions and rents from ecclesiastical property.

The alienation of church wealth by means of a last will was an even more serious matter, because the money here disappeared permanently into the coffers of private families. Attitudes about this also altered during the century, as the social needs of the cardinals caused their fiscal needs to increase. As we have seen, the authors of the *Consilium* of 1537 deplored the granting of licenses to make wills. But cardinals, in order to sustain themselves according to their rank, were also obliged to see to the needs of their families, and, as luxuries increased in Rome, so too did the sums of money churchmen were allowed to bequeath. By 1587, Cardinal Savelli, who clearly thought it would have been an evil thing if he had procreated children, saw nothing amiss about his will. He, along with other men who were leaders of the Catholic reform, thought it a worthy thing that his executors should be allowed to dissolve his ecclesiastical incomes, lump them together with his secular property, and invest all liquid assets in bonds.

The fate of Cardinal Savelli's will is testimony to what was happening. The incomes of our ecclesiastical *rentiers* were being diverted into the hands of lay *rentiers,* who were transforming the social fabric of Italy by buying their way into the nobility.[160] The Savelli were among the oldest nobility in Rome, and it seems more than a coincidence that Pope Sixtus V allowed Bernardino Savelli to subvert the cardinal's will at the very time that the pope's family, the Peretti—non-noble before the success of their papal relative—were negotiating a marriage contract with the same Bernardino. We shall investigate these relationships more fully in the succeeding chapters. As for last wills and testaments, they, like rental agreements, pensions, and other practices, became so customary that they were sanctioned by canon law. The privilege of bequeathing church money, which still required special papal license in the sixteenth century, now accompanies the red hat as a matter of course.[161]

4
The Distribution of Church Property: Sacred Office

The preceding chapters have frequently touched upon practices of patronage and nepotism that were prevalent at the Roman court. This chapter and the next will focus directly upon these problems and examine the ways in which the church was used to further the interests of clients and relatives. First we shall discuss the distribution of moneys and properties with sacred office attached, that is, ecclesiastical benefices and pensions from ecclesiastical benefices; in the following chapter, we shall look at other forms of nepotism.

Nepotism and patronage were not new phenomena at the papal court, of course. Wolfgang Reinhard traced nepotism back to the earliest days of the church, and research has shown that a fifth of the cardinals created at Avignon in the fourteenth century were papal relatives.[1] The schism and the councils of Constance and Basel temporarily altered papal habits, and then, as Denys Hay argued, "a new trend" began with the pontificate of the Spaniard, Calixtus III (1455–1458).[2] Wholesale papal nepotism began in earnest during those years and continued throughout the seventeenth century.[3] Hay also identified two other trends that began in the mid-fifteenth century—the "Italianisation" of the Catholic church and the "Romanisation" of the Italian church.[4] Once the papacy was firmly established in Rome, and once the popes "began to play Italian politics at the dynastic level and on this scale," Italian princely families for the first time found it important, even necessary, to seek the red hat for their members.[5] A further development, which began toward the end of the fifteenth century, was the clericalization of the Roman bureaucracy. That is, offices in Rome were administered in increasing proportions by churchmen—the precise opposite of the trend in other bureaucracies, where laymen were beginning to dominate.[6] All of these developments, relatively new in our period, suggest that patronage and nepotism would be likely to increase during the sixteenth century rather than diminish.

But did contemporaries regard patronage and nepotism as abuses? Were practices that appear, to say the least, odd to the twentieth century considered so in the sixteenth? Reinhard has argued convincingly that they were not, that nepotism was "the accustomed social norm" in Italy.[7] Other evidence, however, suggests that these practices were *not* entirely acceptable. Nepotism came under attack from the fifteenth century. In 1436, for example, the Council of Basel issued a decree forbidding the creation of cardinal nephews or governor nephews for the papal state.[8] The relative absence of papal nepotism during the pontificates of Martin V, Eugenius IV, and Nicholas V from 1417 to 1455 reflects, perhaps, the fear of criticism and an eye toward the decree *Frequens* and a possible future council.[9] The reform program of Domenico de' Domenichi during the pontificate of Pius II (1458–1464) condemned papal nepotism, and the reform bull of 1514 cautioned against nepotism at all levels.[10] The authors of the *Consilium* of 1537 are silent on the subject of relatives, to be sure, but their criticisms of reservations, expectancies, the inheritance of benefices, faculties for making wills, and so forth, all attack patronage and nepotism indirectly.

At the same time, however, a man clearly had obligations to his familiars and to his family. Rewards and favors to faithful servants and relatives were the marks of a gentleman, the measure of his honor. A prince of the church could not, after all, be niggardly toward his own retainers and clients. Still less could he disregard or ignore matters involving the honor and *grandezza* of his own blood family. This is the attitude Reinhard called "piety," *pietas* in the classical, pre-Christian sense of the word—the honoring of one's homeland, one's ancestors, one's family.[11] The apparent tension between the ideal of reform and that of *pietas* can be illustrated from two very different sources: reports of the events surrounding the death of Pope Pius III, and the language of the reform bull of 1514.

On 3 October 1503, Pius III lay dying.[12] A nephew of Pius II, Francesco Piccolomini had been elected only days earlier, and he had promised to be a reforming pope, saying that he would call a council and that he would *not* create a cardinal nephew.[13] The Venetians reported on 14 October that his condition was critical, and that his brothers had visited the cardinal of Naples, Oliviero Carafa, to ask that he support the red hat for the pope's nephew Giovanni Piccolomini, "saying that they ought to have at least this from the tiny papacy of their brother."[14]

On the 17th, the cardinals were called to the papal palace, and there they tried to persuade Pius III to promote this nephew to the purple, but the pope would not do it, "saying that he did not want to break the promise he had made."[15] Nothing daunted, the Piccolomini brothers appeared before the congregation of cardinals that met following the pope's death on the next day, carrying a bull of creation for Giovanni which they claimed to have received from the hand of their defunct brother, "begging the cardinals to accept it." The cardinals rejected this suspicious document, but they did so "with kind words."[16] The incident shows that the Piccolomini family thought that they had some "rights" here and that the cardinals apparently agreed with them, even though they refused to honor the purported post mortem "bull." The pope himself, however, had felt that it was more honorable to keep "the promise he had made" than to support the interests of his family.[17]

Although the reform bull of 1514 was not enforced, its language provides insights into the minds of the fathers at the Fifth Lateran Council as it spells out even more clearly the dilemma between reform ideas and *pietas:*

And, although it is in no way proper to neglect blood relatives and relatives by marriage, especially those deserving and lacking in resources, but rather just and praiseworthy to provide for them, we still do not deem it fitting to shower them with a multitude either of benefices or of ecclesiastical incomes, with the result that others suffer damage from such intemperate largess, and scandal is born. We order therefore that the wealth of churches not be poured out heedlessly, but be placed in pious and holy works.[18]

It was just and praiseworthy to care for poor and worthy relatives, *but* moderation must prevail, and ecclesiastical wealth be put to pious and holy works. As for rewarding servants, the decree stated that cardinals "should act cautiously and with foresight," not providing for too many or too few. "For the house of a cardinal should be a hospitable one, a harbor and shelter for learned and upright men, for impoverished nobles and persons of high repute and esteem."[19] The key here is Christian *charity*—recipients of church moneys must be worthy and also truly poor. Cardinals in the sixteenth century shared remarkably similar values on the duty of charity toward their families and servants. Our cardinals, whether classified as conservative, reactionary, moderate, progressive, zealous, or indifferent as reformers, agreed that they must watch over the interests of their dependents. These must be provided with suitable incomes, either from the cardinal's own pockets or from ecclesiastical benefices under his control.

PATRONAGE

Cardinals had large retinues of retainers serving in a wide variety of capacities for whom they had to find livings. The "family" planned for the newly created Cardinal Ippolito I d'Este in 1493, for example, included some 136 "familiars" and servants.[20] D. S. Chambers has shown that the average cardinalate household in 1509 numbered 154 servants, and even at the end of the century, according to Delumeau, when the number of cardinals had about doubled and the average number of household members had diminished, it was considered only fitting that each cardinal nourish at least twenty "mouths."[21]

Systems of patronage were subject to the fluctuations of fortune. The network of relationships among cardinals and favorites shifted ceaselessly with events, as successions of individuals gained or lost authority. Ecclesiastics and laymen alike did not hesitate to follow the dictates of fortune in asking for aid or pledging support. And those in authority did not hesitate to use it to their own advantage and that of their familiars.

The correspondence of Giovanni Morone between 1555 and 1560 is instructive about the ways of the papal court. Morone was important enough to have been widely considered "papable" in the two pontifical elections of 1555. On 22 March 1555, the duke of Florence, Cosimo I de' Medici, having heard of the "grave indisposition" of Julius III, wrote immediately to offer his support to Morone as a papal candidate.[22] After the election of Marcello Cervini as Marcellus II and his sudden demise on 30 April of the same year, more letters arrived. Morone's friends in Milan and the priors of Perugia sent their best wishes for his election as pope.[23] The duke of Amalfi, Innigo Piccolomini, offered more. Writing from Naples on 3 May, the duke expressed the profundity of his desire for Morone's success in the conclave:

And so, both because of the obligation of my servitude and my wish for such an outcome, in every way that I can, I offer Your Most Illustrious Lordship my state, which you may sell or mortgage or use for any service and dispose of as you please, as the true *Padrona*. And know well that you are equally and fully my *Padrona* and that of my sons and of anything else that I have in the world, and that now and always, we have been, we are, and we shall be prepared to serve you and to put our lives continually at your service. And I kiss the hands of Your Most Illustrious Lordship, praying to Our Lord God for you.[24]

Paul IV's accession to the papacy on 23 May did nothing to detract from Morone's reputation as a powerful force in Rome. Ercole Gonzaga wrote him three letters in the sycophantic style of the day during October

1555, and in November, Ferrante Gonzaga asked Morone to take a young Mantuan into his household, "who, being noble, rich, and of high spirit, wishes to follow that court for some years under your protection and with the example of your noble and holy customs."[25] Others, also convinced of Morone's continuing influence with the new pope, asked ecclesiastical favors. On 6 January 1556 Gianangelo de' Medici, the future Pius IV, asked that one of his familiars be allowed to resign his benefices in favor of a nephew; on 7 September the same duke of Amalfi asked that his illegitimate son be allowed to exchange the bishopric of Lanciano for that of Tropea; on 28 November Girolamo Dandino asked to be given the bishopric of Cesena; on 8 April 1557 Alessandro Farnese asked that he be granted one of the abbeys belonging to Reginald Pole; and on 20 April the same cardinal asked that he be allowed to resign the archbishopric of Benevento in favor of Jacopo Savelli.[26]

These requests remained unfulfilled, and on 1 June 1557, the shocked court learned why when Paul IV announced Morone's arrest and incarceration for heresy.[27] Morone's supporters in the Sacred College and elsewhere proved to be of vital importance to him during the critical years of his imprisonment in the Castel Sant'Angelo. In spite of the pope's urgent insistence, Morone's conviction was repeatedly delayed. His release and absolution, however, had to await the death of the Carafa pope in 1559.[28] With the election of Gianangelo de' Medici as Pius IV on Christmas Day of that year, Morone survived with greater authority and reputation than ever. Letters of congratulation poured in from all over Europe, and on 13 March 1560, in full consistory, the new pope formally absolved Cardinal Morone of any suspicion of wrongdoing.[29]

Morone had already begun to take care of some old business. During a busy consistory held on 26 January 1560, he managed to satisfy some of the preimprisonment entreaties and simultaneously reward two of his faithful retainers. On that day, the pope transferred Pompeo Piccolomini, the son of the duke of Amalfi, from the bishopric of Lanciano to Tropea, reserving a pension of 500 ducats per year for "Filippo Gherio, secretary of Cardinal Morone."[30] Then, with Morone himself acting as cardinal *referente*, the bishopric of Ischia was granted to the same Filippo Gherio.[31] Cardinal Ercole Gonzaga then resigned the bishopric of Fano in favor of *his* principal familiar, Ippolito Capilupi, and reserved a pension of 300 *scuti* for Filippo Gherio. Alessandro Farnese at long last resigned Benevento to Jacopo Savelli, and Savelli in turn resigned Nicastro, reserving a pension of 400 *scuti* of gold for familiars of Cardinal Farnese.[32] Morone began to receive letters of supplication once again in January 1560.[33] The Roman court was back to normal. Paolo Sadoleto expressed a common sentiment in a letter to Morone written from Carpentras on 21 January:

> God be praised that the affairs of the long and confused conclave have been well resolved at last with a good and holy election, pleasing, as one hears, to the universe. I am very happy about it, because of the knowledge I have of the good and very worthy qualities of this pope, and especially because of his great gentleness and kindness, of which your court has more need than anything else in order to be restored and to recover from the rigidity and the strictness of the past.[34]

One sign of the court's recovery was the generosity with which Cardinal Morone rewarded Filippo Gherio, his secretary and familiar.

Familiares continui commensales enjoyed a special status in cardinal-ate households. Originally, one had to live in the patron's house and eat at his table in order to qualify as a true familiar, and these generally held the more important posts in the retinue of servants—major domo, secretary, chamberlain, chaplain. Much of the patronage of cardinals focused upon these servants, and by the sixteenth century they did not necessarily have to be present and attendant upon their patron to keep their status. Popes also had familiars, and, at least from the pontificate of Eugenius IV, all officers of the curia were so designated.[35] Sixtus IV confirmed this privilege in 1472 during his wholesale creation of new offices, and Paul III issued a fresh order in 1534, repeating that all curial officeholders were "true and undoubted familiars and not fictitious" even if they did not reside at the papal palace or eat at the pope's table.[36] As the number of officeholders at the curia increased during the century, so too did the number of papal familiars. When Paul III imposed a special tax of two tenths upon the dominion of Venice in 1536, for example, he sent an additional brief listing twenty-two of his familiars who were to be exempt.[37] A similar exemption accompanied another extraordinary tax on Venice in 1546, this time numbering some forty persons as familiars.[38] By 1560, the number of papal familiars who were exempt from a special Venetian tax had risen to fifty-six.[39]

Cardinals regularly interfered with the administration of the church in favor of their familiars. In late 1530, when Lorenzo Campeggio urged the appointment of one of his familiars as auditor of the Rota, he cited his own services to the pope as justification, and added that besides, he had "never received the grace of putting a man on the Rota, [a grace] which has been conceded, perhaps, to almost all the Very Reverend Cardinals."[40] Sometimes cardinals acted on behalf of familiars in matters that seem to be of minimal moment. Personal pride probably motivated Guido Ascanio Sforza in 1557 when he demanded that the tax collector return the sum of eleven *scuti* and eleven *baiocchi* to one of his servants. "It is the opinion of patrons," wrote the cardinal *camerlengo*, "that familiars of the Very Illustrious and Reverend *camerlengo* are free from paying tenths on their benefices."[41] The most common rewards for familiars of cardinals, however, were ecclesiastical benefices themselves—bishoprics, lesser benefices, and monetary pensions from church benefices.

During our period, relatively few familiars of cardinals received bishoprics. Consistorial records specifically identify twenty-two new bishops as familiars, mostly secretaries, between 1520 and 1563.[42] Familiars other than secretaries who became bishops included Francesco Soderini's physician, Alessandro Farnese's preceptor, and Girolamo Grimaldi's auditor.[43] Cardinals procured these episcopal churches for their familiars either through direct resignations in their favor or by using their leverage in consistory. We have seen Cardinal Gonzaga resigning the bishopric of Fano directly to his familiar in 1560, and Cardinal Morone acting as *referente* for a bishopric for his familiar during the same consistory. Similarly, Alessandro Farnese was *referente* when the diocese of Ravello went to the secretary of his brother Ranuccio in 1549, and Giulio della Rovere did the same in acquiring the bishopric of Forlì for his own secretary in 1563.[44]

Cardinals could be stubborn about their rights in matters involving the conferral of benefices upon familiars. Ercole Gonzaga, for example, withstood considerable pressure from Rome when he determined to resign the bishopric of Fano in 1537 to his man Pietro Bertano, a Dominican monk. Gonzaga wrote to his friend Gasparo Contarini about his decision in late September. Contarini replied on the first of October, saying that he would discuss the fitness of Bertano's nomination with the master of the Sacred Palace, Tommaso Badia.[45] Gonzaga's reaction was stiff: he did not object to the solicitation of Badia's opinion, he wrote, but he had already made up his mind and spoken to Bertano about the matter, and further, "there has never been a more free and holy resignation than this one, because I was not motivated by any human cause to make it, and he [Bertano] knew nothing about it and could not demonstrate ambition with either words or hints."[46] Rome continued to be obstinate, advancing names of other candidates, while Gonzaga, with increasing impatience, continued to insist upon Bertano.[47] "Having already made this deliberation according to my conscience and that which has been inspired in me by God, I cannot change it, nor do I wish to do so," he wrote on 19 October.[48] Contarini then suggested the man who seemed to him best fitted for the office: his own familiar and secretary, Lodovico Beccadelli.[49] But Gonzaga had had enough. He informed Contarini on 3 November that if Bertano were not given the bishopric of Fano, he, Gonzaga, would keep it for himself, "since I have been prevented by His Beatitude from giving it to the person who alone seemed to me worthy of having it because of his wisdom and goodness."[50] This last argument succeeded: Pietro Bertano was named bishop of Fano during the consistory of 28 November 1537,[51] and eventually achieved the cardinal's hat for himself. Lodovico Beccadelli, for his part, found a more influential patron in Paul III's younger grandson Ranuccio Farnese.[52]

Bishoprics entailed considerable incomes, but smaller benefices made up the vast bulk of church properties at the disposition of cardinals and popes. Parish churches, nonconsistorial abbeys, canonicates, prebends—benefices such as these furnished the treasury from which prelates usually provided for their familiars. Cardinals controlled countless such small income-bearing properties, and the primary purpose of this control seems to have been to furnish incomes for faithful servants. Young curialists, then, usually found the first step on the ladder of the church hierarchy to be a minor ecclesiastical office. Jacopo Sadoleto, for example, received his first benefice, a canonicate in the church of San Lorenzo in Damaso, at the hands of his patron, Cardinal Oliviero Carafa, in 1506.[53] The familiar then accumulated a sufficient number of small offices to create a viable annual income.

Indeed, it was not considered fitting for cardinals to hold benefices with tiny incomes. When the ambassador from Ferrara asked the doge of Venice for two vacant benefices in Rovigo for Ippolito I d'Este in 1504, "the Prince said that it was not [right] for a cardinal to take such small benefices, and that they would see," wrote Sanuto.[54] The unpublished reform bull of 1514 forbade the conferral upon cardinals of parish churches or other benefices worth less than 200 ducats per year unless such benefices were vacant because of the death of a familiar, in which case they must be resigned within six months to others worthy and pleasing to the cardinal.[55] And licenses to confer benefices usually stipulated that any vacancies with incomes of less than twenty-four ducats per year must be disposed of by cardinals within four, six, or eight months, depending upon their location.[56] We have established that cardinals were not, in fact, shy about possessing lesser benefices, and it was only in the 1580s that a papal decree required ecclesiastics to resign all small properties (except for abbeys) upon promotion to the cardinalate.[57] Propriety held, nevertheless, that these benefices should be used for the welfare of persons "pleasing and agreeable" (grata et accepta) to the cardinals—that is, for their familiars.

The close relationship among these lesser benefices, cardinal patrons, and client familiars was emphasized by the custom that all possessions of familiars reverted to the disposition of their patrons at death. By the eighteenth century this custom had become a rule, and it obtained even if the familiar had long ceased to act in his patron's service, provided he had originally acquired the property through his status as a familiar; also, although the properties of familiars who died at the Roman curia were at the disposition of the popes, cardinal patrons still retained the power of approval over any new nomination.[58] The documents indicate that the practice was even more direct during the sixteenth century. Popes simply granted to cardinals the benefices and goods of dead familiars or former familiars whether or not they had died at the curia; it was deemed only proper.[59] Papal briefs also show that plural benefices were the norm for familiars as they were for cardinals, and that familiars, like their patrons, received expectancies.[60]

The chief access to the reservoir of small properties was the right to the collation of benefices. This faculty allowed the ordinary—bishop, archbishop, abbot—to confer upon persons "pleasing and agreeable" all benefices falling vacant within his jurisdiction. The only exceptions were benefices that were already reserved to familiars of the pope or living cardinals and those that were vacant because of the deaths of familiars of the pope or living cardinals. Consistorial abbeys were also usually exempt. It was, of course, proper for a bishop, for example, to control the nominations of priests for his own parishes or of canons for his own cathedral. Indeed, the lack of such authority was one of the evils of the time which reformers deplored. The problem was that Italian cardinals tended to collect these faculties just as they collected benefices and regresses to them. One of the most common rights reserved by cardinals when resigning their benefices was the faculty of collation (fig. 4.1).

This meant that the new archbishop, bishop, or abbot did not, in fact, control appointments within his archdiocese, diocese, or abbey, but that they were made by someone in Rome who had servants for whom to provide. Further, during the first three decades of the sixteenth century, curial cardinals—those residing in Rome—counted the faculty of the collation of benefices among their normal privileges. When Pirro Gonzaga left the papal court in the autumn of 1528, for example, the pope authorized him to keep all of his cardinalate privileges, just as if he were still present at the Roman curia. Among these was the license to confer

> any ecclesiastical benefices, secular or regular, belonging to your collation, provision, presentation, institution, or any other disposition . . . by reason of any cathedral churches, even metropolitan, and other churches or monasteries, priorates, and benefices which you possess or will possess in the future, even if they be particularly or generally reserved by apostolic disposition, falling vacant at any time outside the Roman curia.[61]

This state of affairs altered under Paul III—not, as one might suppose, in response to reform agitation, but rather "so that poor men and other clerks, seeking the expectancies which we have granted them for the time being, can derive some profit from such expectancies."[62] The pope too had *personae gratae et acceptae* for whom to provide. The new constitutions about the collation of benefices were issued on 22 August

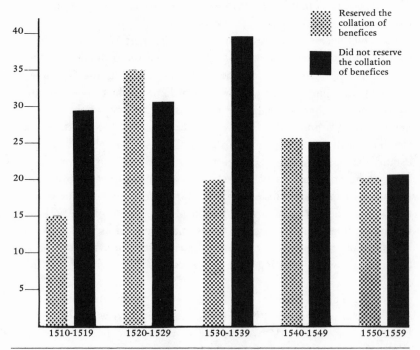

FIGURE 4.1   RESIGNATIONS IN WHICH CARDINALS
RESERVED THE COLLATION OF BENEFICES

1537. Henceforth, all cardinals were required to choose one bishopric and one monastery from which to confer benefices and to abandon the faculty of collation for all their other possessions. Each cardinal had to prepare a document naming his choices and register it with the apostolic chancery within one month.[63]

Apparently this decree was enforced. Rodolfo Pio, at least, who had been absent from Rome when it was promulgated, needed a special dispensation in November 1537 allowing him to choose his church and monastery and register them "just as if you had made the election within the time ordered in the said constitutions."[64] Similarly, in May 1538, Alessandro Cesarini required a special indulgence in order to transfer the right of collation from his former diocese of Jaén to his new diocese of Cuenca.[65] And subsequent popes—Julius III, Marcellus II, and Paul IV—all renewed and revalidated the Pauline order on collation.[66]

Adjustments could be made, of course. International politics probably motivated the indulgence Paul III bestowed upon Ippolito II d'Este in later 1539. Ippolito was considered a member of the French party and was at the French court at the time, and the delicate balance between the French and the imperialists perhaps dictated a favor for the French king. In any case, Ippolito received the right to confer vacancies in his title church of Santa Maria in Aquiro, in the archdioceses of Milan and Lyon, in three Benedictine abbeys in the dioceses of Beauvais, Soissons, and Rouen, "and also any other monasteries, even consistorial, priorates, and ecclesiastical benefices which you possess or will possess in the future."[67] When Ippolito came to Rome in the following year, however, this grant was revoked, and he had to adhere to the 1537 constitutions. He was allowed the right to choose Milan for his cathedral church and Lyon for his monastery nevertheless, not an insignificant concession.[68] The same indulgence—the right to choose a second bishopric from which to confer benefices in place of a monastery—went to other cardinals as well, along with other special graces.[69]

Even with the help of special graces, cardinals apparently felt the restrictions too rigid, and patronage needs extended the system to include alien properties, benefices in the possession of another man. The earliest example of such an indulgence being granted to one of our cardinals was dated 13 June 1536. Alessandro Farnese obtained from his grandfather the license to confer benefices falling vacant during the apostolic months in the diocese of Nantes, a bishopric with which he had no other connection, "as if you presided over the diocese of Nantes."[70] After the decree of 1537 was published, these arrangements became

TABLE 4.1   LICENSES FOR THE
COLLATION OF BENEFICES IN ALIEN DIOCESES

Cardinal	Diocese	Date
Guido Ascanio Sforza	Segovia, Spain	1546
Girolamo Capodiferro	Braga, Portugal	1547
Ercole Gonzaga	Reggio-Emilia, Italy	1550
Ranuccio Farnese	Cuenca, Spain	1550
Girolamo Doria	Urgel and Albarricin, Portugal	1550
Durante Duranti	Cartagena, Spain	1550
Girolamo Verallo	Barcelona, Spain	1550
Alessandro Farnese	Monte Aragona, Spain (abbey in diocese of Huesca)	1550
Giulio della Rovere	Vicenza, Italy	1550
Giovanni Morone	Como, Italy	1560
Ranuccio Farnese	Saragossa, Spain	1560
Carlo Borromeo	Vercelli, Italy	1560
Guido Ascanio Sforza	Segovia, Spain	1560

more common, and more cardinals secured the right to confer benefices in dioceses to which they had no other claim—usually, however, with the consent of the present bishop. The exigencies of the patronage system clearly caused these modifications; the language in the briefs is un-equivocal. Collation in alien dioceses was granted "so that you can provide ecclesiastical benefices to persons deserving and obedient to you and otherwise pleasing and agreeable, and graciously reward them."[71]

Thirteen lengthy and elaborate licenses were issued to the cardinals on our list between 1545 and 1560 authorizing collation in alien benefices (table 4.1). Fully eight of these, interestingly, involved bishoprics and a monastery in Spain and Portugal.[72] On 21 May 1546, for example, Paul III granted Guido Ascanio Sforza the right to confer vacant benefices at the disposition of the bishop of Segovia in all twelve months, and also to confer any vacancies belonging to abbots and lesser collators in the same diocese in the apostolic months, "with the express consent of the Venerable Brother Antonio Ramirez de Garo, Bishop of Segovia."[73] The details of each such indulgence varied, giving the recipient the right of collation in each jurisdiction for six, eight, or twelve months, for some years or for life, with the consent of the ordinary.[74]

Notations on these briefs suggest that such licenses had become customary by the middle of the century. Ercole Gonzaga's indulgence for the bishopric of Reggio-Emilia in 1550, for example, bears the following comment: "For the Cardinal of Mantua. An indulgence for his lifetime to confer benefices belonging to the collation of the Bishop of Reggio with the consent of the same bishop, even those reserved except, *etc.,* and otherwise in the form usually conceded to cardinals. "[75] The identical phrase appears on the back of such an indulgence for Durante Duranti in the same year, and Cardinal Crescenzio himself noted on the back of one for Girolamo Verallo that "similar indulgences were conceded to the Cardinals of Compostela, Burgos, and Carpi."[76] The customary nature of these grants did not imply legality, however. The later licenses, even those awarding the right of collation in dioceses that were not alien but were in the possession of the recipient, include the phrase *adversus regulas Cancellarie.*[77] As the rules became more restrictive, the language of the briefs that circumvented them became more elaborate. Thus Alessandro Guidiccioni, bishop of Lucca, was granted the right to the collation of benefices in his diocese, for alternate months only, by the newly crowned Pope Pius IV on 25 March 1560, "notwithstanding constitutions and apostolic orders and rules of the same Chancery to the contrary, perhaps even [promulgated] by us or by our predecessors."[78]

Monetary pensions from ecclesiastical benefices offered another way to reward faithful servants. Although grants of pensions to familiars were much less frequent than those to cardinals, their steadily increasing use in the later years of the period intimates that patrons became ever more dependent upon them for the support of their clients. Perhaps the average amount of a familiar's pension increased with the years as did the patron's, but this is not demonstrable. Since most of the pensions reserved by cardinals for others were in favor of unnamed persons, it is not possible to be precise about sums. Suffice it to say that the average familiar on a pension seems to have collected between 50 and 100 ducats per year. Two general kinds of consistorial transactions provided the means: (1) the cardinal, in reserving fruits and pensions to himself, could also obtain the faculty to transfer them to one or more persons, or (2) he could assign them directly to others or reserve them for "persons to be named," as Morone did for Gherio and Farnese did for unnamed persons in the consistory of 26 January 1560.[79]

Faculties to transfer pensions to one or more persons were popular early in the century. Almost 60 percent of twenty-three such licenses were conferred between 1519 and 1530.[80] These also seem to have been a kind of insurance for inheritability of the money. Several of the documents state that the pension can be transferred "even at the moment of death to one or more persons, without any other consent."[81] This is an interesting concession, because the church frowned upon deathbed bequests. Indeed, Paul III ordered in 1545 that any Spanish prelate who made a will must live at least twenty days beyond its date for it to be valid. Spanish benefices were singled out as being of the greatest importance, said the pope, "because of the opulence of the churches, monasteries, and benefices" in Spain.[82] These favors to Italian cardinals, then, seem to have been special indeed. In essence they meant that the cardinal could collect the pensions himself until the end of his life and at the same time bind his people, servants and relatives, to himself with the promise of immediate or future reward.

Unlike faculties to transfer, the direct assignment of pensions or reservations for persons to be named became more frequent with the years. The 500 ducats and 300 *scuti* per year that Filippo Gherio obtained at the largess of Cardinal Morone in 1560 were probably unusually munificent.[83] Giandomenico de Cupis reserved a similarly large pension, 400 ducats, for his secretary when he resigned the bishopric of Montepeloso in 1540, but smaller pensions seem to have been the norm.[84] Innocenzo Cibo reserved 100 ducats from the diocese of Volturara in 1537, "that is to say, 50 ducats for Ercole Machiavelli, clerk of Ferrara, and 50 ducats for Eliano Spinola, clerk of Genoa, his familiars."[85] Likewise, Andrea della Valle reserved 100 ducats from Gallipoli in 1529 for a person to be named, and Giovanni Morone reserved 300 ducats from Modena in 1571 for four of his familiars.[86]

Some reservations for unidentified persons carried time limits. Cardinal della Valle had to name the recipient of the pension from Gallipoli within four months. The two extraordinary pensions of 2,500 ducats in all from Naples and Cremona which Alessandro Farnese reserved in 1549 bore the stipulation that he *could* transfer them to persons of his choice within six months; it was not mandatory.[87] The remainder of these pensions seem to have been open and unrestricted, and the moneys so reserved were, in fact, assigned to familiars. Ercole Gonzaga, when he and Agostino Trivulzio began their plan to exchange one of Gonzaga's French monasteries for Trivulzio's bishopric of Reggio-Emilia in 1535, thought that the emperor ought to approve of the arrangement, because he, Gonzaga, asked nothing for himself. He merely wished to place Reggio in the hands of one of his relatives, Agostino Gonzaga, "and, from the pensions I will get, to remunerate some of my other servants, to whom I have long wished to show some gratitude for their service."[88] He supposed that 1,000 ducats in pensions would suffice, but the actual provision, made on 11 April 1537, designated only 800 ducats, for persons to be named by Cardinal Gonzaga.[89]

We saw at the end of chapter 2 that popes also reserved pensions for persons to be named. From Adrian VI on, every pope of our period made large reservations for persons pleasing and acceptable. Although such reservations seem to have diminished temporarily during the last years of Paul IV, his apparent distaste for the practice did not prevent his reserving 1,000 *scuti* of gold from Milan in 1556 and an enormous 16,500 ducats of gold from Toledo in 1557 for persons to be named.[90] The popes of our period, however, seem almost timid in this activity when compared to their successors in the years after the Council of Trent.[91]

All of the foregoing practices drew the bitterest of criticism at the Council of Trent's first sessions. Most outraged among the fathers were the Spanish bishops, whose anger prompted the legates, del Monte and Cervini, to send a summary of their complaints to Rome on 7 March 1546.[92] Concerning the residence of bishops, they wrote, the Spaniards contended that there was no sense in even discussing episcopal residence as long as papal provisions impeded them from exercising authority in their own dioceses. They objected to the proliferating conferral of benefices on aliens, as we have seen; they objected to the exemptions of such beneficiaries from the jurisdiction of the ordinary (archbishop, bishop, abbot); they objected to the granting of expectancies from their territories, "which, besides being prejudicial to the ordinary, engender many scandals, brawls, and enmities" over possession of the properties.[93] Cardinal Farnese replied on 23 March. The pope, he said, could not be deprived of control over the collation of benefices and the various exceptions and still maintain his dignity, and besides, in regard to expectancies, those recently granted had been published the preceding year. "One must avoid eradicating abuses in such a way as to fall into the other extreme," he added.[94] The legates wrote back on 10 April that the fathers totally rejected the arguments from Rome, "replying that experience shows the contrary because of the homicides, brawls, and tumults that are born from the competition of so many in taking possession by means of armed force and in every other evil manner, with unbelievable scandal to the people."[95] The question of impediments to episcopal residence continued to occupy a large part of the correspondence between Rome and Trent during the ensuing months. Alessandro Farnese imagined that the bishops exaggerated the state of affairs, and only wished to enlarge their own authority and deprive the pope of his.[96]

Whatever the motives of the Spanish bishops, their objections to curial practice remained for the most part unanswered. Reservations of pensions from "alien" benefices intensified. As for the right to the collation of benefices, we saw that Paul III restricted cardinals to the reservation of only two, one episcopal see and one abbey, or, with special dispensation, of two bishoprics. Paul IV revoked reservations of the collation of benefices in 1556, "except for the Most Reverend Cardinals."[97] Finally, Pius IV included cardinals in his order revoking concessions of the collation of benefices in 1562, but only those for "alien" benefices.[98] And, as stated earlier, the Council of Trent forbade expectancies and pluralism in benefices with the care of souls.[99]

But the special needs of the curia and its officers required special graces. By the eighteenth century the privileges of familiars were so commonplace that Lucio Ferrari outlined them as canon law. Familiars of cardinals were allowed to hold *incompatibilia,* they were exempt from the obligation of residence, they were exempt from the jurisdiction of the ordinary of the diocese in which their benefices were located, and they were frequently exempt from ordinary and extraordinary taxation. Familiars of popes enjoyed all of these and many additional privileges: exemption from the cost of the expedition of their bulls of promotion, exemption from all ordinary taxes, the faculty to make wills, the faculty to exchange or transfer their benefices, and the license to rent out the fruits of their benefices.[100] Papal constitutions and conciliar decrees to the contrary notwithstanding, the princes of the church were expected to take care of their servants. And, when it came to the sustenance of relatives by blood or marriage, the obligation was only the more compelling.

NEPOTISM

The reform bull of 1514 urged that the wealth of churches "not be poured out heedlessly, but rather placed in good and holy works."[101] Our cardinals, however, adhered to the first part of the injunction, that it was "just and praiseworthy" to provide for worthy and needy relatives. Christian charity, even when it countervailed established rules or proposed reform projects, must begin at home. As one of Paul III's biographers pointed out, the pope felt that it was not only his right but also his duty to use his office for the favor of his children and his grandchildren.[102] To contemporary Italians, kinship by blood or marriage to a member of the church hierarchy in no way disqualified an aspirant to an ecclesiastical career. On the contrary, the repeated identification in the records of the specific family relationship between a new beneficiary and an established churchman shows not only that nepotism was not clandestine, but rather that the very family ties rendered the neophyte the more worthy of sacred office. After all, who could be more trusted to discharge the duties of such office faithfully than one's own son, brother, uncle, nephew, or cousin? The fitness of a four- or five-year-old child might indeed be questioned, but the prevailing attitude was that nobility of blood—and princes of the church were *ipso facto* noble— would ensure the desired traits upon maturity. Bloodlines also took precedence over canonically required legitimacy of birth.

Nepotism in sacred office lasted throughout the period and beyond as a central fact of church life. Almost 90 percent of the 1512–1519 cardinals, 86 percent of the 1520–1539 cardinals, and 90 percent of the 1540–1549 cardinals provided relatives with ecclesiastical benefices (tables 4.2–4.4). They created at least 32 abbots, 148 bishops, 20 cardinals, and 3 popes.

Nepotism fostered the virtual inheritance of ecclesiastical property, with the result that families came to consider certain benefices as belonging to them by right. Pompeo Colonna's family, for example, lacked a suitable "heir" to the possessions of Cardinal Giovanni Colonna early in the sixteenth century. The young Pompeo, having already embarked upon a martial career, stubbornly resisted the family plan that he take holy orders. According to Paolo Giovio, Pompeo gave in only after his dead father appeared to him in a dream "with severe and menacing face" and strongly reproached him.[103] Filial piety was at work again, and considerable property was at stake, including the rich abbeys of Grottaferrata and Subiaco and the bishopric of Rieti.[104] All these went to Pompeo and through him to other members of his family. Subiaco was still a Colonna possession in 1571.[105]

Denys Hay described the establishment of virtual ecclesiastical fiefdoms in Italy during the fifteenth century.[106] The same can be said for the house of Ferrerio in Piedmont and the Grimani family of Venice during the sixteenth century. The Ferreri were bishops of Ivrea from 1497 to 1612, of Vercelli from 1503 to 1572 and again from 1599 to 1611, and also held three important monasteries in their domain for the better part of the century.[107] The Grimani, for their part, possessed three major benefices in the dominion of Venice: the bishopric of Ceneda (1508–1547), the bishopric of Concordia (1533–1585), and the patriarchate of Aquileia (1497–1616).[108]

Lorenzo Campeggio's efforts on behalf of his family illustrate the methods whereby prelates made benefices, in effect, inheritable. Campeggio, created cardinal in the 1517 promotion of Leo X, resigned the

TABLE 4.2   NEPOTISM IN SACRED OFFICE: 1512-1519 CARDINALS

Name of Cardinal, followed by Relatives

NO RELATIVE

Adriano Castellesi
Francesco Armellini
Tommaso de Vio
Egidio da Viterbo
Bernardo Dovizi

ONE RELATIVE

Silvio Passerini
 (Francesco Passerini, ?lb)
Alfonso Petrucci
 Lactanzio Petrucci, c*
Luigi de' Rossi
 Girolamo de' Rossi, ?*
Federico Sanseverino
 Alessandro Sanseverino, n*
G. B. Pallavicino
 (Francesco Pallavicino, ?*)
Franciotto Orsini
 Leone Orsini, gs*
Ferdinando Ponzetti
 Jacopo Ponzetti, n*
Francesco Conti
 (Federico Conti, ?@)
Sigismondo Gonzaga
 Ercole Gonzaga, n**
Marco Cornaro
 Francesco Cornaro, b**
Marco Vigerio
 Marco Vigerio, n*
Ercole Rangone
 Giulio Cesare Rangone, s@

TWO RELATIVES

Cristoforo Numai
 Antonio Ercolani, c*
 Antonio Numai, n*
Giandomenico de Cupis
 Paolo de Cupis, s*
 Bernardino de Cupis, s*
Alessandro Cesarini
 Ascanio Cesarini, s*
 Giovanni Battista Cesarini, s?
Domenico Jacobazzi
 Andrea Jacobazzi, b*
 Cristoforo Jacobazzi, n**
Francesco Soderini
 Giuliano Soderini, n*
 Francesco Tommaso Soderini, n$
Ippolito I d'Este
 Ercole Gonzaga, n**
 Ippolito II d'Este, n**

Nicolò Pandolfini
 (Giovanni Pandolfini, ?*)
 (Ferdinando Pandolfini, ?*)

THREE RELATIVES

Giovanni Piccolomini
 Francesco Bandini, n*
 Bernardo Piccolomini, ?*
 Nicolò Piccolomini, ?lb
Raffaele Petrucci
 Pietro Petrucci, c*
 (Angelo Petrucci, ?*)
 (Rinaldo Petrucci, ?lb)
Andrea della Valle
 Quintus de Rusticis, n*
 Orazio della Valle, n*
 (Nicolò della Valle, ?*)
Lorenzo Pucci
 Antonio Pucci, n**
 Gianotto Pucci, n*
 Antonio Nerli, n*
Leonardo Grosso della Rovere
 Raffaele Riario, c**
 Bartolomeo della Rovere, b*
 Antonio della Rovere, ?*
Sesto Franciotto della Rovere
 L. Grosso della Rovere, c**
 Raffaele Riario, c**
 Francesco della Rovere, ?*

FOUR RELATIVES

Pompeo Colonna
 Francesco Colonna, n*
 Scipione Colonna, n*
 Fabio Colonna, n**
 Marco Antonio Colonna, ?*
Pietro Accolti
 Benedetto Accolti, n**
 Baldovino Baldovinetti, n*
 Francesco Accolti, n*
 Bernardo Accolti, ?$
Nicolò Ridolfi
 (Cosimo Ridolfi, b@)
 (Filippo Ridolfi, ?@)
 Nicolò Lorenzo Ridolfi, n*
 Bernardo Antonio de' Medici, ?*
Giovanni Salviati
 Bernardo Salviati, b**
 Antonio Maria Salviati, n*
 Benedetto Nerli, n*
 Giovanni Battista Salviati, ?*
Bandinello Sauli
 Stefano Sauli, b@

Continued on next page

TABLE 4.2   CONTINUED

Name of Cardinal, followed by Relatives

Girolamo Sauli, ?*
Giulio Sauli, ?$
(Marcantonio Sauli, ?@)
Agostino Trivulzio
  Filippo Trivulzio, b*
  Pietro Trivulzio, b*
  Antonio Trivulzio, c*
  Ambrosio Trivulzio, ?*
Scaramuzza Trivulzio
  Antonio Trivulzio, b**
  Cesare Trivulzio, n*
  Catelano Trivulzio, n*
  Scaramuzza Trivulzio, n@
Domenico Grimani
  Marino Grimani, n**
  Giovanni Grimani, n*
  Pietro Grimani, b@
  Nicolò Grimani, n@
Francesco Pisani
  Luigi Pisani, n**
  Matteo Priuli, n*
  Giorgio Cornaro, n*
  Giorgio's brother, n*

FIVE RELATIVES

Nicolò Fieschi
  Urbano Fieschi, n*
  Jacopo Fieschi, n*
  Giovanni Francesco Fieschi, ?*
  (Lorenzo Fieschi, ?*)
  (Ottobono Fieschi, ?*)
Innocenzo Cibo
  Giovanni Battista Cibo, b*
  Cesare Cibo, ?*
  Ottavio Cibo, ?*
  Andrea Cibo, ?*
  David Cibo, ?$

SIX RELATIVES

Achille Grassi
  Baldassare Grassi, s*
  Corrado Grassi, s@
  Jacopo Grassi, n@
  Ippolito Grassi, n@
  (Giovanni Battista Grassi, ?*)
  (Paride Grassi, b*)

Antonio Maria del Monte
  Gian Maria del Monte, n***
  Cristoforo del Monte, n**
  Gasparo Antonio del Monte, n*
  Pietro del Monte, n*
  Gabriele del Monte, n*
  Antonio del Monte, ?*
Paolo Emilio Cesi
  Bartolomeo Cesi, u*
  Federico Cesi, b**
  Ottavio Cesi, n*
  Pomponio Cesi, ?*
  Ludovico Vespasiano Cesi, b@
  Massimiliano Ottavio Cesi, b*

SEVEN RELATIVES

Bonifacio Ferrerio
  Agostino Ferrerio, b*
  Filiberto Ferrerio, n**
  Francesco Ferrerio, n*
  Pierfrancesco Ferrerio, n**
  Bonifacio Ferrerio, gn@
  (Ascanio Ferrerio, ?*)
  (Vincenzo Ferrerio, ?*)
Lorenzo Campeggio
  Tommaso Campeggio, b*
  Marcantonio Campeggio, b*
  Alessandro Campeggio, s**
  Giovanni Battista Campeggio, s*
  Girolamo Campeggio, u*
  Giovanni Campeggio, n*
  Filippo Maria Campeggio, n*

NINE RELATIVES

Raffaele Riario
  Cesare Riario, b*
  Cesare Riario, n*
  Girolamo Riario, n*
  Ottaviano Riario, n*
  Girolamo Rossi, n*
  Ettore Rossi, gn@
  Girolamo Sansone, n*
  Tommaso Giovanni Riario, ?*
  Francesco Sforza Riario, ?*

ECCLESIASTICAL DIGNITY	FAMILY RELATIONSHIP
lb—Lesser Benefices	u—Uncle
$—Pension	b—Brother
@—Abbot	s—Son
*—Bishop	n—Nephew
**—Cardinal	c—Cousin
***—Pope	gn—Great nephew
( )—No evidence of direct conferral	gs—Grandson
	?—Relationship unknown

TABLE 4.3 NEPOTISM IN SACRED OFFICE: 1520-1539 CARDINALS

Name of Cardinal, followed by Relatives

NO RELATIVES

Federico Fregoso
Nicolò Caetani
Antonio Sanseverino
Dionisio Lorerio
Ippolito de' Medici

ONE RELATIVE

Cristoforo Jacobazzi
  Girolamo Verallo, n**
Benedetto Accolti
  Bernardo Accolti, ?$
Pirro Gonzaga
  Alfonso Gonzaga, b@
Ippolito d'Este
  Luigi d'Este, n**
Gasparo Contarini
  Giulio Contarini, n*
Pier Paolo Parisio
  (Flaminio Parisio, n*)
Ascanio Parisani
  (Giulio Parisani, ?*)

TWO RELATIVES

Uberto Gambara
  Gianfrancesco Gambara, n**
  Cesare Gambara, n*
Alessandro Farnese
  Ranuccio Farnese, b**
  Guido Ascanio Sforza, c**
Rodolfo Pio
  Teodoro Pio, b*
  Gianlodovico Pio, b@
Andrea Matteo Palmieri
  Francesco Palmieri, b*
  Giovanni Vincenzo Palmieri, b@
Jacopo Savelli
  Mariano Savelli, b*
  (Flaminio Savelli, ?@)
Girolamo Aleandro
  Francesco Aleandro, n*
  Claudio Aleandro, slb
Pietro Bembo
  Torquato Bembo, s@
  Carlo Bembo, n@
Girolamo Ghinucci
  Pietro Ghinucci, b*
  Andrea Ghinucci, ?lb

Antonio Pucci
  Roberto Pucci, u**
  Lorenzo Pucci, n*

THREE RELATIVES

Bartolomeo Guidiccioni
  Giovanni Guidiccioni, n*
  Alessandro Guidiccioni, n*
  Pietro Duranti, n*
Gian Vincenzo Carafa
  Francesco Carafa, n*
  Oliviero Carafa, n*
  Ferdinando Carafa, nlb
Agostino Spinola
  Carlo Spinola, b*
  Girolamo Spinola, n@
  (Ambrogio Spinola, ?@)
Guido Ascanio Sforza
  Alessandro Sforza, b**
  Carlo Sforza, b@
  Ottavio Maria Sforza, ?*

FOUR RELATIVES

Girolamo Doria
  (Imperiale Doria, b or c*)
  (Massimiliano Doria, ?*)
  Branco Doria, ?$
  Andrea Grimaldi, ?*
Nicolò Gaddi
  Taddeo Gaddi, n**
  Lorenzo Lenzi, n*
  Girolamo Gaddi, ?*
  Nicolò Gaddi, ?$
Ennio Filonardi
  Ennio Filonardi, n*
  Antonio Filonardi, n*
  Cinzio Filonardi, n*
  (Paolo Emilio Filonardi, gnlb)
Marino Grimani
  Giovanni Grimani, b*
  Marco Grimani, b*
  Giulio Grimani, n$
  Pietro Quirini, n*
Francesco Cornaro
  Andrea Cornaro, n**
  Marco Cornaro, n*
  Giorgio Cornaro, n@
  Giorgio's brother, n@

Continued on next page

TABLE 4.3 CONTINUED

Name of Cardinal, followed by Relatives	
Girolamo Grimaldi	**SIX RELATIVES**
Giovanni Battista Cicada, ?**	Jacopo Sadoleto
Odoardo Cicada, ?*	Paolo Sadoleto, c*
Carlo Grimaldi, n*	Paolo Emilio Sadoleto, n@
Andrea Grimaldi, ?*	Gianfrancesco Sadoleto, blb
	Camillo Sadoleto, nlb
FIVE RELATIVES	Paolo Sacrati, nlb
Jacopo Simonetta	Nicolò Sacrati, nlb
Giovanni Simonetta, n*	
Francesco Simonetta, n*	**SEVEN RELATIVES**
Lodovico Simonetta, n**	Marino Caracciolo
Giulio Simonetta, n*	Scipione Caracciolo, b*
(Alessandro Simonetta, n@)	Luigi Caracciolo, n*
Ercole Gonzaga	Alfonso Caracciolo, n*
Francesco Gonzaga, n**	Nicolò Maria Caracciolo, n*
Federico Gonzaga, n**	Giovanni Tommaso Caracciolo, ?*
Rodolfo Gonzaga, c@	Fabio Caracciolo, ?@
Agostino Gonzaga, ?*	Nicolò Antonio Caracciolo, ?@
Giulio Gonzaga, ?*	

ECCLESIASTICAL DIGNITY	FAMILY RELATIONSHIP
lb—Lesser Benefices	u —Uncle
$—Pension	b —Brother
@—Abbot	s —Son
*—Bishop	n —Nephew
**—Cardinal	c —Cousin
***—Pope	gn —Great-nephew
( )—No evidence of direct conferral	gs —Grandson
	? —Relationship unknown

bishopric of Feltre in favor of his brother Tommaso in 1520.[109] Having acquired the bishopric of Bologna in late 1523, the cardinal resigned it to Cardinal Andrea della Valle in December 1525. Three months later, Cardinal della Valle ceded Bologna in turn to Lorenzo's son Alessandro Campeggio, aged twenty-one.[110] In 1528, the cardinal acted in consistory to provide his brother Marcantonio Campeggio with the vacant bishopric of Grosseto.[111] Then, during the consistory of 28 March 1530, Cardinal Campeggio resigned a monastery in France directly to his son Alessandro and acted as cardinal *referente* to transfer a monastery in the diocese of Martorano from his brother Tommaso to his nephew Filippo Maria, then fifteen years old.[112] In September 1532 the cardinal saw another of his sons, Giovanni Battista Campeggio, named bishop of Majorca. In 1533 he persuaded his septuagenarian uncle Girolamo Campeggio to cede the bishopric of Parenzo to him, and, finally, he resigned Parenzo in 1537 in favor of another nephew, twenty-three-year-

TABLE 4.4   NEPOTISM IN SACRED OFFICE: 1540-1549 CARDINALS

Name of Cardinal, followed by Relatives

NO RELATIVES

Pomponio Cecci
Tommaso Badia

ONE RELATIVE

Cristoforo Madruzzo
   Lodovico Madruzzo, n**
Nicolò Ardinghello
   Luigi Ardinghello, b*
Bernardino Maffei
   Marcantonio Maffei, b**
Francesco Sfondrato
   Nicolò Sfondrato, s***
Ranuccio Farnese
   Alessandro Farnese, b**
Roberto Pucci
   Alessandro Pucci, gslb
Girolamo Capodiferro
   Fabio Mignanelli, ?**
Giulio della Rovere
   Giuliano della Rovere, slb

TWO RELATIVES

Tiberio Crispo
   Tiberio Crispo, nlb
   Gaspare Crispo, ?@
Girolamo Verallo
   Paolo Emilio Verallo, b*
   Giovanbattista Castagna, c***
Marcello Crescenzio
   (Stefano Crescenzio, ?lb)
   (Giuseppe Crescenzio, ?lb)

THREE RELATIVES

Andrea Cornaro
   Marco Cornaro, n*
   Andrea Cornaro, ?$
   (Federico Cornaro, ?*)

Federico Cesi
   Giannandrea Cesi, c*
   Pierdonato Cesi, c**
   Scipione Santa Croce, n*
Giovanni Vincenzo Acquaviva
   Giovanni Battista Acquaviva, c*
   Giovanni Antonio Acquaviva, c*
   Andrea Matteo Acquaviva, n*

FOUR RELATIVES

Gregorio Cortese
   Jacopo Cortese, blb
   Giovanni Livizzani, gnlb
   Lanfranio Cortese, ?lb
   Jacopo Cortese, clb
Giovanni Morone
   Girolamo Galerate, n*
   Galeazzo Morone, n*
   Orazio Morone, n*
   Galeazzo Pallavicino, n@

FIVE RELATIVES

Filiberto Ferrerio
   Sebastiano Ferrerio, n*
   Guido Ferrerio, n**
   Ferdinando Ferrerio, n*
   Cesare Ferrerio, ??
   Rodomonte Ferrerio, n$

SIX RELATIVES

Durante Duranti
   Pietro Duranti, c*
   Vincenzo Duranti, c*
   Bartolomeo Duranti, clb
   Alessandro Duranti, ?*
   Nicolò Duranti, ?*
   Valerio Duranti, ?lb

ECCLESIASTICAL DIGNITY
  lb—Lesser Benefices
  $—Pension
  @—Abbot
  *—Bishop
  **—Cardinal
  ***—Pope
  ( )—No evidence of direct conferral

FAMILY RELATIONSHIP
  u—Uncle
  b—Brother
  s—Son
  n—Nephew
  c—Cousin
  gn—Great-nephew
  gs—Grandson
  ?—Relationship unknown

old Giovanni Campeggio.[113] When he died in 1539, then, Campeggio left two sons as bishops, two brothers as bishops, one nephew-bishop, and one nephew-abbot.[114] His family continued the tenture of these properties: Marcantonio remained bishop of Grosseto to his death in 1553; Tommaso secured Filippo Maria as his coadjutor with the right of succession to Feltre in 1546, and Filippo Maria, succeeding in 1559, kept the diocese until 1580; after being created cardinal in 1553, Alessandro ceded Bologna to his cousin Giovanni, who kept it to his death in 1563; Giovanni Battista resigned Majorca in 1561, reserving a pension.[115]

In all this activity, the Campeggio family used the several available means of providing themselves with ecclesiastical property, of keeping it, and of transferring it to their heirs: (1) the sheer strength of the cardinal-member's curial position, (2) direct conferral, (3) coadjutorship with the right of succession, and (4) the use of an intermediary. The first of these, the most difficult to measure, reveals itself in the numerous transactions in which a nominee's family relationship to a cardinal is cited in the records whether or not the latter was present, or even alive. The three other methods are more easily quantified.

The most common practice was the most direct. Cardinals either resigned their own benefices in favor of relatives or used their authority as cardinals *referenti* to the same end to dispose of benefices otherwise vacated. A survey of some 160 such direct conferrals through the first five decades of the century shows that the practice remained constant throughout the period. Although the absolute number of such transactions diminished, so, proportionately, did the number of surviving cardinals on our list. And, as we have seen in the case of the Campeggio family, the repercussions of these grants could last for decades.

Cardinal Agostino Spinola, for example, took back the bishopric of Perugia when his brother, to whom he had earlier resigned the diocese, died in 1535. He resigned it again at once to his fellow cardinal Jacopo Simonetta, but reserved half the fruits for himself and half for a Girolamo Spinola, his nephew.[116] This Girolamo, who had embarked upon his career in 1531 at the age of four years with five benefices *in commendam* at the hands of his uncle, continued to collect half the fruits of Perugia each year, even after the cardinal's death in 1537. The pension was confirmed in 1538, 1550, and again in 1553 as the diocese changed hands.[117] Giulio Grimani, illegitimate nephew of Cardinal Marino Grimani, was equally tenacious. Cardinal Grimani reserved a pension of half the fruits of the bishopric of Concordia for Giulio in 1537 when he resigned the diocese in favor of another nephew. Giulio thereafter enjoyed half the fruits of Concordia each year at least through 1585, when the pension was confirmed for the last time during the century.[118] Furthermore, Giulio seems not to have been an active servant of the church. Although he had been named coadjutor with the right of succession to the bishop of Torcello in September 1561, Pius IV revoked this grace six months later "with a decree that the same Giulio is perpetually *inhabilis* to possess any sort of ecclesiastical benefice."[119]

Girolamo Garimberti mildly reproved these practices in the section of his work on the cardinals entitled "concerning love for friends and relatives." Cardinal Marco Cornaro, he said, had outstripped all his predecessors in his old and noble family, not because he was the greatest among them but because he had so enriched his family with church benefices and offices. "In a short period of time we have seen three cardinal successors, one brother and two nephews, with bishops, archbishops, abbots, and others placed in dignity through the lovingness of Cardinal Marco."[120] Only an improvident death prevented him from resigning his bishoprics of Verona and Padua, the patriarchate of Constantinople, and the many other important benefices in his possession to his beloved family.[121]

A coadjutor bishop assists the ordinary in the performance of his episcopal duties. In the sixteenth century, the Italian episcopate often used coadjutors to ensure the inheritance of the property by a family member. Cardinals, with greater privileges and powers than bishops, rarely resorted to this device. Direct conferral accomplished the same end, and with greater certainty. Thus only four cardinals on our list seem to have gone to the trouble of providing a relative with the office of coadjutor in their bishoprics: Jacopo Sadoleto, Gasparo Contarini, Bartolomeo Guidiccioni, and Durante Duranti. In the nepotistic appointments of the period, therefore, most of the coadjutors were relatives of bishops, not cardinals. Cardinal Achille Grassi, for example, resigned his diocese of Città di Castello *directly* to his illegitimate son Baldassare in 1515, and the young man presided there until 1534.[122] Meanwhile, the same Baldassare served until 1528 as coadjutor with the right of succession in the bishopric of Pesaro for his uncle, the cardinal's brother and well-known diarist, Paride Grassi.[123] Achille was a cardinal, Paride only a bishop.

It may be significant that three of the four cardinals who used coadjutorships were among the more prominent figures in the reform circles of the sacred college. Jacopo Sadoleto, to be sure, was still two years from his elevation to the cardinalate when his cousin Paolo was named his coadjutor with the right of succession at Carpentras.[124] Both Contarini and Guidiccioni were already cardinals, however, and in the years of their deaths, 1542 and 1549 respectively, when they asked for and received special dispensations for their chosen successors. Giulio Contarini, who replaced his uncle as bishop of Belluno, required dispensations for both illegitimacy and youth; Alessandro Guidiccioni, who succeeded his uncle as bishop of Lucca, required a dispensation for youth alone.[125] It is not surprising that Paul III should comply with the last wishes of two of his most faithful servants. What is interesting, and striking evidence of the strength of the family bond, is that even these reforming prelates, both of whom had argued at length about the central importance of the episcopal office to the health of the church, should feel compelled at the last to circumvent the church's rules in the interests of their young nephews. Indeed, their use of the coadjutorship instead of the more common direct conferral probably reflects a distaste for the resignation-with-reservation system so widely used by their colleagues. They thus assured the pope at least the opportunity to accept or reject their choices after their deaths.

In fact, for most of the college, a major drawback to the use of coadjutors was precisely this uncertainty of the inheritance. It was understood that these offices carried the right of succession, but the pope still had to make the necessary promotion in consistory following the death of the incumbent, and it was always possible that he would balk.[126] This happened to the chosen successor of Cardinal Duranti. Paul IV consented to the designation of Duranti's nephew Alessandro as coadjutor with the right of succession to the diocese of Brescia in 1557, but he had second thoughts after the cardinal's death in 1558.[127] Alessandro Duranti's claim to the bishopric was not wholly clear; when Julius III conferred Brescia on Cardinal Duranti in 1551, he had also given the right of *accessus* to Alvise Priuli of Venice.[128] Paul IV stepped to the center of the ensuing controversy, annulled the rights of both claimants, and on 15 March 1559 granted Brescia to a third person, Domenico Bolano.[129] The new bishop's impediment to the holding of sacred office was not of the sort to disturb the Carafa pope: Bolano needed a dispensation for having judged criminal cases and imposed sentences of blood, including dismemberment and death.[130]

As with coadjutors, the use of intermediaries to ensure the inheritance of benefices was primarily confined to noncardinalate families. Only two cardinals transferred bishoprics to members of their families through intermediaries: Lorenzo Campeggio, as outlined above, and Girolamo

TABLE 4.5   INHERITANCE OF BISHOPRICS THROUGH INTERMEDIARIES

Diocese	Old Bishop	Cardinal	New Bishop
Giovanazzo	Vincenzo de Planca	L. Pucci April-Aug. 1517	Marcello de Planca d. 1528
Potenza	Jacopo Nini	P. Colonna 1521-1526	Nino Nini d. 1564
Fano	Gregorio Gherio	E. Gonzaga 1528-1530	Cosimo Gherio d. 1537
Bologna	Lorenzo Campeggio	A. della Valle 1525-1526	Alessandro Campeggio res. 1553
Nicotera	Giulio Cesare de Januario	P. Colonna 1528-1530	Princivallo de Januario d. 1539
Alatri	Filippo Ercolani	A. M. del Monte Feb.-July 1530	Filippo Ercolani res. 1535
Bitetto	Lorenzo Serristori	G. Salviati 1532-1539	Lodovico Serristori d. 1584
Crete	Giovanni Lando	L. Campeggio 1534-1536	Pietro Lando res. 1576
Vaison	Tommaso Cortese	G. Salviati 1535-1536	Jacopo Cortese d. 1570
Conza	Camillo Gesualdo	A. M. Palmieri Sept.-Oct. 1535	Trioano Gesualdo d. 1539
Camerino	Giovanni Buongiovanni	G. de Cupis 1535-1537	Bernardo Buongiovanni d. 1574
Catanzaro	Angelo Geraldino	A. Cesarini May-Aug. 1536	Sforza Geraldino d. 1550
Lacedogna	Antonio Dura	A. Sanseverino Feb.-Sept. 1538	Scipione Dura d. 1551
Cavaillon	Girolamo Ghinucci	A. Farnese 1540-1541	Pietro Ghinucci d. 1569 (?)

Ghinucci. Probably some consistorial impediment to direct conferral prompted these actions, accompanied perhaps by private agreements between cardinals and intermediaries. For the most part, the cardinals themselves were the intermediaries, and these maneuvers worked to the satisfaction of all. A bishop resigned in favor of a cardinal, the cardinal resigned in favor of the bishop's relative, usually reserving the regress and sometimes pensions as well. Although the precise kinship between the original resigner and the new bishop was usually unspecified, we do know that Alessandro Campeggio was Lorenzo's son, that Jacopo Cortese was Tommaso's son, and that Nino Nini was Jacopo's nephew (see table 4.5). Whatever the degree of consanguinity of the others, it is clear that the system worked to keep the property in the family, and that families needed close contacts with the powers in Rome who could facilitate this form of inheritance. In addition, nearly all the new bishops needed dispensations for youth. The old bishop, in effect, entrusted his property to a cardinal until his heir had reached some semblance of canonical age.[131]

There were other advantages. Angelo Geraldino, for example, reserved the administration, the episcopal palace, the collation of benefices, and two-thirds of the fruits of Catanzaro when he resigned it in favor of Cardinal Cesarini in May 1536. To all intents and purposes, he was still the bishop. He also assigned a pension of 160 ducats from his reserved fruits, "80 for Alessandro Geraldino . . . and the remaining 80 for Ascanio, also Geraldino, to be paid after the death of the said Angelo and not otherwise."[132] When Cardinal Cesarini ceded Catanzaro to Sforza Geraldino three months later, Angelo, the old bishop, had accomplished much. He had provided for his own old age, bequeathed his diocese to one heir, and provided future pensions from the diocese for two more. For his part, Cardinal Cesarini had acquired a new regress.[133] In a similar transaction, Giovanni Lando, archbishop of Crete, reserved 500 ducats for a Giulio Lando and 200 ducats for one of his familiars when he resigned in favor of Cardinal Campeggio in 1534.[134] Campeggio, however, exacted more profit than Cesarini when he resigned in 1536 to a Pietro Lando. The cardinal reserved for himself not only the regress and the collation of benefices but also all the fruits of the archdiocese of Crete until Pietro, then seventeen years old, should reach the age of twenty-two.[135]

The preceding pages examined the distribution of church benefices at the disposition of living prelates. The notion that families had certain rights over benefices was so strong that it extended beyond the grave, even after death had removed the influence and authority of the prelate-relative. This attitude was expressed and acted upon so frequently that it seems to have been a principle for proper conduct, a principle we may label here the "dead hand" of nepotism. We saw in discussing last wills and the diversion of church incomes to the estates of laymen that "spoils" and other goods attached to the benefices of a deceased prelate were frequently granted by popes to lay relatives. Here we address the benefices, the sacred offices themselves, and their inheritance by relatives in holy orders or by children who were destined for a clerical career. In cases where there was more than one clerical heir to be satisfied, the obvious course was the inheritance of the benefice itself by one and a pension from it by another.

TABLE 4.6   THE DEAD HAND OF NEPOTISM

Dead Prelate	Benefice or Pension	Date	Beneficiary
Cristoforo Numai	Bpric of Alatri	April 1528	Filippo Ercolani (cousin or nephew)
Gianotto Pucci	1/3 fruits of bprics of Melfi and Rapallo	1537	Roberto Pucci (father)
Pietro Duranti	Bpric of Termoli	July 1539	Vincenzo Duranti (nephew)
Filippo Trivulzio	Mon in diocese of Tarbes, France	March 1544	Agostino Trivulzio (brother)
Filiberto Ferrerio	(1) Bpric of Ivrea	1549	Sebastiano Ferrerio (nephew)
	(2) 600 ducats from bpric of Ivrea		Rodomonte Ferrerio (nephew)
Nicolò Ridolfi	Mon of Avellana, diocese of Gubbio	1550	Filippo Ridolfi (?)
Andrea Cornaro	500 ducats from bpric of Brescia	1551	Andrea Cornaro (nephew)
Bernardino Maffei	Archbpric of Chieti	July 1553	Marcantonio Maffei (brother)

Gasparo Contarini elucidated the principle of the dead hand of nepotism in his correspondence with Ercole Gonzaga about the bishopric of Fano in 1537. Two things were necessary in the nomination of a new bishop, wrote Contarini, first, to satisfy the honor of God and the needs of the city, and second, "as much as possible, to satisfy also the family of the dead bishop [Cosimo Gherio] and of the earlier one [Gregorio Gherio] who committed it to your trust solely in the interests of his family."[136] What Gonzaga held with his right of regress to the bishopric of Fano was a sacred trust, not only to the honor of God, but also to the house of Gherio. Years later, Ercole Gonzaga explained the common feeling more fully. In August 1550 his familiar Ippolito Capilupi wrote the cardinal to ask for an abbey that had fallen vacant. Gonzaga replied:

As for the abbey of Lamoli, vacant because of the death of that son of our Messer Guidobaldo, you may be certain that if I had not pledged my faith, I would not fail to keep you in mind for all the reasons you have adduced in your [letter] and for many others, but as you know, I was a very great and intimate friend of Messer Guidobaldo, and he had such faith in me that he wanted me to have the regress to the said abbey, knowing that whatever happened, I would always return it to his house, and that I, wanting the world to know that whosoever deals with me, deals with a gentleman and a sincere and faithful man, would not fail to give it to another of his sons, not only this time, but every time it should return to my person.[137]

The records show many examples of ecclesiastical benefices transferring to heirs of dead churchmen who had made no such provision while living (table 4.6). Cardinals and popes alike followed the principle. In 1524, for example, nine days after the death of Cardinal Nicolò Fieschi, Clement VII gave four monasteries and a priorate in the dioceses of Rossano, Arezzo, Tortona, and Fréjus to Jacopo Fieschi, the six-year-old nephew of the late cardinal. The briefs of conferral noted that the cardinal of blessed memory had attempted to resign these properties in Jacopo's favor earlier and that Pope Adrian VI had consented, but that both had died before the bulls could be expedited.[138] It was therefore fitting and proper for the new pope to carry out the wishes of the dead pope and the dead cardinal. Federico Cesi may also have acted on the principle of the dead hand when he resigned the bishopric of Cremona to Nicolò Sfondrato, the son of his predecessor in the diocese, Cardinal Francesco Sfondrato. Apparently there had been no formal pact or agreement between Cesi and the elder Sfondrato, but it seemed right to all parties that the son should have it. The conferral took place on 13 March 1560, and Nicolò Sfondrato, the future Pope Gregory XIV, was launched upon his career.[139]

Lay rulers likewise subscribed to the rule. During the early months of 1547, Duke Cosimo I of Florence expressed the greatest concern over the disposition of some benefices that were vacant following the death in January of twenty-three-year-old Lorenzo Pucci, bishop of Vannes. This unexpected loss was a severe blow to the Pucci family, because their last cardinal of the century, Roberto Pucci, had also recently died. Duke Cosimo hastened to send condolences to Pandolfo di Roberto Pucci in Rome, now head of the clan, and to offer his assistance.[140] In February, Paul III gave Pandolfo, a layman, the right of collation to all the benefices left vacant by the young Lorenzo, with the single exception of the bishopric of Vannes. Cosimo wrote again, repeating his close interest in the matter.[141] By 1 March 1547 the nominations had been made, and the duke was satisfied. He was very happy, he wrote, that Pandolfo's son Alessandro Pucci had been awarded all of the benefices, "and for that which is expected of us," he added, "we shall not fail to admit that provision since we approve of it, knowing that it will be to the honor and utility of your son, and consequently to your [honor and utility] and that of your house."[142]

The principle of the dead hand was long-lived. Cardinal Antonio San-severino, for example, had died in 1543, but as late as 15 January 1561 his name was invoked in consistory. "The bishopric of Agde was pro-vided in the person of Amerigo Sanseverino, Neapolitan clerk, nephew through the brother *germanus* of Cardinal Sanseverino of blessed mem-ory," recorded the secretary.[143] Even Garimberti supported the rule:

Although the imperfection of Pope Alexander VI, or, to speak more precisely, his shameful life, was a dreadful example to our age; nevertheless, in order not to deprive him of the honor by which he merits to be numbered among the grateful princes, . . . I shall say something about his gratitude.[144]

Garimberti then recalled that the pope had created Nicolò Fieschi a cardinal in grateful memory of Fieschi's uncle, who had been instrumen-tal in the election to the papacy of the pope's uncle, Calixtus III.[145] By this measure, Paul III equally deserved to be numbered among the grate-ful princes. Owing his own elevation to the purple to the favor of Alexander VI, Paul III paid homage to his memory in his third promotion of cardinals, on 22 December 1536. One newly created prince of the church was "Lodovico Borgia, the nephew of Alexander VI, the pro-moter of His Holiness."[146] And a Don Juan Borgia collected a pension of 100 *scuti* of gold each month from the dataria from September 1537 to the death of Paul III.[147]

Popes combatted these practices throughout the period. In 1530 Clement VII issued a bull that prohibited sons "born from the fornication of prelates and priests" from obtaining any benefices or pensions from their fathers, "even through the interposition of another person."[148] Paul IV struck at the same problem, among others, in 1555 with a decree forbidding further dispensations for defect of age, and Pius IV annulled all indulgences of legitimization on 1 January 1561.[149]

Another set of orders was designed to curtail private maneuvers and agreements among prelates about the disposition of church property. Julius III ordered that cessions and resignations of cathedral churches and monasteries must not be made in favor of anyone, but "must be made freely and purely into the hands of His Holiness."[150] In 1557 Paul IV ruled that no monasteries could henceforth be granted, even to cardinals, by means of any "pact."[151] And in 1562 Pius IV revoked all "confidences" concerning ecclesiastical benefices except for those granted by himself, and ordered that all existing agreements be made public and refuted within two months.[152] This last measure caused so much debate that its implementation was repeatedly postponed. It was accepted, finally, on 10 October 1564, but its effectiveness must be questioned, because confidences were still under debate in subsequent pontificates.[153]

However effective these measures may have been in regard to lesser clergy, cardinals seem to have been able to get around them easily. Sons of priests, legitimate or otherwise, along with brothers, nephews, uncles, and cousins, continued to acquire and to keep ecclesiastical benefices. The Campeggio brothers and Nicolò Sfondrato were legitimate in birth, their fathers having enjoyed lawful marriage before embracing ecclesiastical careers. Illegitimate sons of cardinals, despite the language of the canons, also discovered few obstacles to inheriting church property. Their fathers could and did obtain bulls of legitimization on their behalf, and it was always possible to get simple dispensations for defects of birth attached to each ecclesiastical transaction. Bulls of legitimization could be very comprehensive. Clement VII, the author of the order prohibiting inheritance by sons of priests, issued two such legitimizations for the sons of Pietro Bembo, in January 1530 and January 1532, when the Bembo children, Lucilio and Torquato, were each about six years old. The pope not only pronounced them legitimate and able to inherit property from both parents and other ancestors, he also declared them able to hold any "honors, dignities, and offices, public or private, ecclesiastical and secular." They could be promoted to any grade of priest and hold benefices *in commendam,* and, finally, they were not to be held to mention their defect of birth in curial documents.[154] Lucilio Bembo died shortly thereafter, but Torquato, as we have seen, pursued a career in the church founded upon his father's resignations in his favor.[155]

These graces continued under succeeding pontificates. Paul III granted to one of Cardinal Alessandro Cesarini's illegitimate sons all the concessions his predecessor had given the young Bembos. The pope even extended his initial favors to Giovanni Battista Cesarini in 1538 by allowing the boy to accept and keep Italian benefices directly resigned to him by his father—one of the more blatant examples of nepotistic inheritance of church property during the period.[156] Cardinal Cesarini was also allowed to resign the bishopric of Oppido directly in favor of Ascanio Cesarini, another of his "spurious" sons, on 20 February 1538.[157] Cardinal Giandomenico de Cupis likewise found it possible to favor his illegitimate sons with direct resignations. Paolo de Cupis—already a canon in the cathedral of St. John Lateran and the beneficiary of a pension of twenty *scuti* from the diocese of Macerata in 1546—then became the bishop of Montepeloso at the cession of his father.[158] Two years later, with his father the cardinal acting as *referente*, Paolo transferred to the diocese of Recanati, reserving for himself a pension of 100 *scuti* from Montepeloso.[159] He either transferred, resigned, or died in 1552, and the bishopric reverted to Cardinal de Cupis.[160] The other son, Bernardino de Cupis, fared better. His father gave him the abbey of Santa Maria della Strada in Bologna in 1547, and then procured the bishopric of Osimo for him in 1551, reserving the fruits for himself. Sole beneficiary after the cardinal's death in 1553, Bernardino kept the bishopric until 1574, when he resigned, reserving the denomination and an annual pension of 1,050 ducats. After his own death in 1588 and a new conferral of Osimo, new pensions from its fruits of 500 ducats each were assigned to a Cristoforo de Cupis and a Septimio de Cupis, identified as Roman clerks.[161]

The final years of our period saw no diminution of nepotism in sacred office. Paul IV, the avid reformer, established Girolamo Aleandro's illegitimate son Claudio as his own familiar and provided him with benefices in 1558, and, in spite of his own order against dispensations for youth, the same pope in early 1556 created his great-nephew Alfonso Carafa, then seventeen years old, a cardinal, and named him archbishop of Naples three weeks later.[162] During the following pontificate, Cardinal Francesco Pisani persuaded Pius IV to accept a nepotistic disposition of the bishopric of Nemosia on the island of Cyprus, vacant, ironically, because its last bishop had been removed for heresy. In June 1560, with Pisani acting as *referente*, the pope conferred the diocese upon a Venetian, Andrea Mocenigo, who received a dispensation for defect of birth and the right to retain at least five other benefices and pensions. Half the fruits of Nemosia, however, were reserved as a pension for Matteo Priuli, a nephew through the sister of Cardinal Pisani.[163] Then, in September 1561, the same pope allowed Cardinal Pisani to confer the bishopric of Città Nova directly upon the same nephew.[164] During the same month, Pius IV also granted Giovanni Battista Campeggio, son of the late cardinal, license to reserve several pensions when resigning the bishopric of Majorca: 200 ducats for himself; 500 ducats for his cousin, Annibale Campeggio, "Bolognese clerk"; 500 more for a Gualengo Ghislieri, another Bolognese clerk and probably kin to Cardinal Michele Ghislieri, the future Pius V; and four more pensions for nominees of Philip II.[165] Finally, as pope, Ghislieri legitimized Giuliano della Rovere, son of Cardinal Giulio della Rovere, and started him on an ecclesiastical career.[166] These are but a few examples of papal violations of their own rules.

The popes of our period thus approached questions concerning patronage and nepotism obliquely, and, confronted with individual cases, they made exceptions. Attempts to restrict regresses, the collation of benefices, pacts and "confidences," were all indirect attacks upon practices of patronage and nepotism. Decrees about legitimacy of birth and canonical age addressed the problem more directly, but here again, as in the matter of personal pensions, papal reformers tended to focus upon the seemliness of the beneficiary rather than the health of the benefice. Canonical age certainly appears a valid reform goal to us in the twentieth century, but the extirpation of illegitimacy seems less compelling. Prohibitions for "defect of birth," however, were designed to prevent the inheritance of ecclesiastical benefices, the very practices which we have outlined in this chapter.[167] In any case, the repeated violations of the injunctions suggest that they remained ineffective.

If popes were hesitant in coming to grips with the problem of patronage and nepotism, the fathers at Trent were not. The decree issued from the last sessions of the council in 1563 forbade bishops, including cardinals, to "seek to enrich relatives or familiars with incomes from [episcopal] churches," and enjoined them from giving ecclesiastical properties, "which are of God," to relatives.[168] Whereas the fathers at the Fifth Lateran Council had deemed it just and praiseworthy to provide for poor and worthy relatives, the fathers at Trent ordered churchmen to "put aside all human feelings towards brothers, nephews, and relatives according to the flesh."[169] The decree of 1563 still permitted succor for poor relatives, to be sure, but only in the form of charity, as in the distribution of alms to any other paupers. Nepotism and patronage, accoring to the fathers at Trent, were the sources, the nourishers, of "many evils in the church."[170]

The uncompromising language of the Tridentine decree weakens Wolfgang Reinhard's repeated assertion that nepotism was not scandalous to contemporaries but rather the accepted social norm. Reinhard attributed the decree's rigor to its origin with a strict Portuguese reformer, the archbishop of Braga.[171] Insofar as the decree diverged from Roman tradition, he thought, it must have appeared strange in Rome.[172] Our evidence supports this view, but, if Roman practices appeared scandalous to non-Italian Catholics, they cannot be considered the customary norm. Further, the papal edicts designed to restrict patronage and nepotism attest to a consciousness in Rome, however dim, that the system permitted abuses. The uneasiness, the tensions, between the ideal of *pietas* for the family and the ideals of the reformers were still present in 1563, but they may well have faded away by the pontificate with which Reinhard is most concerned, that of Paul V (1605–1621).[173] Paul III, after all, was severely criticized in 1534 when he gave the purple to his schoolboy grandsons; by 1605 and the election of Paul V, however, the "Cardinal Nephew" was institutionalized. Whether or not they were accustomed norms, the suspicion that networks of patronage and nepotism broadened and deepened with the years finds support in Reinhard's own work on the Borghese family.[174]

In fact, it is difficult to imagine that the Tridentine decree found much application at the Roman court. The notion that church office, including sacred office, was primarily a source of income was still pervasive. As the Roman curia grew more and more Italian, and more and more clerical, patronage practices became regularized. Privileges of familiars of cardinals and popes expanded and took on the aspect of law. Consistorial records for the years following the Council of Trent show little alteration in the manner of papal provisions of benefices.[175] The ideal expressed by Cardinal Gonzaga, that he wanted the world to know that whoever dealt with him dealt with a gentleman and a sincere and faithful man, was the ideal of the good *signore* all Italians shared. The honor of a gentleman was even more at stake when it came to family matters. In the next chapter we shall examine means other than sacred office by which Italians used the church to aid their families.

5
The Distribution of Church Property: Secular Office and Families

The church controlled vast properties other than ecclesiastical benefices which could be used to support papal and cardinalate families. New methods of financing the Holy See which were introduced and developed from the late fifteenth century brought the Italian laity fresh and ever-expanding opportunities for profitable investment in the church. These devices also produced fresh incomes from which popes could support dependent relatives and advance the interests of their families. In addition, the steady expansion and consolidation of the temporal states of the church created a host of lucrative positions to be filled by papal appointment. The administration of the state required soldiers, governors, and castellans, tax collectors, financiers, and treasurers, and an increasingly complex bureaucracy in Rome.[1]

Secular office could serve as a stepping-stone to high church office, the red hat, even the triple crown, and high church office offered a means to promote family interests in other secular offices, advantageous marriages, and the procurement of landed property with titles of nobility attached.[2] Leafing through the pages of Pompeo Litta's *Famiglie celebri italiane,* one is struck by the number of celebrated Italian families which owed their rise to service in the church, and particularly to the possession of the cardinalate, in the sixteenth century.[3] Nepotism in the sixteenth and seventeenth centuries, as Reinhard pointed out, became an instrument of upward social mobility.[4]

NEPOTISM AND SECULAR OFFICE

Predictably, many secular offices of the church were filled with members of papal and cardinalate families. Nepotistic patterns were reciprocal. Many of our cardinals began their careers under the protection of an elder relative who worked for the Roman curia as bureaucrat, merchant, or soldier. But this worked both ways. Once in possession of the red hat, the cardinal was expected to facilitate whatever dealings his family had with the papal government. A look at some of the personnel occupying such secular positions can provide clues to the economic and social connections among the Italian laity, the Italian cardinalate, and the administration of the church.

The burgeoning administrative apparatus in Rome offered Italians opportunities in several areas. The growth of the bureaucracy was not owed solely to the church's territorial expansion in Italy, but also to an increase in the curia's business in spiritual as well as temporal matters.[5] It was, in addition, directly tied to the economic necessities of the popes. Several fiscal developments, new in our period, allowed growing numbers of Italians to invest in the church at interest.

The sale of curial offices, "venal offices," for example, underwent a major metamorphosis during the pontificate of Sixtus IV (1471–1484) and became institutionalized.[6] The rise in numbers was dramatic: Sixtus IV increased them from 300 to 625; by the end of Julius II's pontificate there were some 936 venal offices; and during the reign of Leo X the figure rose to 2,232.[7] By 1521, purchasers had invested some 2,485,150 ducats of gold in these offices for an annual return of some 325,000 *scuti* in interest.[8] Thereafter the number of venal offices remained fairly steady throughout the century: there were some 2,900 in 1599, at a reputed value of some 3,800,000 *scuti* of gold.[9]

Three other developments of singular importance to the administration and finance of the church also took place early in our period. First, the dataria separated from the camera apostolica as a distinct treasury under Sixtus IV; second, Leo X invented a totally new category of venal offices, the honorary "knighthoods" or *cavalierati*; and third, in 1526 Clement VII instituted the *Monte della fede*, the first public offering of shares in the church.[10]

The datary originated in the medieval past as the official who actually placed the date on papal indulgences and dispensations.[11] The office, the dataria, only became one of major importance during our period, however, and it remained so for centuries.[12] The venal offices were responsible for this newly found importance. All the income from the sale of offices flowed into the dataria, as did all the income from compositions, the moneys paid by petitioners for all manner of papal indulgences. Furthermore, the interest, "rents," paid out to the title-holders of the venal offices were drawn from the older treasury, the camera apostolica.[13] The datary was responsible to the pope alone, and the funds of the office were directly at his disposal. The dataria thus had the characteristics of a "secret" treasury, a private purse for the popes. Cameral funds were also at the disposition of the popes, but those transactions were more public in nature. The head of the apostolic camera, the camerarius or camerlengo, had a certain independence as well. His appointment, for example, did not cease with the death of the reigning pope, as did that of the datary. This important difference between the two departments meant that the popes of the sixteenth century gained a new freedom to support their families and friends with funds from their private treasury.[14] The amounts were not small. Peter Partner found that the income of the dataria averaged more than 140,000 gold *scuti* per year between 1534 and 1564, an average that fell drastically —but only temporarily—after the Council of Trent. After 1585 the income revived until it reached about 200,000 gold *scuti* annually at the beginning of the seventeenth century, according to Professor Partner's estimates.[15]

The introduction of the honorary offices, the knighthoods, was a brilliant fiscal innovation and another device through which Italian families could invest in the papacy at interest and improve their social status at the same time. Leo X created the first, the *Cavalieri di San Pietro*, in 1520 with 401 positions at a price of 1,000 ducats each, with an annual interest of about ten percent.[16] Clement VII confirmed these *cavalieri* in 1526, and in 1534 Paul III put up 151 new offices of St. Peter for sale at 500 ducats each. This proved so satisfactory a money-raiser that the same pope inaugurated a whole series of "colleges" of knights—the Knights of St. Paul in 1540, the Knights of Loreto in 1545, and the Knights of St. George and the Knights of the Lily in 1546.[17] Julius III and Paul IV increased the number of honorary posts, and, finally, Pius IV created the largest college of all, the *Cavalieri Pii*, in 1560, with a total of 535 offices at 500 *scuti* of gold each.[18] For the office-holder, the purchase of a *cavalierato* was not only an investment at interest but also an automatic improvement in social rank. Knights of St. Peter, for example, were named counts palatine, with attendant rights to coats-of-arms and the like, and Knights of St. Paul had their names inscribed in the "golden book" of the Roman nobility and used the Farnese lily on their escutcheons.[19] For the popes, knighthoods were a means of securing large loans at minimal interest, 10 to 12 percent, because the initial purchasers were, in fact, bankers.[20]

All venal offices had to be purchased with gold, and those that were not honorary but carried the burden of work, such as abbreviator, writer of briefs, or secretary, were much more expensive than the *cavalierati*. Clerks of the camera apostolica, for example, paid 10,000 *scuti* for the office in 1514, 14,000 *scuti* in 1526, 19,000 *scuti* in 1551, and an astonishing 30,000 *scuti* in 1561.[21] Not all offices saw such inflation. The prices of some even diminished during our period, but they were all high, beginning at about 800 *scuti* of gold.[22] The highest offices of the church were dear indeed. Francesco Armellini outbid Innocenzo Cibo's 40,000 ducats with 50,000 paid to Leo X for the *camerlengato* in 1521, and in 1564, Vitellozo Vitelli paid 70,000 for the same office.[23]

These investments in venal offices by curial servants opened the door to many other Italians with money on hand to put out at interest. Having purchased a position, the new title-holder then offered to "share" it with others for a fixed price at a fixed annual return. In 1515, for example, Filippo Sauli, bishop of Brugnato, agreed to pay Gian Pietro Cesi 700 ducats of gold, for an interest of 15 percent over eighteen months, for a share in his office of writer of apostolic letters.[24] Curial officials also invested in each other's offices, and outsiders participated as well.[25] Such contracts were usually drawn for eighteen months, but this was not mandatory. Filippo Ridolfi, "Florentine citizen," invested 400 ducats in an office of *scutifer apostolicus* (shield-bearer) in 1516 for the monthly return of "half of all the income of the said office," in perpetuity "or at the good pleasure of the parties."[26]

The vested interest in venal offices thus spread far beyond the title-holders themselves to a numberless public of Italians—clergy, laymen, bankers, citizens, anyone with money to invest. Offices could be acquired for anyone, regardless of qualification, and the system was flexible. One could buy an office for persons under age, as the thirteen-year-old Gian Pietro Cesi under Julius II or fourteen-year-old Ottaviano Bartolomeo della Valle under Leo X; one could hold plural offices, as did Ottaviano Cesi under Leo X; one could obtain dispensations to possess curial office and sacred office simultaneously.[27] Elevation to the cardinalate usually vacated these positions, but the succession of relatives could be arranged. When he received the red hat in 1517, for example, Giovanni Battista Pallavicino saw to it that his office of apostolic secretary was taken by an Antoniotto Pallavicino, and Ferdinando Ponzetti left his lucrative post as treasurer general to his nephew Jacopo Ponzetti on the same occasion.[28] Even women apparently partook: in August 1547 the datary paid 150 *scuti* of gold to "Madonna Bernardina Capodiferro . . .

by order of His Holiness for the full value of half of the offices left vacant
by the death of her grandson (nephew), Giulio Mignanelli."[29]

Possession of curial office, then, offered much more than simple em-
ployment, and it is not surprising that almost 50 percent of the cardinalate families on our list had members among the curialists (table 5.1).
Real venal offices also represented the means of advancement in the
church hierarchy. Persons with talent, energy, and imagination could
achieve signal success by exploiting the Roman bureaucracy. Reinhard
traced the rise of the Borghese family in the sixteenth century through
the work at the Roman curia of Paul V's father, Marcantonio Borghese.[30]
Many other families sought their fortunes through curial careers and
achieved nobility, even without a papal election.

One such family was the Cesi of Umbria, whose history offers us a
concise portrait of the rise to *grandezza* in the service of the Holy See.
Pietro Chitani da Cesi, born in 1422, was the first of the clan to establish
himself in Rome. He adopted the name of his *patria* and prospered at
the papal court, holding such diverse offices as consistorial advocate,
podestà of Perugia, and senator of the *alma urbs* of Rome.[31] One of
his sons, Angelo Cesi, was born in Rome in 1450. He became a noted
jurist, held the offices of apostolic secretary and auditor of the apostolic
camera under Julius II, fathered thirteen children, and died in 1528.[32]
One of the thirteen children was Paolo Emilio Cesi, the first cardinal
of the family and the man who firmly established its fortunes. Born in
1481, Paolo Emilio entered the service of the church at an early age as
canon and archpriest of Santa Maria Maggiore and St. Peter's. He
distinguished himself as a curial official and was rewarded in 1517 with
the cardinal's hat.[33] His brother Lodovico Vespasiano was a consistorial
advocate; another brother, Massimiliano Ottavio, and a cousin, Giannandrea, were abbreviators of the major parc; another brother, Federico,
was a cameral clerk.[34] With Paolo Emilio's help, Lodovico Vespasiano
became an abbot, and Massimiliano Ottavio, Giannandrea, and Federico
all became bishops. Federico also achieved the cardinalate in 1544, and
accumulated a rich patrimony in landed property, palaces, villas, and
collections of antiquities for his heirs before he died in 1565. The recipients of this inheritance, however, were not the many abbots, bishops,
archbishops, and cardinals of the Cesi family who followed Federico in
succeeding centuries. His heirs were the children of his married brother
Giangiacomo Cesi. Giangiacomo's wife was Isabella, daughter and
heiress of the *condottiere* Bartolomeo d'Alviano. He exchanged her
inheritance with Pier Luigi Farnese for the territories of Acquasparta

TABLE 5.1 CURIAL OFFICERS FROM CARDINALATE FAMILIES

UNDER ALEXANDER VI
Jacopo Caetani
Paolo Pietro Farnese
Lodovico Spinola
Nicolò Conti
Giovanni Battista Ferrerio
Francesco Spinola
Onofrio Giovanni Orsini
Francesco Savelli
Antonio Grassi
Agate de Cupis

UNDER JULIUS II
Angelo Cesi
Ottaviano Massimo Cesi
Gian Pietro Cesi
Clemente Cesi
Thesio de Cupis
Tancredi de Cupis
Orlando della Rovere
Cesare Riario
Lorenzo Fieschi
Giulio Cibo
Gianfrancesco Conti
Alfonso Carafa

UNDER LEO X
Antonio della Rovere
Antoniotto Pallavicino
Francesco Pallavicino
Domenico Conti
Nicolino Ferrerio
Giannandrea Cesi
Lorenzo Grassi
Paride Grassi
Ippolito Cesi
Andrea Cibo
Ottaviano Bartolomeo della Valle
Clemente Cesi[1]
Gian Pietro Cesi[1]
Ottaviano Cesi[1]
Mario Maffei
Giovanni Jacopo Gambara
Massimiliano Ottavio Cesi

UNDER CLEMENT VII
Jacopo Ponzetti
Gasparo del Monte
Francesco della Rovere
Galeazzo della Rovere
Lorenzo Nicolò Jacobazzi
Curzio Crescenzio
Ambrosio Doria
Ugo Rangone
Antonio Filonardi
Girolamo Campeggio
Antonio Numai
Rainaldo Petrucci
Ramondo Capodiferro

Lodovico Vespasiano Cesi
Jacopo Cesi
Clarissimo de' Medici
Giovanni Antonio Ghinucci
Ippolito Cesi[1]
Francesco Pallavicino[1]
Ottaviano Cesi[1]
Cesare Riario[1]
Antonio della Rovere[1]

UNDER PAUL III
Giulio Cesare Piccolomini
Jacopo Cortese
Jacopo Crescenzio
Pascascio Savelli
Adriano de Cupis
Giovanni Grimaldi
Quintus Rustici (Valle)
Imperiale Doria
Giovanni Gaddi
Giuliano Ardinghello
Bernardo Piccolomini
Pietro Duranti
Girolamo Gambara
Giulio Gonzaga
Lodovico Vespasiano Cesi[1]
Lorenzo Nicolò Jacobazzi[1]

UNDER JULIUS III
Virgilio Capodiferro
Gasparo del Monte
Girolamo del Monte
Girolamo Gambara[1]
Pascascio Savelli[1]
Giulio Cesare Piccolomini[1]
Giuliano Ardinghello[1]
Gian Pietro de Cupis

UNDER PAUL IV
Marcantonio Sauli
Tiberio Capodiferro
Jacopo Jacobazzi
Raynerio Libicino Cesi
Alessandro Sforza
Achille Maffei
Giulio Sauli
Pascascio Savelli[1]
Giulio Cesare Piccolomini[1]

UNDER PIUS IV
Marcantonio Simonetta
Paolo Pallavicino
Lodovico Simonetta
Pietro Bembo
Claudio Aleandro
Girolamo Gambara[1]
Giulio Sauli[1]
Alessandro Sforza[1]
Raynerio Cesi[1]

[1]Continued from an earlier pontificate.

and Procaria and became the *signore* of Acquasparta. His daughter married an Orsini, and his son, invested in 1550 as *signore* of Monticelli, married Beatrice Caetani, daughter of the duke of Sermoneta.[35] The family now numbered among the Italian nobility, and the Cesi intermarried in later generations with the Colonna, Conti, Orsini, Savelli, among Roman families, and produced counts, *marchesi*, dukes, and princes until they died out in the nineteenth century.[36] They had accomplished their rise in only three generations.

Venal offices as papal fiscal policy have received ample attention elsewhere.[37] Our sole concern has been their use as opportunities for secular nepotism and lay investment in the sixteenth century. The picture is one of countless Italians taking advantage of the new fiscal systems in order to buy their way into the patriciate with a *cavalierato*, or, if they were lucky enough to obtain a red hat, into the nobility. The high cost of real venal offices led to further investment, division, and "sharing" of the incomes from the offices with larger populations. Indeed, perusing these documents, one wonders who actually did the work. At any rate, the stakes were high. Angelo Cesi invested large sums in venal offices for his sons, and his investment paid off.

Italian bankers were key figures in Rome.[38] Besides managing the affairs of individual prelates and the sale of the venal offices, they acted as banks of deposit for the apostolic camera and the camera of the college of cardinals; they farmed taxes and duties in Rome and throughout the states of the church; they acted as treasurers for the several provinces; they effected the international exchange and transfer of moneys; they contracted to provide the eternal city with grain; and, most important, they were the principal lenders to the pope and funders of the church debt. And after the creation of the *Monte della fede* in 1526, bankers managed the shares (*luoghi*) of the papal debt, and another vast opportunity opened to Italian investors.[39]

The presence of bankers at the papal court was certainly not new. Their title, *mercatores romanam curiam sequentes*—merchants following the Roman curia—derives, as Melissa Bullard remarked, from merchants following popes to Avignon, Florence, and elsewhere.[40] What does seem to be new is the acquisition of the cardinalate by members of banking families. Among the many banking firms who appear in the fiscal records of the curia, seventeen had cardinal relatives (table 5.2). For fourteen of the seventeen, the cardinal on our list was the first of his family to wear the purple, and the cardinal predecessors of the three who were not the first date only from the fifteenth century—Pallavicino,

TABLE 5.2   MERCHANTS FOLLOWING THE ROMAN CURIA:
RELATIVES OF CARDINALS

Family	City	Family	City
UNDER ALEXANDER VI		**UNDER PAUL III**	
Sauli	Genoa	Sauli	Genoa
Ghinucci	Siena	Grimaldi	Genoa
Medici	Florence	Spinola	Genoa
Gaddi	Florence	Pallavicino	Genoa
Pucci	Florence	Gaddi	Florence
Pandolfini	Florence	Pucci	Florence
		Salviati	Florence
UNDER JULIUS II		Ardinghello	Florence
Sauli	Genoa	Bandini[1]	Florence
Ghinucci	Siena	Grassi	Bologna
Gaddi	Florence		
Pandolfini	Florence	**UNDER JULIUS III**	
Soderini	Florence	Sauli	Genoa
		Grimaldi	Genoa
UNDER LEO X		Ardinghello	Florence
Sauli	Genoa	Bandini[1]	Florence
Ghinucci	Siena	Rossi[1]	Florence
Gaddi	Florence	Grassi	Bologna
Salviati	Florence		
Ridolfi	Florence	**UNDER PAUL IV**	
Ardinghello	Florence	Sauli	Genoa
Della Valle	Rome	Pallavicino	Genoa
		Ardinghello	Florence
UNDER CLEMENT VII		Bandini[1]	Florence
Sauli	Genoa		
Grimaldi	Genoa	**UNDER PIUS IV**	
Spinola	Genoa	Sauli	Genoa
Ghinucci	Siena	Pallavicino	Genoa
Gaddi	Florence	Bandini[1]	Florence
Salviati	Florence		
Ridolfi	Florence		
Ardinghello	Florence		
Della Valle	Rome		

[1]Family connection not clear

Piccolomini, and Medici.[41] This is true even for banking families such as the Ghinucci, whose mercantile connections with the Holy See dated back for more than a century.[42] It suggests a new consciousness on the part of merchant families that the cardinal's hat could be useful, and that nepotistic connections could bring lucrative contracts while simultaneously advancing the social status of the family. Of the Florentine bankers, the most obvious example is Ippolito de' Medici's predecessor among cardinalate families, Leo X himself, the first Medici cardinal.

Similarly, Nicolò Pandolfini, Nicolò Ardinghello, Francesco Soderini, Lorenzo Pucci, Nicolò Gaddi, Luigi de' Rossi, Nicolò Ridolfi, and Giovanni Salviati were the first cardinals of their families. The same is true of the Genoese, Bandinello Sauli, Girolamo Grimaldi, and Agostino Spinola; the Sienese, Girolamo Ghinucci; the Bolognese, Achille Grassi; and the Roman, Andrea della Valle.[43]

Some of these merchant families seem to have had only sporadic business with the church and do not appear frequently in the records. Bartolomeo della Valle and Company, for example, farmed the lucrative *dogane* (customs duties) of Rome in partnership with Filippo Strozzi from 1521 to 1526, a privilege for which they advanced 36,000 ducats, but I did not find further mention of the della Valle bank.[44] Virgilio Grassi sold fabrics and other goods to the popes in 1545 and 1551, and the cardinals named Girolamo Rossi *depositario* of the Sacred College during the vacant see of January 1550; again, I did not see further activities.[45] The Bandini of Florence, possibly relatives of the Piccolomini, appear more frequently. Pietro Antonio Bandini was among the merchants who loaned Paul III 10,000 *scuti* of gold in 1543 and 100,000 in 1546, and he was also the *depositario* of the camera of the college of cardinals from 1559 to 1591.[46] The Ardinghello and Gaddi firms of Florence seem to have profited from the position of their cardinal relatives. Nicolò Ardinghello, our cardinal, began his career as a secretary to Leo X, but his principal patron was Paul III, who raised him to the cardinalate in 1544. His brother Giuliano Ardinghello, the banker, joined him in working for the Farnese family, and was still dealing with the curia in 1558.[47] The Gaddi, who had been established in Rome at least from the days of Alexander VI, were headed under the Medici and Farnese popes by Luigi Gaddi, and it was through him that the family attained the status of nobility.[48] Luigi loaned Clement VII 30,000 ducats in 1526 for the disastrous League of Cognac, and in 1527, reportedly for a gift of 40,000 ducats, he saw his brother Nicolò elevated to the cardinalate.[49] Thereafter his business with the Holy See became more extensive, and he put his profits to good use.[50] He bought the *feudo* of Riano and Casal Dragoncelli; his second wife was Claudia Savelli of the old Roman nobility; his daughter Costanza married Nicolò Caetani, the duke of Sermoneta; his son Alessandro became the *marchese* of Riano and married Silvia Savelli; and another son, Taddeo Gaddi, was created cardinal by Paul IV in 1557.[51] The Gaddi had arrived, and I found no notice of banking activity beyond that of Luigi.

Other Florentine bankers enjoyed the protection of the Medici family.

The Medici bank itself, of course, had failed in 1494, but Giovanni de' Medici was already a cardinal, and his election as Leo X in 1513 brought opportunities to his adherents.[52] Piero Ridolfi and Jacopo Salviati, the fathers of our cardinals, were the new pope's brothers-in-law, and both bankers were prominent during the pontificates of Leo X (1513–1521) and Clement VII (1523–1534).[53] The heirs of Jacopo Salviati continued business in Rome under Paul III, but seem to have closed their bank thereafter; the Ridolfi bank, quiescent during the middle years of the century, became important in Rome again at its end.[54] Another Florentine bank, the Pucci, rose to prominence earlier as adherents of the Medici. Our cardinal, Lorenzo Pucci, professor of civil and canon law at the University of Pisa and counselor to Lorenzo the Magnificent in Florence, went to Rome during the pontificate of Innocent VIII (1484–1492), whose son Franceschetto Cibo had recently married Lorenzo the Magnificent's daughter Maddalena.[55] Lorenzo Pucci began his career at the curia as an apostolic notary, and his brothers followed him to Rome.[56] Alessandro Pucci, the father of our Cardinal Antonio Pucci, was the banker of the family, with extensive business at the Roman court during the pontificate of Alexander VI (1492–1503).[57] The Medici protection was probably not very helpful to the family during the Borgia years, but the judicious marriage of another of the brothers undoubtedly was. Puccio Pucci married Girolama Farnese, the sister of the future Paul III and of the fabled beauty Giulia Farnese Orsini, inamorata of Alexander VI.[58] The family bank seems to have ceased with this pontificate, but now they had the protection of another powerful cardinal, Alessandro Farnese. During his reign as Paul III (1534–1549), we find two banking firms identified by Bullard as new: those of Bartolomeo Pucci and Giovanbattista Pucci.[59]

Genoese bankers who boasted cardinal relatives display a different pattern. The Sauli, Grimaldi, Spinola, and Pallavicino families did not need to rise to prominence—they numbered among the oldest nobility in Genoa. What is interesting is that they only felt the need to acquire the purple for a family member during our period. Agostino Spinola, for example, was the first of a series of eleven cardinals in his family down to the nineteenth century, and Giovanni Battista Pallavicino was only the second of his family to bear the honor. His uncle Antoniotto Pallavicino had been created cardinal in 1489 by his fellow Genoese, Innocent VIII.[60] Bankers from these families, along with other Genoese, rivaled the Florentines in Rome, and almost succeeded in monopolizing curial business later in the century.[61]

A brief list of Genoese banking firms and activities suggests the breadth and variety of the work and their close involvement with the Holy See. Damiano and Tobia Pallavicino worked for Rome from 1542, and after 1543 they formed a new partnership, Tobia Pallavicino, Luca Giustiniani, and Company.[62] Girolamo and Pasquale Spinola were bankers of the Roman curia from 1546 to 1548.[63] Ansaldo Grimaldi and Company farmed the alum mines at Tolfa from 1533 to 1550, after 1540 as the heirs of Ansaldo Grimaldi.[64] Other Grimaldi bankers included Paolo Grimaldi (1532), Domenico and Stefano Grimaldi (1534–1538), and Girolamo Grimaldi (1546–1547).[65] The Sauli clan provided both the most bankers and the most varied business with the church. They were lenders, depositors general, tax farmers, treasurers of the patrimony of Peter and of Perugia and Umbria, and, finally, farmers of the alum at Tolfa under Paul IV. From at least 1493 to 1557, Paolo Sauli, Vincenzo and Sebastiano Sauli, Sebastiano, Giovanni, and Agostino Sauli, Girolamo Sauli, Pasquale Sauli, Cristoforo Sauli, and Agostino Sauli junior were *mercatores romanam curiam sequentes*.[66] Continuing prosperity for these families called for an authoritative voice in the Roman curia, and what could be of more use than a cardinal, perhaps a pope?

The perceived need for a cardinal-member put banking families in disadvantageous positions from time to time. Patronage and nepotism worked both ways, and when popes brought pressure on bankers for loans of prodigious size, how could they refuse? According to Professor Bullard, the Bini family of Florence "practically ruined themselves" through unsecured loans to Leo X in hopes for the red hat, and her account of Filippo Strozzi's frantic attempts to gain the cardinalate for his son during the last days of Clement VII shows that Filippo realized how vulnerable he would be without a protector at court.[67] The close connection between the great bankers at Rome and the college of cardinals continued throughout the century. Delumeau listed the following banking houses with cardinal members at the end of the sixteenth century: Bandini, Lomellini, Giustiniani, Bonvisi, Pinelli, Spinola, Sauli, Spada, Bianchetti.[68]

Another broad category of remunerative secular positions for family members was that of governors and soldiers, all at the disposition of the popes. The expanding states of the church, for example, required temporal governors. During conclaves, cardinals divided these offices among themselves, and by 1550 it was customary that each cardinal should possess at least one.[69] These had to be confirmed by the pope after his election, but this seems to have become customary by the

TABLE 5.3   GOVERNORS AND CASTELLANS
FROM CARDINALATE FAMILIES

Name	Jurisdiction	Kinship to Cardinal*
UNDER ALEXANDER VI		
Urbano Vigerio	Cas. Viterbo	Brother
UNDER LEO X		
Guido Rangone	Gov. Modena	Brother
Sigismondo Rangone	Gov. Modena	?
UNDER CLEMENT VII		
Gian Giorgio Cesarini	Gov. Spoleto	?
Alberto Pio	Gov. Bertinoro	Uncle
Alessandro de' Medici	Gov. Spoleto	Cousin
Giovanni Marco Pio	Cas. Faenza	?
Guido Rangone[1]	Gov. Modena	Brother
Luigi Ridolfi	Gov. Orvieto	Brother
Giovanni Jacopo Gambara	Gov. Marches of Ancona	?
Lorenzo Salviati	Gov. Campagna	?
Leonello Pio	Gov. Bertinoro	Father
Lorenzino and Giuliano de' Medici	Gov. Fano	Cousins
UNDER PAUL III		
Leonello Pio[1]	Gov. Bertinoro, Cas. Rimini, Lt. Gov. Marches of Ancona	Father
Cesare Trivulzio	Gov. Perugia and Umbria	Nephew
Ferrante Gonzaga	Gov. Benevento	Brother
Baldassare Grassi	Gov. Faenza and Brisigella	Son
Antonio Grassi	Cas. Imola	?
Giovanni Guidiccioni	Gov. Rome	Nephew
Giannandrea Duranti	Cas. Parma, Cas. Camerino	Brother
Ambrogio Spinola	Lt. Gov. Benevento	?
Paolo Pallavicino	Gov. Campagna	?
Camillo Orsini	Gov. Parma	?
VACANT SEE		
Giovanni Campeggio	Gov. Patrimonio	Nephew
Francesco Orsini	Col. of Rome	?
Orazio Farnese	Prefect of Rome	Grandson[2]
UNDER JULIUS III		
Leonello Pio[1]	Gov. Bertinoro, Gov. Meldola	Father
Giannandrea Duranti[1]	Cas. Camerino	Brother
Ambrogio Spinola[1]	Gov. Camerino	?
Giovanni Campeggio[1]	Gov. Patrimonio	Nephew
Giovanni Battista del Monte	Gov. Fermo, Gov. Nepi	Nephew[2]
Baldovino del Monte	Gov. Narni, Gov. Nepi	Brother[2]
Giovanni Brandino del Monte	Cas. Ostia	?
Antonio Maria Ferrio del Monte	Cas. Civitavecchia	?

Continued on next page

TABLE 5.3 CONTINUED

Name	Jurisdiction	Kinship to Cardinal[*]
UNDER PAUL IV		
Leonello Pio[1]	Gov. Bertinoro, Gov. Meldola	Father
Giovanni Carafa	Gov. Spoleto	Nephew[2]
Carlo Carafa	Gov. Ceretti	Nephew[2]
Alfonso Carafa	Gov. Benevento	Great-nephew[2]
Antonio Carafa	Gov. Patrimonio	Nephew[2]
UNDER PIUS IV		
Giovanni Battista Doria	Gov. Campagna	?
Federico Borromeo	Gov. Spoleto, Gov. Tassignani	Nephew[2]

[*]? = Kinship assumed on basis of same family name.
[1]Continued from an earlier pontificate.
[2]Kinship to the pope.

middle of the century. The post of governor usually included that of castellan of the fort attached to the jurisdiction, but this office could be separated off for special security reasons.[70] These were not sinecures. The governor or his lieutenant was responsible for the defense, peace, and prosperity of his area. He was the final authority in all matters spiritual and temporal if a clergyman, in all matters temporal if a layman. He drew up laws and regulations; judged all manner of litigation, ecclesiastical, civil, and criminal; saw to the sufficient provision of grain and wine; provided for the common defense.[71] He also received the privileges and immunities, the fruits and emoluments of office. The briefs of commission and confirmation do not specify the amounts of the stipends that went with these jobs, but some evidence indicates that the sums were substantial. Leonello Pio, for example, collected 1,200 *scuti* of gold each year as lieutenant governor of the Marches of Ancona under Paul III.[72] Anticipated incomes from the area must have been much larger for the actual governor, however. Benedetto Accolti paid Clement VII 19,000 ducats for the governorship and legation of the Marches in 1532, and in 1533 he paid an additional 5,500 *scuti* for the governorship of Fano.[73] Accolti surely expected some profit.

Besides the cardinals themselves, members of their families sought and obtained posts as governors and castellans, and the records indicate that this was more than coincidence (table 5.3). Cardinal Ridolfi, for example, was the author of his brother Luigi's appointment as castellan of the city and fortress of Orvieto in 1531, and Giannandrea Duranti's nominations as castellan of Parma in 1540 and of Camerino in 1550

TABLE 5.4   CONDOTTIERI PAID FROM THE CAMERA:
100-1,000 *SCUTI* OF GOLD PER MONTH

Name	Kinship
UNDER ALEXANDER VI	
Giulio Orsini	Uncle of Franciotto Orsini
Nicolò Orsini	?
Orsino Orsini	Husband of Giulia Farnese
Carlo Orsini	?
Giovanni Battista Conti	?
Antonello Savelli	?
Mariano Savelli	?
Gasparo Sanseverino	Brother of Federico Sanseverino
Angelo Farnese	Brother of Paul III
UNDER LEO X	
Jacopo Savelli	?
Giovanni Maria Varano	Brother-in-law of Innocenzo Cibo
UNDER CLEMENT VII	
Luigi Gonzaga	Brother of Pirro Gonzaga
Giovanni Battista Savelli	Father of Jacopo Savelli
UNDER PAUL III	
Giovanni Battista Savelli[1]	Father of Jacopo Savelli
Morello Farnese	?
Giuliano Cesarini	Nephew of Alessandro Cesarini
Alessandro Colonna	?
Girolamo Orsini	?
Sforza Sforza	Grandson of Paul III
Pier Bertoldo Farnese	Nephew of Paul III
Sforza Pallavicino	Grandson-in-law of Paul III
UNDER JULIUS III	
Giuliano Cesarini[1]	Nephew of Alessandro Cesarini
Alessandro Colonna[1]	?
Camillo Orsini	?
Antonio Maria del Monte	?
Vincenzo Tibaldesco del Monte	?
Giovanni Battista del Monte	Nephew of Julius III
UNDER PAUL IV	
Giovanni Savelli	?
Giovanni Antonio Orsini	?
Giovanni Carafa	Brother of Paul IV
Orazio Farnese	Grandson of Paul III
UNDER PIUS IV	
Alessandro Colonna	?
Leonardo della Rovere	?
Aurelio Fregoso	?
Orazio Trivulzio	?
Nicolò Gambara	?

[1]Continued from an earlier pontificate.

both note specifically that he was the brother *germanus* of Cardinal Duranti.[74] The diligence with which Cardinal Rodolfo Pio pursued the interests of his family is well documented. In 1534, Pio obtained the position of castellan of the city and fortress of Rimini and the presidency of the Romagna for his father, Leonello Pio. At the same time, Paul III confirmed Leonello's governorship of Bertinoro.[75] The elder Pio encountered setbacks during the following year, however, and his son wrote to Rome from France in some bitterness on 23 September 1535. His family had reproached him for abandoning their interests for those of the church, he said, but "if it is a sin to love one's family and desire that they should not suffer, I recognize and confess myself to be the equal of any great sinner and even greater, because I intend always to remain so."[76] But Pio had not yet heard the worst; four days earlier Paul III had deprived Leonello of both Rimini and the Romagna. The papal secretary apologized on 14 October and offered reassurances to the nuncio: "I understand that Our *Signore*, in taking that *Rocca* away from your father, has done so with the greatest displeasure, fearing to give you cause for unhappiness, and he has resolved to find a way to compensate him with another."[77] Leonello Pio did indeed receive compensation. With the help of his son's influence at the curia, Leonello was governor of Bertinoro from 1531 to at least 1555, he was the *signore* of Meldola, he was lieutenant of the Marches of Ancona while his son was legate there, and, finally, he was the count of Carpi.[78]

Sensitive military positions were filled with members of papal and cardinalate families to an even greater extent than governorships or castellanies (tables 5.4–5.8). Seasonal captains (*condottieri*) and persons holding the standing military positions in the church—captain of the triremes, captain of the palace guard, castellan of Sant'Angelo, and captain general and standard-bearer (*gonfaloniere*) of the church—were figures of vital importance to the security of the papal state, indeed to the personal safety of the pope himself. Popes thus tended to choose, as soldiers who could be considered reliable, men from their own families or their own *patriae*.

Two popes who were exceptions to this general rule about military appointments encountered considerable difficulty with their soldiers. Tables 5.4 and 5.8 show that Alexander VI depended heavily upon the Roman nobility for *condottieri,* and, in the person of Nicolò Orsini, for a captain general and *gonfaloniere* from 1493 to 1494.[79] During the last years of his reign, however, the Borgia pope and his son Cesare became so disgruntled with their mercenaries that they attempted to

TABLE 5.5 CAPTAINS OF THE TRIREMES:
500 *SCUTI* PER SHIP PER MONTH

Name	Kinship
UNDER CLEMENT VII	
Antonio Doria	?
Bernardo Salviati	Brother of Giovanni Salviati
Andrea Doria	Uncle of Girolamo Doria
UNDER PAUL III	
Marco Grimani	Brother of Marino Grimani
Pietro del Monte	Nephew of Antonio Maria del Monte
Ranuccio Farnese, later card.	Grandson of Paul III; brother of Alessandro Farnese
Girolamo Fieschi	?
Carlo Sforza	Grandson of Paul III; brother of Guido Ascanio Sforza
Pier Luigi Farnese	Son of Paul III
UNDER JULIUS III	
Carlo Sforza[1]	Grandson of Paul III; brother of Guido Ascanio Sforza
UNDER PAUL IV	
Carlo Sforza[1]	Grandson of Paul III; brother of Guido Ascanio Sforza
UNDER PIUS IV	
Carlo Sforza[1]	Grandson of Paul III; brother of Guido Ascanio Sforza

[1]Continued from an earlier pontificate.

TABLE 5.6 CAPTAINS OF THE PALACE GUARD:
100 *SCUTI* PER MONTH

Name	Kinship
UNDER JULIUS II	
Nicolò Doria	?
UNDER LEO X	
Annibale Rangone	Brother of Ercole Rangone
UNDER CLEMENT VII	
Lorenzo Cibo	Brother of Innocenzo Cibo
UNDER PAUL III	
Giovanni Battista Savelli	Father of Jacopo Savelli
Giovanni Francesco Orsini	?
UNDER PAUL IV	
Antonio Carafa	Nephew of Paul IV
UNDER PIUS IV	
Gabriele Serbelloni	Nephew of Pius IV

TABLE 5.7   CASTELLANS OF SANT'ANGELO: 110 *SCUTI* PER MONTH
(CARDINALS AND RELATIVES OF CARDINALS AND POPES)

Name	Kinship
UNDER JULIUS II	
Marco Vigerio[1]	Nephew of Julius II
Giovanni Lodovico della Rovere	?
Giovanni Francesco della Rovere	?
UNDER LEO X	
Raffaele Petrucci[1]	
UNDER CLEMENT VII	
Guido de' Medici	?
UNDER PAUL III	
Ennio Filonardi[1]	
Giovanni Vincenzo Acquaviva[1]	
Tiberio Crispo[1]	
UNDER JULIUS III	
Pietro del Monte	Cousin of Julius III
UNDER MARCELLUS II	
Giovanni Battista Cervini (April-May 1555)	Nephew of Marcellus II
UNDER PAUL IV	
Diomede Carafa[1]	Great-nephew of Paul IV
UNDER PIUS IV	
Giovanni Battista Serbelloni	Nephew of Pius IV

[1]Later created cardinal.

destroy the entire Orsini clan. The interests of the Orsini, and those of the Conti and Savelli for that matter, as Roman nobility, did not depend upon or coincide with the interests of the pope and his son. Clement VII was the only other pope of the period to entrust a papal army to a captain general who not only lacked blood ties but even had a personal history of enmity toward the papal family. Francesco Maria della Rovere had been forcibly expelled from his territory and deposed as duke of Urbino in 1517 by Clement's cousin Leo X. When, almost a decade later, Francesco Maria headed the papal army that faced the invading imperial forces, he employed tactics that, at the least, did nothing to delay or obstruct the sack of Rome in May 1527. The celebrated soldier had no cause to love the house of Medici.

Other popes saw to it that *condottieri* in the service of the Holy See, and particularly the captains general, were more dependable. It seems

TABLE 5.8 CAPTAINS GENERAL AND GONFALONIERI OF THE CHURCH:
1,000 *SCUTI* OF GOLD PER MONTH

Name	Kinship
UNDER ALEXANDER VI	
Nicolò Orsini	?
Cesare Borgia	Son of Alexander VI
UNDER JULIUS II	
Francesco Maria della Rovere	Nephew of Julius II, father of Giulio della Rovere
UNDER LEO X	
Giuliano de' Medici	Brother of Leo X
Lorenzo de' Medici	Nephew of Leo X
Giovanni Maria Varano	Brother-in-law of Innocenzo Cibo
UNDER CLEMENT VII	
Francesco Maria della Rovere[1]	Nephew of Julius II, father of Giulio della Rovere
UNDER PAUL III	
Pier Luigi Farnese	Son of Paul III
Ottavio Farnese	Grandson of Paul III
Sforza Sforza	Grandson of Paul III
VACANT SEE	
Sforza Pallavicino	Grandson-in-law of Paul III
UNDER JULIUS III	
Ottavio Farnese[1]	Grandson of Paul III
Guidobaldo della Rovere	Brother of Giulio della Rovere
Ascanio della Corgna	Nephew of Julius III
Cesare della Corgna (lt.)	Nephew of Julius III
UNDER PAUL IV	
Antonio Carafa	Nephew of Paul IV
UNDER PIUS IV	
Federico Borromeo	Nephew of Pius IV
Gabriele Serbelloni (lt.)	Nephew of Pius IV
Annibale d'Altemps	Nephew of Pius IV

[1]Continued from an earlier pontificate.

likely, then, that nepotistic military appointments were made as much in the self-interest of the pontiffs as in the interest of promoting particular families. Some of the Farnese grandsons seem to have been exceptions, to be sure: it is difficult to imagine that Ranuccio Farnese was an effective admiral of the triremes at the age of nine.[80] Other military men, however, seem to have been experienced soldiers.

Regardless of the contemporary diplomatic situation, military positions drew handsome stipends from the coffers of the camera apostolica or the dataria. *Condottieri* normally received 100 *scuti* per month, but on occasion these payments could rise dramatically: Giulio Orsini, for example, was paid 4,200 florins in gold by Alexander VI between May and August of 1493 alone.[81] The captain of the papal fleet, which numbered from two to seven triremes with an occasional brigantine or frigate added, was supposed to maintain the ships as well as himself from the 500 ducats per month per trireme he collected.[82] The captain general and *gonfaloniere*'s ordinary provision was 1,000 ducats of gold per month. This sum was also subject to change depending on circumstance. As captain general, Pier Luigi Farnese received some 20,445 ducats during the year 1539, and in 1545 his stipend rose to 23,100 ducats.[83] However necessary his services were to his father, the pope, they were also of clear benefit to him.

POPES, CARDINALS, AND KINSHIP

Bureaucrats, including *cavalierati*, merchants, governors, and soldiers, all had distinct functions in the administration of the Holy Roman Church. The overriding importance of the family was such, however, that the distribution of church property extended to another class of stipendiary, which owed its existence solely to its family status. Women and children required support, suitable marriages had to be arranged, dowries provided, and land with appropriate titles of nobility acquired— all matters of central interest to popes and cardinals.

As the dataria developed into a major and private treasury of the popes, it became the source of regular monthly pensions for increasing numbers of cardinals. It also became the primary source of regular subventions for members of papal families. The records of the datary that survive cover the years 1531–1534, 1535–1550, and 1554–1555. They show that each of the popes of those years, Clement VII, Paul III, and Julius III, consistently used these moneys in the interests of their kinfolk.

Most of the papal pensioners, interestingly, were women.[84] Barred by their sex from sacred or secular office, they turned to their patron for ordinary and extraordinary provision. Their pensions therefore lasted either for their lifetimes or that of the pope, sometimes even beyond. Payments to the household of Paul III's daughter, Costanza

Farnese, continued for seventeen months after her death, and two other Farnese pensioners, Isabella Farnese and Giulia Acquaviva, collected their stipends as late as January 1550, two months after the death of their benefactor.[85] Male pensioners were mostly children, and they generally lost their datarial incomes when they took up an assignment in the service of the church which carried its own salary. Pier Luigi Farnese, for example, gave up his pension from the dataria when he was named *gonfaloniere* of the church and duke of Castro in 1537.[86] Jacopo Savelli did the same when he was created cardinal in 1539; papal nephew Pier Bertoldo Farnese and papal grandson Sforza Sforza did so when they contracted to take up arms for the church in 1541; and Ottavio Farnese, Pier Luigi's son, did so when he succeeded as *gonfaloniere* and duke of Parma and Piacenza in 1548. Thereafter they all received funds from the apostolic camera.[87]

This pattern probably derives from the developing nature of the dataria as the popes' private treasury. Unlike gifts or grants of money from the camera apostolica, few people were involved in administering grants of money from the dataria. The pope simply ordered the datary to pay out moneys directly to the recipient or to his or her agent. Disbursements from the apostolic camera were not so simple. There the *camerlengo,* on the authority of the pope, ordered the treasurer general to order the depositor general or another treasurer or a collector to pay someone a certain sum for a particular reason, and the cameral records reveal that the particular reason usually involved some sort of service, at least nominal, to the Holy See. Women and children performed no useful function and thus drew incomes from the dataria, while adult males took on responsibilities that carried traditional stipends from the apostolic camera or other sources. The dataria thus provided a less visible means of providing for functionless relatives, and, paralleling the use of ever larger ecclesiastical pensions as incomes for churchmen, the increasing use of datarial moneys for relatives helped to conceal the practice somewhat from the public eye.

The extant records of the dataria show that papal habits varied and that the use of datarial funds altered with the years. Clement VII appears almost hesitant in comparison with his successors. He authorized only three nepotistic pensions from the dataria, and only two were for lay relatives. The pope's niece Catherine de' Medici drew 250 *scuti* per month from the department between 1531 and 1533. Her pension ceased, however, in August 1533 on the eve of her marriage to the duke of Orléans, the future Henry II of France. The pope felt, perhaps, that her extraordinary dowry of 130,000 *scuti* would suffice for her support.[88] Her cousin, the young Duke Alessandro de' Medici of Florence, received 735 *scuti* per month from March to May of 1531; thereafter his pension reduced to 500 *scuti* per month for the remainder of the pontificate.[89] Ippolito de' Medici, the cardinal nephew, who certainly did not lack ecclesiastical incomes, benefited the most from the dataria. He received 7,096 *scuti* in 1531, 11,580 *scuti* in 1532, and 4,200 *scuti* in 1534, all "extraordinary" provision.[90] Otherwise, Clement VII used the surpluses in the dataria for himself. Between May 1533 and August 1534, he sent more than 88,091 *scuti* of gold from the dataria to his own treasure-box in the Castel Sant'Angelo.[91]

The next pontificate saw a veritable explosion in the number of papal pensioners (table 5.9). The utility and convenience of the private treasury had become apparent to Paul III, and he used its moneys lavishly in support of his family. Indeed, Paul III emerges (thanks probably, however, only to the complete records surviving from his fifteen-year pontificate) as the most generous pope of the period in his use of the dataria. Furthermore, the figures presented in table 5.9 represent the "ordinary" provisions alone. The particular or "extraordinary" grants rose to immense sums.

Many of the extraordinary subsidies bear an aura of frivolity as the pope sought to please his young grandchildren: 710 *scuti* in December 1536 "for the gifts for the grandchildren and relatives of His Holiness"; 574 *scuti* and 94 *bolendini* for "silver and clothing made for the Most Illustrious *Signore* Ranuccio Farnese, prior of Venice and grandson of His Holiness" in August 1541 (probably for his eleventh birthday); 10 *scuti* and 50 *bolendini* for a ruby for granddaughter Vittoria Farnese in December 1540, and 100 *scuti* for another jewel for her in December 1541; 200 *scuti* "to give to *Signora* Vittoria to go to the hunt with *Madama*" in January 1542; another 50 *scuti* to Vittoria in May 1544, "which Our *Signore* gives her for a coach Her Excellency is having made"; 600 *scuti* to grandson Ottavio Farnese in January 1540, "to spend for his pleasure this Carnevale"; 471 *scuti* and 20 *bolendini* in January 1543, for "a belt of lapis lazuli and other things purchased and taken to *Madama* the Duchess of Camerino for gifts for the present New Year"; and 450 *scuti* in June 1546, for a diamond ring for "one of the sisters of the *camerlengo*" (another granddaughter).[92]

In addition to special gifts, Paul III's ordinary provisions for members of his immediate family were very substantial, but they were never enough. The pope's daughter Costanza, for example, had a regular

TABLE 5.9 FARNESE PENSIONERS: 1535-1550

Name	Kinship to Pope	Scudi per Month	Dates
EXTENDED FAMILY			
Isabella Farnese	Niece	100	1535-1550
Hortensia Farnese	Kin	50-75	1535-1549
Contarina Farnese	Kin	50	1535-1549
Beatrice Farnese	Kin	50-75	1535-1549
Ambrogio Farnese	Kin	70	1535-1549
Antonia Caetani	Kin	12	1539-1549
Emilia of the counts of Marciano	Kin	10	1539-1549
Girolamo Mariscotto, count of Marciano	Husband of Hortensia Farnese	33-1/3	1540-1549
Girolama Savelli	Wife of Paolo Savelli	15	1541-1549
Virginia Pallavicino	Widow of son, Ranuccio Farnese, wife of Brunoro Gambara	50-75	1544-1549
Giulia Acquaviva	Wife of nephew, Pier Bertoldo Farnese	60	1544-1549
Marcantonio Mariscotto	Son of Hortensia Farnese	8	1546-1547
Alfonso Mariscotto	Son of Hortensia Farnese	8-16	1546-1549
SCHOOLBOYS			
Pier Bertoldo Farnese	Nephew	33-1/3	1535-1541
Jacopo Savelli	Kin	33-1/3	1535-1539
Luca Savelli	Son of Paolo Savelli	33-1/3	1538-1547
Alfonso Mariscotto	Son of Hortensia Farnese	33-1/3	1539-1546
Paolo Sforza	Grandson	100[1]	1545
Alessandro Sforza	Grandson	100[1]	1545
IMMEDIATE FAMILY			
Pier Luigi Farnese	Son	500	1535-1537
Girolama Orsini	Daughter-in-law	150-240	1535-1549
Countess of Santa Fiore	Daughter's mother-in-law	10-15	1535-1547
Costanza Farnese	Daughter	300	1540-1547
Giulia Sforza Pallavicino	Granddaughter	80	1545-1549
		800[1]	1545
		300[1]	1545
Vittoria Farnese	Granddaughter	50[1]	1545
		80[1]	1545
Sforza Sforza	Grandson	100	1538-1541
Mario Sforza	Grandson	200	1549
Orazio Farnese	Grandson	666-2/3	1541-1549
Ottavio Farnese	Grandson	1,500-2,000	1540-1548
Margaret of Austria	Granddaughter-in-law	666-2/3	1540-1549

[1]Particular as opposed to regular subsidy.

annual income of 480 *scuti* of gold from the Marches of Ancona from 1535 to 1547, 3,600 *scuti* annually from the dataria from 1540 to 1547, and 1,200 ducats of gold annually from the tax on the *patrimonio* from 1545 to 1547.[93] This would not do. The apostolic camera assisted her with 500 *scuti* of gold in March 1539 and 1,000 *scuti* of gold in May 1541 "for satisfying some of her ancient debts and many extraordinary expenses."[94] Eight months after her death, the treasurer of the Marches paid 510 *scuti* to the creditors of the late Costanza.[95] Her son Sforza Sforza, count of Santa Fiore, also received extraordinary funds: the pope gave him 2,000 *scuti* from the dataria in 1540 "to spend on his marriage" to Luisa Pallavicino, and on 1 January 1541 an additional 1,500 *scuti* went to pay for some cloth materials "which the Most Illustrious Count of Santa Fiore has selected to give to his consort."[96]

The secular sons of Pier Luigi Farnese, destined to carry on and perpetuate the house of Farnese, received even more in ordinary and extraordinary incomes. Orazio Farnese, the younger son, spent 3,699 *scuti* in July 1541 in preparation for his journey to the French court at the age of nine.[97] Orazio still found it necessary to borrow 2,000 *scuti* in Lyon from the Florentine banker Giovanni Francesco Bini. In December, the datary reimbursed Bini and simultaneously transferred another 2,000 *scuti* to Orazio in France.[98] Even with his more or less regular 8,000 *scuti* per year from the dataria and an additional pension of 6,000 francs from Francis I, Orazio continued to run out of money, and his grandfather continued to order more.[99] By the death of Paul III in 1549, Orazio had collected at least 80,999 *scuti* of gold from the dataria alone.[100]

Orazio's older brother Ottavio Farnese, however, was the principal heir of the family and the figure upon whom the pope's hopes for the family depended. His subventions were correspondingly greater than those for the other young men of the family. His ordinary pension from the dataria began in early 1537, when he was thirteen years old, at the semiregular rate of 100 to 165 *scuti* per month.[101] Ottavio's marriage to the daughter of Charles V, Margaret of Austria—the "Madama" who received New Year's gifts in 1543—occasioned a true shower of gold. The wedding took place in November 1538, and between October and December of that year, the datary paid out 13,768 *scuti* directly to Ottavio and Margaret for their ordinary provision and also for furnishings, tapestries, clothes, gifts, and the refurbishing of Margaret's house.[102] The total subsidy rose to 23,246 *scuti* in 1539, 25,747 *scuti* in 1540, and 34,833 *scuti* in 1541, all from the dataria.[103] In addition, the camera apostolica provided 6,000 ducats of gold *della camera* in June 1541 for Ottavio's trip to the court of the emperor.[104] Like his brother, however, Ottavio ran out of money en route and borrowed 1,000 *scuti* in Genoa from the archbishop of Bari and another 2,500 *scuti* from a merchant in Barcelona, both debts later paid from the dataria.[105] Subsequent years saw the same scale of munificence, with a reduction after 1546 that reflected the growth of Ottavio's temporal fortune.[106] He received his last payment from the dataria in April 1548; he was now duke of Parma and Piacenza and *gonfaloniere* of the church.[107] His wife continued to collect her "ordinary" provision.[108] Ottavio and his wife and his brother Orazio alone received a total sum in excess of 375,425 *scuti* in gold from the dataria, or the purchase price of 751 *cavalierati*, all in the interests of the magnificence of the Farnese family.

The sole extant volume of dataria records for the pontificate of Julius III covers the year from March 1554 to March 1555, and it shows that important developments had taken place. Previously, expenditures had been recorded daily, that is, the *depositario* had written, "On the seventh day of July" and then described the several payments. Also, the earlier records usually included some reason, some justification for the disbursements. By 1554 the bookkeeping had altered. The *depositario* now listed all transactions at the same time under the simple heading, "Expenditures for March," and so forth. "Ordinary" pensions were recorded first, and in July 1554 "extraordinary" grants began to be listed under a separate heading.[109] There were sixty-two ordinary pensioners by that time. Indeed, the number of ordinary pensioners had expanded so much that for the first ten months of the year, expenditures exceeded income in amounts ranging from 2,099 to 7,825 *scuti*.[110] In those instances the datary himself made up the difference from his own pocket and paid himself back at the beginning of the following month. No reason was given for ordinary pensions beyond the simple "for his provision," or "for his usual (*solita*) provision for the present month."[111] Pensions from the dataria had become so standardized, so regularized, that they were paid whether or not funds were available.

As we saw in chapter 2, regular pensioners now included twenty-two cardinals. Eleven members of the family of Julius III were also ordinary pensioners, and between March 1554 and March 1555, they collected 20,760 *scuti* of gold from the dataria (table 5.10). The pope's brother Baldovino del Monte happened to be building a palace at Monte Sansovino that year, and thus he received extraordinary provision as well.

TABLE 5.10   DEL MONTE PENSIONERS: 1554-1555

Name	Kinship to Pope	*Scuti* per Month
Baldovino del Monte	Brother	600
Orsola del Monte	Niece	50
Cristofana del Monte	Niece	50
Vincenzo de' Nobili	Nephew	200
Lodovica del Monte	Sister	100
Jacoma del Monte	Sister	100
Laura della Corgna	Niece	40
Ersilia del Monte	Niece-in-law	500
Lorenza del Monte	?	25
Cornelia Tibaldescha del Monte	?	25
Fabiano del Monte	?	15

The datary paid at least 6,725 *scuti* of gold for this enterprise, either to Baldovino himself or to his *provveditore* of the building, to his architect, to his artist, and even to his stable-master.[112] If the other four years of Julius III's pontificate produced similar subventions, the del Monte relatives collected some 103,800 *scuti* from the dataria in ordinary provision, or the purchase price of 207 *cavalierati*.

During the years of reform, then, the dataria became the principal source of papal nepotistic subventions. From the timid support of Catherine, Alessandro, and Ippolito de' Medici under Clement VII, through the lavish and colorful expenditures of Paul III for the Farnese family, to the almost laconic ordinary support of Julius III's family during the last year of his reign, we see the use of datarial moneys for nepotistic ends becoming, like so many other practices at the curia, traditional and customary in Rome. We can also see why projects for reforming the dataria had to be abandoned in 1539, and why the restricted income of the office following Trent was only temporary. The Council's activities provoked some uneasiness in Rome in 1546, but no reduction in revenues materialized.[113] It seems safe to assume that subsequent popes used the moneys of the dataria for the same purposes, although the absence of the account books renders this assumption conjectural. The records of the camera apostolica for the pontificates of Paul IV and Pius IV, however, suggest that papal nepotism increased during the last years of our period along with the enhanced standards of luxury and magnificence in Rome. If, as we have supposed, the dataria continued to be the major source of nepotistic moneys, the accounts of the camera apostolica represent mostly *extraordinary* grants, and what we see is a mere glimpse of papal benevolence, the tip of the iceberg, from 1555 to 1565.

TABLE 5.11   CARAFA PENSIONERS: 1556-1559

Name	Kinship to Pope	Scuti	Dates
Countess of Montorio	Sister-in-law	100[1]	1556-1558
Brianna Carafa, marchesa	Niece	200[1]	1556-1559
of Polignano		400	1557
		400	1557
		400	1557
		50	1557
		150	1557
		200	1557
		75	1558
		290	1558
		280	1558
		500	1558
		250	1558
		200	1558
		200	1558
Giovanni Carafa, duke of	Nephew	1,000	1557
Palliano		3,093	1557
		1,000	1558
		6,000	1558
		10,000	1558
Pietro Carafa	Great-nephew	300	1557
Giovanni Battista Carafa	Kin	60	1557
Giovanni Francesco Carafa	Kin	200	1558
Giovanni Antonio Carafa	Kin	16½	1558
Vincenzo Carafa	Kin	200	1558

[1]Per month—regular as opposed to particular subsidy.

Cameral records show that the Carafa family profited through the pontificate of their kinsman even though Paul IV was one of the strictest of reforming popes. Volume 902 of the account books, the Mandati Camerali, suggests that some of this generosity was perhaps unknown to the pope. It differs from other volumes in several respects: it is entitled "Secret Mandates, 1556–1560" (Mandati Secreti); it is written in Italian instead of Latin; its orders were recorded in the house of the *camerlengo,* Guido Ascanio Sforza, by Guido Ascanio himself with no countersignatures; and the orders derived for the most part not from the pope but from his nephews Cardinal Carlo Carafa and Giovanni Carafa, the duke of Palliano, on the pope's authority. The volume may represent a method through which the Carafa nephews, in league with Guido Ascanio, attempted to conceal some of the cameral business from their reforming uncle. In any case, when its evidence is coupled with that from Volume 904, cameral mandates from 1557 to 1559 which are *not* labeled "secret," we find that nepotistic grants from the camera apostolica had escalated in number over those in previous pontificates (table 5.11). If ordinary pensions were, in fact, still being assigned from the dataria, the scale of papal largess (or that of the papal nephews) had increased considerably.

The only Carafa who received regular monthly pensions from the camera apostolica were women—Paul IV's sister-in-law, the countess of Montorio, and his niece, Brianna Carafa, *marchesa* of Polignano. Brianna, however, along with several male members of the family, also enjoyed a series of extraordinary subventions in 1557 and 1558, all ordered in the book of secret mandates.[114] Of the others, Giovanni Carafa collected the largest sums, although 2,000 of his 21,093 *scuti* were compensation for a tax he had paid on his duchy of Palliano, because "he has not been able to enjoy the income of his state because of the malignity of the times."[115] Altogether, the church paid members of the Carafa family 33,606 *scuti* from 1556 to 1559 from the camera alone. Other members of the family also prospered under Paul IV.[116] Indeed, in comparison with earlier pontificates, it appears that the level of magnificence deemed necessary for a papal family increased. Clement VII had ordered 1,000 gold ducats each for Alessandro and Ippolito de' Medici in 1529 for their journey to meet Charles V.[117] Paul III ordered 6,000 ducats of gold for Ottavio Farnese in 1541 for his journey to meet Charles V in Spain.[118] For his own journey to the court of Philip II in late 1557, Cardinal Carlo Carafa ordered 14,165 *scuti* of gold and spent an additional 1,963 on the trip, while his personal treasurer received at the same time another 19,291 *scuti* on the order of Giovanni Carafa, duke of Palliano.[119]

The use of cameral funds for the papal family rose to new heights under the next pope, Pius IV (table 5.12). Giangangelo de' Medici, coming from an obscure Milanese clan unrelated to the Florentine Medici, sought to establish his nieces and nephews among the Italian nobility through splendid marriages. Within a year of his election, in fact, he had arranged "so many and so honorable *parentadi* with the *signori* of Italy," that Ercole Gonzaga feared that the Catholic king, Philip II, had taken umbrage.[120] Moneys from the camera apostolica provided dowries and wedding gifts. In 1561, Pius IV ordered the payment of 20,000 *scuti* from the camera to Fortunato Madruzzo, nephew of Cardinal Cristoforo Madruzzo, for the dowry of his wife, Margarita d'Altemps, the pope's niece.[121] The pope then ordered 40,000 *scuti* from the camera for the dowry of another niece, Camilla Borromeo, who married Cesare Gonzaga, the nephew of Cardinal Ercole Gonzaga.[122] One of the pope's

TABLE 5.12   MEDICI PENSIONERS: 1560-1565

Name	Kinship to Pope	*Scuti*	Dates
Margarita d'Altemps (dowry)	Niece	20,000	1561
Camilla Borromeo (dowry)	Niece	40,000	1561
Virginia della Rovere	Niece-in-law	5,500	1561
Ortensia Borromeo (dowry)	Niece	20,000	1565
Annibale d'Altemps	Nephew	400[1]	1561-1564
		500[1]	1565
		2,000	1565
		5,000	1565
		100,000	1565
Gabriele d'Altemps	Nephew	2,000	1565
Gabriele's wife	Niece-in-law	200	1565
Agosto de' Medici	Brother	10,000	1565
Gabriele Serbelloni	Nephew	10,000	1565
Fabrizio Serbelloni	Nephew	10,000	1565
Cecilia de' Medici (dowry)	Niece	40,000	1565

[1]Per month—regular as opposed to particular subsidy.

nephews, Count Federico Borromeo, married the daughter of the duke of Urbino, Virginia Varana della Rovere. The apostolic camera facilitated this union as well, not by providing the dowry but with rich gifts: 5,000 *scuti* entrusted to Cardinal Carlo Borromeo in September 1561, for gifts and services for Donna Virginia, and 500 of gold in gold the following month, "which, for worthy causes, Our *Signore* gives her [Virginia] as a gift."[123] Count Federico himself was named captain general of the church and collected his stipend from the camera as was customary.[124] His cousin Count Annibale d'Altemps sought his fortune at the court of the king of Spain at the end of 1561 and was supported by a monthly stipend of 400 ducats of gold from the camera.[125]

During the last year of his reign, Pius IV quickened his activity on behalf of his family. He had lost his captain general of the church with the premature death of Federico Borromeo in late 1562. Perhaps his own failing health prompted his decision to honor another nephew in 1565. In January of that year, Count Annibale d'Altemps was released from a marriage he had contracted with an Isabella of Aragon, married the pope's niece, the thirteen-year-old Ortensia Borromeo, and was named captain general of the church.[126] In February, Pius IV assigned 500 *scuti* of gold from the camera as a monthly pension for Annibale, and in March the pope granted him 2,000 more *scuti* for extraordinary provision.[127] At the end of the same month, Cardinal Carlo Borromeo conveyed 20,000 *scuti* of cameral gold for his sister's dowry to Count Annibale.[128] Nor did Pius IV neglect his other nephews.[129] In addition to the income from his benefices and other offices, Carlo Borromeo received 7,500 *scuti* of gold in 1562, 8,500 *scuti* of gold in 1563, and in April 1565, 10,000 *scuti* of gold "which His Holiness gives him as a gift so that he can more easily pay some of his debts."[130] This was not enough, apparently, for in May the pope ordered gifts of 4,000 *scuti* for Cardinal Carlo Borromeo, 4,000 *scuti* for Cardinal Mark Sittich d'Altemps, and 5,000 *scuti* for Count Annibale d'Altemps, his nephews.[131]

Pius IV still worried about his family at the end of his life. He called a consistory on 8 December 1565, which met in his bedroom because he was too ill to rise, and made the following bequests: 100,000 *scuti* to Count Annibale d'Altemps, 40,000 *scuti* to Donna Cecilia, daughter of the pope's brother, "so that she can more easily marry," 10,000 *scuti* to brother Agosto de' Medici, 10,000 *scuti* to nephew Gabriele Serbelloni, 10,000 *scuti* to nephew Fabrizio Serbelloni, and 12,000 *scuti* to his family.[132] Later during the consistory, after conducting other business, the pope returned to the question of his "donations" and urged the cardinals to proceed with the payments if he should die. Cardinal Morone reassured the pope, saying that since he was the lord of his blood relatives, he could arrange their affairs according to his own will, and that he must not fear that the cardinals would do anything against his orders; on the contrary, they would always carry them out.[133]

Pius IV died the following day. During the almost six years of his pontificate, he had disbursed some 334,400 *scuti* of gold and silver from the camera apostolica to members of his family, almost ten times the sums distributed by his predecessor. If the pope was still using the funds of the dataria in the manner of Paul III and Julius III, we are beginning to approach the level of luxury for papal families which Reinhard described for the pontificate of Paul V (1605–1623) and which apparently continued through the seventeenth century.[134] And, by 1565, this seemed perfectly proper to the members of the Sacred College of cardinals. One of them, after all, would be elected in the next conclave.

It is significant that Pius IV spent 125,500 *scuti* for dowries and wedding gifts. Indeed, one of the most common uses of the church's wealth and prestige to assist papal and cardinalate families was precisely that made by Pius IV—the arrangement of favorable marriage alliances. We have repeatedly seen members of new cardinalate and papal families using their positions to contract marriages with the older nobility, and the inflation in dowries during the sixteenth century signifies the importance of these alliances. One result of this pattern of intermarriage is

startling: by the second half of the century, three-quarters of our cardinals, either directly or posthumously, were related to each other by
blood (consanguinity) or marriage (affinity). Figure 5.1, the kinship
chart (in pocket), has the popes from Julius II to Pius IV in chronological
order from left to right across the top. The cardinals appear in chronological order of promotion, clockwise from the top right of the circle. Each
connecting line represents a kinship among the papal and cardinalate
families. The chart shows the web of family relationships more graphi-
cally than genealogical tables, and it shows an intricate network indeed.
Marriages produced affinities, but these turned into consanguinities, of
course, in a single generation. Ercole Gonzaga, for example, had an
affinity with the Rovereschi through the marriage of his sister Eleanora
to Francesco Maria della Rovere, but he was the uncle by blood of the
fruits of their union.

The attempt to describe family connections among Italian cardinals
results in almost immediate chaos. A single genealogical example suf-
fices. Through his paternal aunt, Cardinal Franciotto Orsini was a first
cousin of Leo X and a first cousin once removed of cardinals Giovanni
Salviati, Nicolò Ridolfi, Innocenzo Cibo, and Ippolito de' Medici. Franciotto's daughter Cecilia Orsini married Count Alberto Pio of Carpi
and thus became the aunt by affinity of Cardinal Rodolfo Pio. Cecilia's
daughter Caterina Pio married Bonifacio Caetani of Sermoneta and thus
became the sister-in-law of Cardinal Nicolò Caetani. The mother of
Nicolò and Bonifacio Caetani was Flaminia Savelli Caetani, niece of
Jacopo Savelli and Camilla Farnese Savelli. Camilla Farnese Savelli was
a first cousin once removed of Paul III and the grandmother of Cardinal
Jacopo Savelli. The entangling relationships already grow difficult to
grasp, but it is clear from the records that these family ties, *parentadi*,
were matters of great moment to the principals—such ties are always
noted in letters and documents. After being widowed in 1531, for example, the same Cecilia Orsini Pio found protection with both Clement
VII and Paul III because of her connections. Clement VII called her his
affinis according to the flesh, and Paul III declared that she was tied to
him by a double affinity, "since one of her daughters has recently married
the son of our beloved son and nobleman, Camillo Caetani, Lord of
Sermoneta and our *affinis*."[135]

We have seen that membership in the college of cardinals had only
become important for the Italian ruling classes in the fifteenth century
after the popes returned to Rome. Only eight of the families of our
prelates could boast cardinal ancestors prior to the fifteenth century

TABLE 5.13   CARDINALATE FAMILIES PRIOR TO THE
SUBJECTS OF THIS STUDY

13th Century	14th Century	15th Century	16th Century
Savelli	Fieschi	Cibo	Trivulzio
Caetani	Caracciolo	Cornaro	Ferrerio
Orsini	Carafa	Cesarini	
Colonna	Sanseverino	Piccolomini	
		Gonzaga	
		Rovere	
		Fregoso	
		Medici	
		Farnese	
		Pallavicino	
		Conti	

(table 5.13).[136] Furthermore, for 73 percent of the families, our cardinals were the first to wear the purple. This was true both for old, established families, such as the Grimaldi of Genoa or the Estensi of Ferrara, and new families, such as the Gaddi of Florence or the Cesi of Umbria. For old and new families alike, the cardinal's hat had become one way to establish, continue, or enhance honor and fortune.

Marriages among cardinalate and papal families tended to effect a nationalizing of the Italian ruling classes. That is, cardinals looked for alliances with families of high status from without their own *patriae*, Florence, Genoa, Venice, or elsewhere. We noted that Pius IV married his nephew and nieces, from Milanese families, to the Rovereschi of Urbino, the Madruzzi of the Trentino, and the Gonzaga of Mantua. Another example is the house of Grimani of Venice. They were members of the closed Venetian patriciate but not wealthy by Venetian standards before the mercantile successes of Antonio Grimani in the late fifteenth century.[137] Antonio's son Domenico Grimani, making good use of this prosperity, became the first cardinal of the family under Alexander VI. New status brought new ambitions. After the cardinal's death in 1523, his nephews worked for another red hat and a marriage alliance with the Medici, the new papal family. They achieved the former dignity in 1527, when Clement VII created Marino Grimani a cardinal. The negotiations over the prospective marriage, between a Grimani niece and a Ridolfi nephew, never succeeded, but the Grimani persisted in them from 1525 to 1534.[138]

Cardinal Gregorio Cortese had a different goal. His pedigree was excellent, but that of his niece was not. Ersilia Cortese was the illegitimate daughter of the cardinal's brother Jacopo, and they offered her hand to the nobility of their *patria,* Modena, with a handsome dowry. Even though she had been legitimized by Paul III in 1541, "all refused," wrote Pompeo Litta, "to marry the fruits of the adultery of *Monsignore* Cortese."[139] The Cortese brothers then turned to the scion of a distinctly new family, Giovanni Battista del Monte, nephew of Cardinal Gian Maria del Monte, who willingly allied himself with the more ancient lineage, adultery or no. When Cardinal del Monte was elected to the papacy as Julius III in 1550, the Cortese compromise had turned into a brilliant stroke: Ersilia Cortese del Monte was a papal niece and pensioner.[140]

Marriage contracts were used as bargaining tools in papal elections. During the conclave that elected Leo X, one of his conclavists, Bernardo Dovizi, negotiated a match between a Medici nephew and the niece of Cardinal Francesco Soderini in return for Soderini's influence and vote. Soderini, a political antagonist of the Medici in Florence, apparently felt that the fortunes of his family were more important than the election of the Vicar of Christ.[141] Similarly, Innocenzo Cibo tried to win votes for himself during the conclave of 1534 by offering the hand of his niece Giulia Varana, heiress to the duchy of Camerino, to Ascanio Colonna in a fruitless attempt to gain the support of the Cesarini–Colonna forces.[142]

On one occasion, a marriage contract even took precedence over the work of the Council of Trent. Vittoria Farnese, for whom a variety of negotiations had failed since 1535, was still unmarried in 1547.[143] At the age of about twenty-eight years, she was on the verge of permanent spinsterhood and the object of cruel pasquinades by Roman wits, when the sudden death of the duchess of Urbino, Giulia Varana, opened the way to honorable marriage.[144] Cardinal Alessandro Farnese wrote urgently to Marcello Cervini, a legate at Trent, on 23 February 1547. He instructed Cervini to approach the bishop of Fano, Pietro Bertano, about the desirability of a match between his sister, Vittoria, and the recently stricken duke, Guidobaldo della Rovere. Cervini was not to mention the Roman origin of this enterprise, but subtly to persuade Bertano to leave Trent and broach the matter to the duke, to his mother, Eleanora Gonzaga, and to his uncle, Cardinal Ercole Gonzaga.[145] Vittoria's hand ought not to be refused, Farnese thought, "especially by the mother of the duke of Urbino, who, having another son as she does, and perhaps consequently desiring to honor him with ecclesiastical rank, will agree with us the more willingly."[146] As an old and trusted retainer of the Gonzaga, Bertano was the ideal man for the delicate diplomacy.

But the business of the Council was also at a delicate, even critical stage in the acerbic deliberations on episcopal residence and pluralism, and Pietro Bertano was one of the most faithful supporters of the Roman point of view and that of the embattled legates. Nevertheless, it did not seem inappropriate to Bertano, Cervini, Farnese, or the pope that the bishop should absent himself from Trent on such a mission. As it happened, the matter was quickly concluded. The marriage took place in June, and on 27 July 1547 Paul III elevated to the cardinalate the twelve-year-old brother of the bridegroom, Giulio della Rovere, reserving the nomination *in petto* temporarily.[147] The pope published his creation on 9 January 1548, and on 10 April Cardinal Jean du Bellay ceded to Giulio the title church of St. Peter in Chains, the traditional title of the Rovereschi, first held by Sixtus IV.[148] All parties were satisfied.

Beyond the exalted social position that accompanied brilliant marriages, Italian prelates sought something more concrete for their families—temporal sovereignty, *un bello stato.* The success of the Cesi and Gaddi families in this endeavor has already been outlined. The Campeggi of Bologna also achieved noble rank through the efforts of their first cardinal. Lorenzo Campeggio bought the county of Dozza for his soldier son Rodolfo Campeggio, and after the latter died without issue in 1548, Paul III invested the late cardinal's brother Antonio Maria Campeggio as the count of Dozza. The county was raised to a *marchesato* by Urban VIII in 1633 and remained in the family until the male line ran out in 1725. It then went to Emilio Malvezzi, the son of Francesca Campeggio, sister of the late *marchese,* and of Matteo Malvezzi of Bologna.[149] These examples could be multiplied almost *ad infinitum.* The top three categories of social class outlined in chapter 1—noble, patrician, and new—steadily merged and expanded with additional new men during the century, as cardinals used their wealth to establish primogenitures in "beautiful states" all over Italy, but particularly in the Papal State, Lombardy, and Naples.[150] Perhaps, as Peter Partner suggested, the creation of this new nobility accelerated at the end of the century, but the process was well under way long before then.[151] While papal families present the most dramatic examples of such sudden rise to perpetual nobility, as Reinhard has shown, cardinalate families did equally well by their heirs.[152]

Ercole Gonzaga expressed a common assumption about the uses of ecclesiastical power. Paul III, he remarked in 1535, urgently required temporal states for his family, "because, although ecclesiastical privileges in families are easily lost at the death of the pope who conceded them, temporal possessions remain."[153] Gonzaga elaborated upon this theme twenty-five years later in some advice to his nephew Cesare Gonzaga, who was about to join the papal court for the first time as a nephew-in-law of Pius IV:

> The other thing that you must attempt to effect with Our *Signore* and the *signori* [Borromei] your brothers-in-law, is that whatever is to be done for their comfort and *grandezza* be done soon, because, even should the pope live for many years (which is, however, uncertain and resting in the will of God), much time is needed before a house of private gentlemen can be established in the position of a prince with a state and jurisdiction of some importance and new. Therefore time must not be lost, and it seems to me that there is no more likely state than Camerino, which Our *Signore* could give to Count Federico [Borromeo]. . . .
>
> There is also Salerno, which is a lovely piece and brings with it the title of prince, suitable for the nephew of a pope, and it would be a simple matter to get it through the grace and courtesy of His Majesty [Philip II], and also because it is not sold but only pawned to the *Marchese* of Pescara, who would be very well satisfied at any time if his money were restored to him and his brother made cardinal.[154]

Professor Partner pointed out that the same families that produced the financiers of the papacy also produced the curialists who ran the church.[155] The same families produced governors, soldiers, and cardinals, to say nothing of wives. The venal offices, as we saw, allowed laymen to invest in the church in new ways and to new extents. The purchase of venal office offered ingress to the inner circles of the curia and the possibility of the red hat. *Cavalierati* brought new opportunities for investment and new social status for Italians. Italian bankers rivaled each other for the lucrative positions in Rome, and they bought up the successive bond issues—venal offices, *cavalierati*, and *monti*—with alacrity for resale to the laity. They also sought the cardinalate for members of their families for the first time. The incomes from the sale of these bonds went into the treasuries of the church, to be used to support ever-higher levels of grandeur for papal families and cardinals. Accumulated incomes provided dowries for splendid marriages and moneys with which to buy landed properties and titles of nobility. The proliferation of marriages among new and old Italian families produced a college of cardinals that, by mid-century, was largely one big family.

No attempt was made to alter these practices; indeed, they seem to have intensified during the century. Professor Partner suggested that the fiscal systems of the papacy may have been unacceptable to reformers, but some of the greatest reformers of the century participated in them.[156] When Pope Julius III spoke of the "reform" of the *monte* in 1550, he meant the launching of a new loan, the *Monte Giulio,* with a capital of 150,000 *scuti.*[157] The revenues of the dataria fell off after Trent, but soon regained their strength. The new fiscal systems were too convenient, and they touched too many people, to be seriously tampered with. The network of relationships—social, political, and economic—among the ruling classes, the papacy, and the college of cardinals grew broader and at the same time stronger during the century. And the health and *grandezza* of the family continued to be a central preoccupation for Italians, ecclesiastics and laymen.

6
Cardinals, Reform, and Church Property

At the outset of this inquiry, we proposed to explore the nature of Catholic reform in the sixteenth century, and specifically the reform of the classical property-related abuses of pluralism, simony, and nepotism. The investigation has been narrowly circumscribed in that it dealt only with questions of money and property, and it approached these questions only through the activities of 102 Italian cardinals as they acquired, alienated, and distributed church money and property. At the same time, the investigation has ranged widely. The pursuit of the cardinals led us from the corridors of the Roman curia to a far greater population, not only the clients and relatives of the cardinals but also the silent shareholders in the church, the moneyed classes of Italy. It is time to summarize the findings.

Reform, as envisioned by the authors of the *Consilium de emendanda ecclesia* of 1537, seems largely to have failed where money and property were involved. First, pluralism in sacred office was abolished only in its most public manifestation, the holding of more than one bishopric. Pluralism in lesser benefices, particularly multiple abbeys *in commendam,* continued throughout the century and beyond, despite the efforts of reforming popes and the decrees of Trent. Even in the case of bishoprics, the eradication of pluralism resulted in the exchange of titles for annual cash payments from the same sacred offices. Furthermore, Italian cardinals retained a large measure of control over the properties they relinquished, through the use of the regress, the access, and the collation of lesser benefices. All of these devices came under attack during our period, and the right of the *regressus* was temporarily restricted to two (it is not clear that this order remained in effect). Restrictions on the collation of benefices may have been effective, but the patronage needs of cardinals brought them special privilege. After mid-century, it became

customary to grant licenses to cardinals allowing them to confer benefices in "alien" dioceses. Pius IV revoked these licenses in 1561, to be
sure, but the patronage needs of cardinals remained urgent enough to
result in the codification over the years of extraordinary privileges for
their familiars and the familiars of popes.

The assignment of annual pensions from resigned benefices and from
"alien" benefices increased dramatically in both number and amount,
after the middle of the century. This method of enhancing the incomes
of cardinals and others continued after Trent, and it became customary
for popes to reserve huge sums "for persons to be named" with each
new provision, particularly from benefices in the Iberian peninsula.
Pensions from sacred offices were still considered benefices as late as
the eighteenth century, requiring duties of and dispensations for pensioners. In Rome, however, they came to be regarded as private property
belonging to the personal fortunes of cardinals and others, who could
bequeath them to lay heirs by means of a last will. Pensions could also,
of course, be used along with other cardinalate incomes to buy landed
properties, titles of nobility, and movable goods for the benefit of lay
heirs. And, while the bequeathing of pensions to laymen occurred only
once, on the death of the cardinal, the power to transfer pensions to
clients and relatives could perpetuate them for a generation or more.
Further, the change we detected in the attitudes of reformers about the
reservation of pensions between the pontificate of Paul III and those of
Pius V and Sixtus V suggests that the practice had become rooted in
Roman custom. While the earlier reformers deplored the granting of
pensions as detrimental to the benefice and its beneficiary, later reformers worried about the personal probity of the pensioner.

The renting out of all manner of church benefices to bankers continued, so deeply entrenched that Paul IV's attempt to restrict rental
leases to three years failed. His decree caused such chaos that it had to
be revoked by Pius IV, and later restrictions from Trent resulted in the
customary use of multiple *triennii* in rental agreements as *not* contrary
to the holy decrees and sacred canons. The close connections among
the popes, cardinals, and Italian bankers surely had some effect upon
this practice and upon the ease with which the three-year limit was
circumvented.

These practices—the collection of multiple lesser benefices *in commendam* or otherwise, the collection of pensions from multiple benefices
and the right to transfer them or bequeath them to heirs, the right to
rent out benefices held in title or *in commendam* or in any other way—

must have damaged the health of the church. Indeed, it is difficult to imagine that the episcopate in Italy, Spain, or Portugal was strengthened during the years of reform when episcopal incomes were siphoned off into the pockets of cardinals and their retainers and families, or rented out to bankers, or both. Nevertheless, these usages, which had seemed abusive in the early years of reform, became so customary that they were affirmed as lawful by the jurists who revised canon law after the Council of Trent: multiple benefices held *in commendam* are not pluralistic, because properties held *in commendam* are no longer benefices; multiple pensions from ecclesiastical benefices are not pluralistic, because pensions are no longer benefices; the right to bequeath property by means of a last will is now one of the normal privileges accorded to cardinals; and the rental of church property is still lawful if it is done for urgent necessity, the utility of the church, or for piety.

Second, simony, the buying and selling of sacred office and graces, seems to have disappeared in the technical sense. After the pontificate of Clement VII we do not see the popes "selling" red hats, for example. But arrangements, exchanges, "pacts," and "confidences" concerning ecclesiastical benefices all persisted. These seemed simoniacal to reformers, and successive popes tried to stop them. For those involved in the transactions, however, confidences and agreements were not a matter of simony, but rather methods through which ecclesiastical benefices could be safely secured for relatives and familiars. Resignations in favor, the use of intermediaries, appointments of coadjutors, all continued throughout the century. The payment of compositions, a major source of income for the department of the dataria, was also considered simoniacal by Contarini and his friends in the 1530s, as we saw, although it was defended vigorously by others at the time. Compositions were of two kinds: money paid for dispensations and indulgences, and money paid as fines for criminal or other wrong behavior. It was probably the restriction on the payment of the first kind of composition that caused the temporary decline in the datary's revenue under Pius V. Compositions that were fines, however, were not considered simoniacal. Presumably the composition Bernardino Savelli was compelled to pay in 1592 for breaking the last will of his brother the cardinal falls into the latter category.

If outright simony disappeared from the Roman court, the venal atmosphere in Rome assuredly did not. The new fiscal systems that developed from the pontificate of Sixtus IV brought new credit mechanisms to the popes and probably reduced the temptation to sell cardinal's hats, but probably they also enhanced the aura of venality surrounding the court as the century progressed. The sale of venal offices, of *cavalierati*, of shares in the successive *monti* opened opportunities for investment to numberless Italians through the bankers who were the initial purchasers. Gold from these sales poured into the treasuries of the dataria and the camera apostolica, and the popes of our period drew on them in increasing amounts to enrich their families. The cash nexus permeated the hierarchy from top to bottom.

Third, nepotism and patronage may have been the keys to the failure to reform in any substantive way the fiscal abuses at the curia. When pressures for reform came face-to-face with Italian ideas of duty and obligation, with the ideals of the good *signore*, the faithful son, the grateful prince, the notion of nepotism and patronage as abuses faded beyond recognition. The compelling need to provide for one's *gens*, to maintain it or to establish it among the nobility, to see to its grandeur and endurance, flooded the consciousness of Italian prelates and took precedence over other sorts of obligations. As Italians, our cardinals owed the first allegiance to their families and familiars; as cardinals, they owed their first allegiance to the church. When these allegiances clashed, our cardinals tended to act as Italians. Reinhard's assertion that *pietas*, the devotion to one's clan, was a paramount sentiment among Italians, is certainly true. On the other hand, the repeated attempts to curb the *instruments* of nepotism and patronage—regresses, accesses, the collation of benefices, "pacts," "confidences," legitimization—suggest that tensions between the ideal of *pietas* and the ideals of reform did not vanish altogether and that these practices were not simply commonly accepted norms, at least not by 1563. Yet, when faced with the drastic curtailment in income and influence that would have resulted from a reform on the outline of the *Consilium* of 1537, the cardinals recoiled. The needs of their families and familiars, and, of course, their own needs as princes of the church rendered any such program impossible. And it remained a primary goal of many Italian cardinals to found a rich legacy for the lay heir of the family, a primogeniture that was intended to continue in perpetuity.

More and more Italians sought their fortunes in Rome from the fifteenth century on. Through the open door that high church office represented, new families emerged, intermarried with the established ruling classes, and formed a new nobility. This group, along with its clients, purchased venal offices or invested in them. They bought *cavalierati* and "places" in the *monti*. They turned themselves into a

class of *rentiers* with direct, vested interests in the welfare of the Holy
See. In this they corresponded to their cardinal relatives, who were
turning into *rentiers* as well—clerical *rentiers*. As the taste for luxury
in Rome increased during the second half of the sixteenth century—
stimulated, perhaps, by the presence of new families—the needs of cardinals and popes correspondingly increased. Any reform directed toward
the reduction of incomes would have been incompatible with the private
interests of their families. Any serious tampering with the fiscal practices
and bureaucratic systems at the Roman curia would inevitably have
disrupted private ambitions. Any diminution of the powers of the popes
would have deprived Italians of their principal patron.

The realities of the time, then, deflected the reform efforts of the
cardinals away from material matters, and focused them upon things
spiritual: the delineation of correct doctrine and the repression of error,
the education of priests and the propagation of correct doctrine, personal
piety and charitable works, and the glorification of the true faith. Italian
cardinals worked at the several sessions of the Council and in the Holy
Office of the Inquisition. They visited and reformed monasteries and
convents. They held diocesan synods, examined priests, founded
seminaries, and supported the new religious orders. They founded charitable hospitals and orphanages and led groups of the faithful on pilgrim-
ages through the holy city to the seven churches. Finally, to celebrate
the Holy Mother Church, they patronized the construction and embellishment of the churches, palaces, and fountains that transformed the
face of the eternal city in the years following the last sessions of the
Council of Trent.

Appendix
A Note on the Currency

The frequent mention of different denominations of money makes a special note on currency desirable. Since the thirteenth century, the principal gold coins of Italy had been the florin of Florence and the ducat of Venice. The Holy See had followed with a gold coin first known as the "papal florin" and later called, by the end of the fourteenth century, the "papal ducat." By the end of the fifteenth century—that is, by the period under consideration in this work—the papal ducat had been largely displaced by the gold ducat *della camera,* which contained slightly less gold. In the fiscal records of the dataria and the camera apostolica, the ducats *della camera* were measures roughly equivalent to the large gold florin, introduced in Florence in the mid-fifteenth century. In 1531 the *scuto* of gold, money of French origin, was introduced in Rome, and it was valued at about 7 percent less than the cameral ducat. The *scuto* of *moneta,* silver, was worth even less—about 15 percent behind the *scuto* of gold.

In addition, there existed a wide variety of provincial moneys, both real and imaginary, known as pounds, ducats, and florins; their worth bore little relationship to other moneys with the same names. In 1537, for example, a florin of the province of the Marches was valued at only half of a Roman *scuto* and less than half of the Florentine florin. The situation was further complicated by the steady inflation of the period and the constant depreciation of silver in relation to gold. Seasonal and regional fluctuations also confuse assessments.

Nevertheless, if we follow the fiscal records of the curia, we can arrive at some estimates of the relative value of the most common currencies. The gold ducat *della camera* was the strongest money in use at Rome during our period. The Spanish large ducat was equivalent to the ducat *della camera* by mid-century. The *scuto* of gold, as noted, was about 7 percent less valuable. The Neapolitan gold ducat was worth about 15 percent less than the gold *scuto,* being equal to the *scuto* of *moneta;* the pound of Tours was worth about half of a gold ducat *della camera;* the pound of Bologna was worth about a third of a gold ducat *della camera;* the imperial pound, a Milanese money of account, was worth about one-sixth of a Roman *scuto* of *moneta.*

On these matters, see Raymond de Roover, *The Rise and Decline of the Medici Bank: 1397–1494* (Cambridge Mass. 1963) 31–34; Carlo M. Cipolla, *Mouvements Monétaires dans l'Etat de Milan (1580–1700)* (Paris 1952); Amintore Fanfani, *Indagini sulla "Rivoluzione dei Prezzi"* (Milan 1940); G. Garampi, *Saggi di Osservazioni sul valore delle antiche monete pontificie* (Rome 1766); Delumeau; Partner, "Papal Financial Policy"; and Reinhard, *Papstfinanz und Nepotismus.*

Notes

1. CHURCH PROPERTY, ABUSE, AND CARDINALS

1. See the survey by John W. O'Malley, *Giles of Viterbo on Church and Reform: A Study in Renaissance Thought* (Leiden 1968) 1–3.

2. For a general account of the growth of papal government, see Geoffrey Barraclough, *The Medieval Papacy* (London 1968) 118–196. See also his *Papal Provisions* (Oxford 1935).

3. John Dillenberger, ed., *Martin Luther: Selections from His Writings* (Garden City N.Y. 1961) 417–431; Olin 182–197; CT 10.410–411, 426–427. For an example of prior German *gravamina*, see Gerald Strauss, trans. and ed., *Manifestations of Discontent in Germany on the Eve of the Reformation* (Bloomington Ind. 1971) 35–63.

4. Olin 186–187.

5. Olin 187–197; Hubert Jedin, *A History of the Council of Trent*, trans. Dom Ernest Graf (2 vols. London 1957) 1.423–428.

6. William J. Bouwsma identified this distaste for the material aspects of papal government with Venetian evangelism. See his *Venice and the Defense of Republican Liberty: Renaissance Values in the Age of the Counter-Reformation* (Berkeley and Los Angeles 1968) 123–133. On the *Consilium*, see also Richard M. Douglas, *Jacopo Sadoleto, 1477–1547: Humanist and Reformer* (Cambridge Mass. 1959) 99–114. In addition to Contarini, the commission included Cardinal Gian Pietro Carafa, later Pope Paul IV; Cardinal Jacopo Sadoleto; Cardinal Reginald Pole of England; Federigo Fregoso, archbishop of Salerno and later cardinal; Girolamo Aleandro, archbishop of Brindisi and later cardinal; Gian Matteo Giberti, bishop of Verona and earlier the datary under Clement VII; Gregorio Cortese, abbot of San Giorgio in Venice and later cardinal; and the Dominican Tommaso Badia, master of the Sacred Palace and later cardinal. Most of these men have been described as members of the "Erasmian," "Mediatist," or "Moderate" school of Catholic reformers. See Frederic C. Church, *The Italian Reformers, 1534–1564* (New York 1932) 20–33; G. K. Brown, *Italy and the Reformation to 1550* (Oxford 1933). Jedin (n. 5 above) 1.419–423 classified curial reformers as moderate or conservative. He specifically excluded Aleandro from the ranks of the reformers altogether, somewhat unfairly in my view. Philip McNair, *Peter Martyr in Italy: An Anatomy of*

Apostasy (Oxford 1967) 1–10, worked out a provocative formula of six degrees of reform thought from conservative to radical. All of the members of the reform commission are on the list of cardinals to be investigated below, with the exceptions of Carafa, who became pope, Giberti, who never became cardinal, and Pole, the Englishman.

7. Olin 188.

8. Jedin (n. 5 above) 1.410–445; Ludwig Pastor, *The History of the Popes from the Close of the Middle Ages,* trans. Ralph Francis Kerr (2d ed. 40 vols. St. Louis and London 1923–1928) 11.182–217. The committee that Paul III chose to reform the dataria, for example, was composed of Contarini, Carafa, Aleandro, Badia, and also cardinals Girolamo Ghinucci and Jacopo Simonetta, a pair of jurists. One of the major quarrels surrounded "compositions," payments for papal dispensations and indulgences which, along with the sale of offices, constituted the major source of income for the department. Contarini and his allies considered them simoniacal; the lawyers saw them simply as court costs. Compositions were defended on philosophical grounds by two men who were raised to the cardinalate in 1539—Bartolomeo Guidiccioni, another lawyer, and Dionisio Lorerio, general of the Servites. Their principal argument was that the *graces* were freely granted by the pope, the *payments* were unconnected. Contarini found this unconvincing; see his arguments in CT 12.215–226. On Guidiccioni, see Hubert Jedin, "Concilio e riforma nel pensiero del Cardinale Bartolomeo Guidiccioni," RSCI 2 (1948) 33–60.

9. See the standard works and also *The Reformation: 1520–1559,* ed. G. R. Elton, vol. 2 of *The New Cambridge Modern History* (Cambridge 1958); G. R. Elton, *Reformation Europe: 1517–1559* (New York 1963); H. Outram Evennett, *The Spirit of the Counter-Reformation,* ed. John Bossy (Cambridge 1968); Henri Daniel-Rops, *The Catholic Reformation,* trans. John Warrington (2 vols. Garden City N.Y. 1964).

10. Hay 1–8. See also the articles by Eric Cochrane, "New Light on Post-Tridentine Italy: A Note on Recent Counter-Reformation Scholarship," *Catholic Historical Review* 56 (1970) 291–319, and "What is Catholic Historiography?," ibid. 61 (1975) 169–190.

11. Partner, "Papal Financial Policy" 17–18.

12. CT 10.161: "Guardate, se potete, più alle mani degli homini che alla bocca." Cervini was elected to the papacy in 1555, and had a very brief pontificate as Marcellus II.

13. Some examples follow. The starting point for Roman studies is still Ludwig Pastor, *The History of the Popes* (n. 8 above). Jedin's work on the Council of Trent must also be cited again (n. 5 above). On Rome during the period, see Pio Pecchiai, *Roma nel Cinquecento* (Rome 1948), and Peter Partner, *Renaissance Rome: 1500–1559* (Berkeley and Los Angeles 1976). The most thorough study of the latter half of the century is Delumeau's *Vie économique et sociale de Rome dans la seconde moitié du XVIᵉ siècle* (2 vols. Paris 1957–1959). Denys Hay recounts the condition of the church in Italy for the century preceding the years included in the present study, with some overlapping; he found the church of the fifteenth century "singularly unfit to meet the challenge of the reformers" (109). Several current scholars argue for a "long" sixteenth

century, extending well into the seventeenth century, as a logical periodization of church history, among them Peter Partner in "Papal Financial Policy," Eric Cochrane in the essays he edited in *The Late Italian Renaissance: 1525–1630* (New York 1970), and more recently Paolo Prodi, *Il sovrano pontifice: un corpo e due anime: la monarchia papale nella prima età moderna* (Bologna 1982).

14. See Adolf Gottlob, *Aus der Camera Apostolica des 15. Jahrhunderts: ein Beitrag zur Geschichte des päpstlichen Finanzwesens und das endenden Mittelalters* (Innsbruck 1889); Emil Göller, *Die päpstliche Pönitentiarie von ihrem Ursprung bis zu ihrer Umgestaltung unter Pius V* (2 vols. Rome 1907–1911); Léonce Celier, *Les Dataires du XVᵉ siècle et les origines de la Datérie Apostolique* (Paris 1910); Walter von Hofmann, *Forschungen zur Geschichte der kurialen Behörden vom Schisma bis zur Reformation* (2 vols. Rome 1914). In 1931 appeared the work of Bruno Katterbach, *Referendarii utriusque Signaturae a Martino V ad Clementem IX et Prelati Signaturae Supplicationum a Martino V ad Leonem XIII*, Studi e Testi 55 (Vatican City). These works largely cover the earlier period, and they concentrate upon constitutions, personnel, and rights and duties of the offices. More helpful about actual curial practices are the works of William E. Lunt, *Papal Revenues in the Middle Ages* (2 vols. New York 1934) and *Financial Relations of the Papacy with England: 1327–1534*, vol. 2 of *Studies in Anglo-Papal Relations during the Middle Ages* (Cambridge Mass. 1962); these also cover the earlier period. The works on the dataria do focus on the sixteenth century, and both are very enlightening: Nicola Storti, *La storia e il diritto della Dataria Apostolica dalle origini ai nostri giorni* (Naples 1969), and Felice Litva, "L'attività finanziaria della Dataria durante il periodo tridentino," *Archivum Historiae Pontificiae* 5 (1967) 79–174. On the departments of the curia in general, see Niccolò del Re, *La curia romana: lineamenti storico-giuridici* (3d ed. Rome 1970).

15. Peter Partner, "Papal Financial Policy" 17–19, summarized the bibliography of works on papal finances. See also Clemens Bauer, "Die Epochen der Papstfinanz: ein Versuch," *Historische Zeitschrift* 138 (1927) 457–503, and the same, "Studi per la storia delle finanze papale durante il pontificato di Sisto IV," ASRSP 50 (1927) 319–400. See also Michele Monaco, "Le finanze pontificie al tempo di Clemente VII (1523–1534)," *Studi Romani* 6.3 (1958) 278–296, and "Il primo debito pubblico pontificio: il Monte della Fede (1526)," *Studi Romani* 8.5 (1960) 553–569. The recently published books of Melissa M. Bullard, *Filippo Strozzi and the Medici: Favor and Finance in Sixteenth-Century Florence and Rome* (Cambridge 1980), and Felix Gilbert, *The Pope, His Banker, and Venice* (Cambridge Mass. 1980) concern papal finance for the early years of the century. Reinhard, *Papstfinanz und Nepotismus*, examines papal finance at the beginning of the seventeenth century in a work that Peter Partner calls the "light . . . at the end of the tunnel" ("Papal Financial Policy" 18). See also the works of Delumeau and Litva cited in nn. 13 and 14 above.

16. For example, see the exhaustive work of F. Gillmann, "Die Resignation der Benefizien," *Archiv für katholisches Kirchenrecht* 80 (1900) 50–79, 346–378, 523–569, 665–788; and 81 (1901) 223–242, 433–460; also Pier Giovanni Caron, *La Rinuncia all'Ufficio Ecclesiastico nella storia del diritto canonico*

dalla Età Apostolica alla Riforma Cattolica (Milan 1946), who assumes that the reform was complete with the Council of Trent. G. Mollat discussed expectative graces for an earlier period: "Les graces expectatives sous le règne de Philippe VI de Valois," *Revue d'histoire ecclésiastique* 32 (1936) 303–312; and "Les graces expectatives du XIIᵉ au XIVᵉ siècle," *Revue d'histoire ecclésiastique* 42 (1947) 81–102. For the law on last wills, see Friedrich Merzbacher, "Das Testamentsrecht des Corpus Juris Canonici," *Österreichisches Archiv für Kirchenrecht* 19 (1968) 289–307.

17. Giuseppe Alberigo, *Cardinalato e collegialità: Studi sull'ecclesiologia tra l'XI e il XVI secolo* (Florence 1969) discusses doctrine concerning the functions of the college, not individual cardinals. The only collective study of the cardinals of which I am aware is the brief and interesting article by A. V. Antonovics, "Counter-Reformation Cardinals: 1534–90," *European Studies Review* 2 (1972) 301–328. Biographical works of individual cardinals abound, and much of the literature is cited in the present work, but the college as a group remains to be dealt with.

18. Evennett (n. 9 above) 114–115. In 1492 there were 27 living cardinals.

19. On reform efforts under Alexander VI, see Léonce Celier, "Alexandre VI et la réforme de l'église," *Mélanges d'archéologie et d'histoire* 27 (1907) 65–124. See also Hay 87, where he analyzes the proposals for reform from the pontificates of Pius II and Sixtus IV.

20. See table 1.1, compiled from Ciacconius vols. 3 and 4. See also Giuseppe Alberigo, *I Vescovi italiani al Concilio di Trento (1545–1547)* (Florence 1959) 443–468; and Hay 41–48, who speaks of the "Italianisation" of the Roman curia in the years following the pontificate of Martin V (1417–1431).

21. Only cardinals resident in Rome were considered members of the papal court and entitled to the cameral "divisions."

22. The old Roman aristocracy cannot qualify as city people—burghers—of course. The Colonna, Conti, Orsini, della Valle, Caetani, and Savelli represent the landed, military nobility.

23. DBI 1.106–109.

24. Lauro Martines, *Lawyers and Statecraft in Renaissance Florence* (Princeton 1968) 502–503. Cardinal Pietro's grandfather, Michele di Santi Accolti, also practiced law in Florence.

25. All of the new men in the last group owed their success to ecclesiastical careers, either their own or those of relatives. See Wolfgang Reinhard on the rise of the Borghese family, "Ämterlaufbahn und Familienstatus: Der Aufstieg des Hauses Borghese, 1537–1621," *QFIAB* 54 (1974) 328–427.

26. See chapter 5 below.

27. Vincenzo Pacifici, *Ippolito II d'Este, Cardinale di Ferrara* (Tivoli 1920) 5–6.

28. Alessandro Ferrajoli, "Il ruolo della Corte di Leone X (1514–1516)," *ASRSP* 36 (1913) 555.

29. Ciacconius 3.683–685; Josephus Cominus, *Gregorii Cortesii Monachi Cassinatis, S. R. E. Cardinalis, omnia quae huc usque colligi potuerunt, sive ad illum spectantia.* 2 vols. (Padua 1774) vol. 1 passim. He was one of the authors of the *Consilium*, later theological adviser to Tommaso Campeggio at the Colloquy of Worms in 1540.

30. Arturo Segre, "Un registro di lettere del cardinale Ercole Gonzaga (1535–36) con un'appendice di documenti inediti," *Miscellanea di storia italiana, R. Deputazione sovra gli studi di storia patria per le antiche provincie e la Lombardia,* terza serie 16 (1913) 275–276.

31. Gonzaga was the penultimate president of the Council of Trent.

32. Antonovics found the same proportions in his article "Counter-Reformation Cardinals" (n. 17 above) 313: "Probably the largest single category of cardinals were lawyers by training."

33. See Amintore Fanfani, *Indagini sulla "Rivoluzione dei Prezzi"* (Milan 1940) and *Storia del lavoro in Italia dalla fine del secolo XV agli inizi del XVIII,* vol. 3 of *Storia del lavoro in Italia* (Milan 1959). Also Delumeau and Partner, "Papal Financial Policy." See Appendix, below.

34. Giuseppe Baraldi, *Elogio del cardinale Tommaso Badia di Modena* (Modena 1830) 17; Ciacconius 3.685; DBI 5.75.

35. MC, vol. 862, fol. 224r and passim.

36. Vat lat 10600, fols. 102r–126r.

37. Vat lat 10602, fol. 55r: "Ad Egidio Zephyro, cento doro sonno per sua provisione di uno anno finito il presente mese per ordine di Nostro Signore." More on the *depositario* of the dataria in Litva (n. 14 above) 103–112.

38. AM, vol, 3, fol. 49r: "Et per Capitula facta in Conclavis in assumptione dilectae recordationis Julii 2 declaratum fuit ut omnibus Cardinalibus dictum annum redditum non habentibus de pecuniis Apostolicae Sedis et Camerae Ducati 200 auri quolibet mense et pro quolibet Cardinale eos non habentes darentur." See Pastor (n. 8 above) 7.20; and Antonovics, "Counter-Reformation Cardinals" (n. 17 above) 325. Pecchiai (n. 13 above) 21–22 lists the incomes of cardinals (in ducats) at the time of the conclave which elected Clement VII in 1523:

Medici	50,000
Cibo	26,000
Cornaro	24,000
Farnese	15,000
Colonna, Gonzaga	12,000
Fieschi, Passerini, Soderini	10,000
Accolti, Scaramuzza Trivulzio	9,000
Del Monte, Pucci, della Valle, Armellini, Vich, Salviati	8,000
Grassi, Cesarini, Ridolfi	7,000
Rangone, Agostino Trivulzio	6,000
Piccolomini, de Cupis, Jacobazzi, Egidio, Orsini, Cesi	4,000
Campeggio, Ponzetti, Pisani	3,000
Numai, Vio	2,000

Later in the century, cardinals were much richer. See Delumeau 1.433–469.

39. A. V. Antonovics, "A Late Fifteenth-Century Division Register of the College of Cardinals," *Papers of the British School at Rome* 35 (n.s. 22) (1967) 87–101; D. S. Chambers, "The Economic Predicament of Renaissance Cardinals," *Studies in Medieval and Renaissance History* 3 (1966) 289–313.

40. Delumeau 1.20.

41. See chapter 2 below and table 2.8.

42. See E. Delaruelle, R. R. Labande, and Paul Ourliac, *L'Église au temps du Grand Schisme et de la crise conciliaire (1378–1449)*, vol. 14 of *Histoire de l'église depuis les origines jusqu'à nos jours* (2 vols. Paris 1962–1964) 2.v–xiv, 209–215, 295–313.

43. ANG 3, *Correspondance des nonces en France Capodiferro, Dandino et Guidiccione: 1541–1546*, ed. J. Lestoquoy (Rome 1963) 116: "Si non de solo pane vivit homo, multo fortius non de solis verbis."

2. THE ACCUMULATION OF INCOME

1. Jules Paquier, *Lettres familières de Jérome Aléandre (1510–1540)* (Paris 1909) 101–103: "A cardinali, a Principi et altri qualunque grandi che dimandono gratia responde *videbimus*, et fa poi quello li pare. . . . Laudatur Deus."

2. Ibid.: "La prepositura vale in portatis ducati cinque cento d'oro como dicono molti, altri dicono 400; . . . Il canonicato vale in absentia duc. 36, in residentia CLXX como si dice, ma io gia ho trovato da piu di sei persone che me daran recompensa duc. CC d'oro portati in Roma. Un altro me ha offerto un Episcopato nel Reame de duc. CCCC solum per il Canonicato; un altro me offerisce una scriptoria apostolica che si vende ducati tre milia. Se io faro qualche cosa, pigliaro questo ultimo partito per molti ragioni, ma non bisogna, per amor del Papa, che si presto faci alcuna innovatione et cossi me consiliano li amici, poi sei o 7 mesi permutare il Canonicato; la Prepositura che vale in portatis tenirlo per me." A prepositure is the office of provost, the head of cathedral chapters.

3. Vat lat 3913, fol. 113r, 17 October 1540.

4. Vittorio Cian, *Un decennio della vita di M. Pietro Bembo (1521–1531)* (Turin 1885) 211: "Queste non sono, Mons. mio, di buono e di leal Signore opere. Non così la benivolenza e l'amistà deli uomini si procura, nè le belle ed immortali fame s'aquistono. . . . Dico adunque che io mi doglio di voi, e della vostra ingratitudine, e dello inganno che fatto m'avete, e dorromene la vita mi durerà. E come che io non abbia da voi quella Badia, che io aver dovea per ogni conto, non per questo rimarrà che io Pietro Bembo non sia. Il quale pure di quella picciola fortuna, che la felice memoria di S.S. Leone m'ha data, ho maritate due mie nipoti pupille in gentiluomini della mia Patria; e fo pensiero di maritar anco la terza, che mi resta, se io potrò."

5. Cian (n. 4 above) 210–213.

6. Hay, 16–20, 44–45, 104.

7. Ferraris 1.394–401.

8. Ferraris 1.394: "Quia nullus in duobus locis simul existere, atque personaliter residere potest, sequitur evidenter, quod sint incompatibilia."

9. Ferraris 1.395: "Unde retinens sine justa dispensatione plura Beneficia, quorum unum sufficiat ad sui honestam sustentationem, peccat mortaliter, et est in statu damnationis aeternae."

10. Ferraris 1.397: "Unde cum Papa secundum plenitudinem potestatis de Jure possit supra Jus dispensare, . . . stat clarum quod Papa ex rationabili, et justa causa possit super pluralitate quorumcumque Beneficiorum dispensare."

11. BR 6.81–87, 254–255, 286–298.

12. Paul Kalkoff, *Aleander gegen Luther: Studien zu Ungedrückten Aktenstücken aus Aleanders Nachlass* (Leipzig 1908) 35.

13. AC, vol. 2, fol. 134v: "donec provideatur ei de persona idonea." See Hay 16–20.

14. Eubel 3.81–84; Willim E. Lunt, *Financial Relations of the Papacy with England: 1327–1534*, vol. 2 of *Studies in Anglo-Papal Relations during the Middle Ages* (Cambridge Mass. 1962) 247–275; Walter von Hofmann, *Forschungen zur Geschichte der kurialen Behörden vom Schisma bis zur Reformation* (2 vols. Rome 1914) 2.209–226. The cardinal-promoter, or *referente*, was the man who proposed the nomination in consistory.

15. Arm. 41, vol. 8, fols. 257r–258r: "Volentes autem providere ne dum dicte littere expediuntur possessio dicte plebanie occupetur aut illius fructus distrahuntur eidem Circumspectione Tue corporalem possessionem dicte plebanie iurumque et pertinentiarum suarum per te vel alium seu alios quem vel quos duxeris deputandum seu deputandos libere capiendi et apprehendendi et illius fructus redditus et proventus praecipiendi et levandi licentiam et facultatem concedimus per presentes." Other such licenses: Arm. 41, vol. 10, fol. 220r; vol. 22, fol. 263r; vol. 27, fols. 222r–223r; vol. 33, fol. 39r; vol. 38, fols. 300r, 315r; Arm. 42, vol. 10, fols. 68r, 69r, 81r–82v, 184r–185v, 230r–231v; vol. 13, fols. 72r, 251r–252v, 403rv; vol. 16, fols. 163r–164v. This practice continued throughout our period. The last citation is dated 10 October 1561, and is labeled "For the Bishop of Belluno, suffragan of the Cardinal of Trent; Third prorogation over not expediting the bulls of his provision to six months *etc.*, and as soon as it lapses, it is conceded again" ("Pro Episcopo Bellinensi suffraganeo Cardinalis Tridentini Tertia prorogatio de non expediendis ad sex menses bullis suae provisionis etc. et quatenus lapsi sint de novo conceditur").

16. Arm. 41, vol. 36, fol. 129v; "Volumus autem quod litteras sub plumbo predictas infra sex menses a dato presentium computandas expedire omnino tenearis."

17. Eubel 3.29, 140; Paolo Guerrini, "L'ingresso episcopale a Brescia dei due cardinali veneti Francesco e Andrea Cornaro," *Brixia Sacra* 8 (January–April 1917) 12; Arm. 40, vol. 41, fols. 109r, 115r; Arm. 41, vol. 49, fol. 135r.

18. Arm. 41, vol. 10, fol. 413rv; vol. 12, fol. 85r; vol. 19, fol. 205r; vol. 22, fol. 235rv; vol. 24, fol. 114r.

19. AV, vol. 3, fol. 46r; Arm. 40, vol. 8, fols. 192r, 217r; vol. 18, fol. 127rv; vol. 28, fol. 6rv: "propter bella pestem et alia impedimenta."

20. Arm. 41, vol. 6, fols. 267r–268r.

21. Eubel 3.142; AC, vol. 5, fol. 49rv.

22. Arm. 42, vol. 54, fol. 238rv.

23. See Hay 16–20; on resignations, see F. Gillmann, "Die Resignation der Benefizien," *Archiv für katholisches Kirchenrecht* 80 (1900) 50–79, 346–378, 523–569, 665–788, and 81 (1901) 223–242, 433–460; and Pier Giovanni Caron, *La Rinuncia all'Ufficio Ecclesiastico nella storia del diritto canonico dalla Età Apostolica alla Riforma Cattolica* (Milan 1946).

24. See Gasparo Contarini, *De officio episcopi* of 1516, and Gian Matteo Giberti's *Constitutions* of the diocese of Verona, trans. John Monfasani, in

Olin, 93–106 and 136–148 respectively; Hubert Jedin, *Geschichte des Konzils von Trient* 3 (Freiburg, Basel, Vienna 1970) 119–140; H. Outram Evennett, *The Spirit of the Counter-Reformation*, ed. John Bossy (Cambridge 1968) 97.

25. Evennett (n. 24 above) 97.

26. Olin 88–191.

27. Rossi, a nephew through the sister of Leo X, was accused of chasing women; Conti, a member of the old Roman nobility, left four illegitimate sons. On Rossi, see Ciacconius 3.389, Gaetano Moroni, *Dizionario di erudizione storico-ecclesiastica da S. Pietro sino ai nostri giorni* (103 vols. Venice 1840–1861) 59.176, and Girolamo Garimberti, *La prima parte delle vite overo fatti memorabili d'alcuni papi, et di tutti i cardinali passati* (Venice 1567) 484–485; on Conti, see Ciacconius 3.347 and Lorenzo Cardella, *Memorie storiche de' Cardinali della Santa Romana Chiesa* (10 vols. Rome 1792–1797) 4.15.

28. On Ponzetti, see Moroni (n. 27 above) 54.133, Garimberti (n. 27 above) 477, and Alessandro Ferrajoli, "Il ruolo della Corte di Leone X (1514–1516)," ASRSP 36 (1913) 553–574. Ferrajoli finds the man praiseworthy.

29. Garimberti (n. 27 above) 473: "In un Concistorio dove per alcuni bisogni della Sede Apostolica, si trattava di certe imposizioni proposte da lui, fu proposto da Pompeo Cardinal Colonna, che la piu utile, piu honesta e piu spedita di tutte sarebbe, che facendosi scorticare il Cardinal Armellino, mandar la pelle per lo stato Ecclesiastico, far pagare un quattrino a chiunque volesse vederla."

30. DBI 4.234–237.

31. On Pandolfini, see Ciacconius 3.349; on Vio, see P. Angelo Walz, *I cardinali domenicani: note bio-bibliografiche* (Rome 1940) 30–31, and Aluigi Cossio, *Il cardinale Gaetano e la riforma* (Cividale 1902).

32. Ciacconius 3.394; Eubel 3.99, 214, 284.

33. Eubel 3.335, 215, 217; AV, vol. 3, fol. 13v; Arm. 40, vol. 41, fol. 114r; AV, vol. 4, fol. 60v.

34. AC, vol. 3, fol. 45v. He had been patriarch since August 1524. AV, vol. 3, fol. 46r. See John W. O'Malley, *Giles of Viterbo on Church and Reform: A Study in Renaissance Thought* (Leiden 1968) for Egidio's ideas.

35. Eubel 3.168, 300.

36. Eubel 3.269.

37. Eubel 3.300.

38. Eubel 3.260.

39. AM, vol. 6, fol. 356r; AV, vol. 3, fol. 99v.

40. AV, vol. 4, fols. 27v–28r, 29r, 30v.

41. AV, vol. 4, fol. 16r; Eubel 3.99; AV, vol. 4, fol. 53r; AC, vol. 3, fol. 39r. This was one of the nepotistic devices discussed below, chapter 4. Filippo Ercolani, cousin or nephew of Cardinal Numai, was named bishop of Alatri when his cardinal relative died, 20 April 1528. He resigned to Cardinal del Monte in 1530 so that the cardinal, in turn, could resign it in favor of Ercolani's brother. In this instance, however, the diocese was ceded back to Filippo, because his brother "does not wish to be bishop" ("non vult esse episcopus").

42. AV, vol. 3, fols. 46r–47r.

43. AM, vol. 6, fol. 329rv; Eubel 3.240.

44. AV, vol. 3, fols. 47v, 48v, 50v–51r, 52v.

45. AM, vol. 6, fol. 185v: "ita quod non desinat esse Electus Forojuliensis."

46. Arm. 40, vol. 8, fol. 237r; AV, vol. 3, fol. 59v: "Providit Ecclesie Saris-buriensi vacanti per obitum Edmundi olim episcopi extra Romanam Curiam defuncti de persona Reverendissimi Domini Cardinalis Campegii ita quod non desinat esse episcopus Bononiensis et retentione benefitiorum suorum."

47. AV, vol. 4, fol. 48v.

48. See Ludwig Pastor, *The History of the Popes from the Close of the Middle Ages*, trans. Ralph Francis Kerr (2d ed. 40 vols. St. Louis and London 1923–1928) 11.133–181; Frederic C. Church, *The Italian Reformers, 1534–1564* (New York 1932) 20–33; Hubert Jedin, *A History of the Council of Trent*, trans. Dom Ernest Graf (2 vols. London 1957) 1.410–445.

49. Jedin (n. 48 above) 1.419–432; Philip McNair, *Peter Martyr in Italy: An Anatomy of Apostasy* (Oxford 1967) 181–182, for reformers in general and Gonzaga in particular.

50. Caracciolo was a member of the old Neapolitan nobility; Cornaro was a Venetian patrician; Pirro Gonzaga, brother of the famous beauty Giulia, was from a lateral branch of the Mantua family; Parisio was a lawyer from Calabria; Filonardi was a student of humane letters who had started his career as an agent of Cesare Borgia.

51. AC, vol. 2, fol. 113v; vol. 5, fol. 52v; Eubel 3.171, 228.

52. AC, vol. 5, fol. 52v: "Cum occupationibus publicis assidue impeditus Ecclesiam Aprutinam cui preerat, visitare non posset, eamque illius curam sus-cipere, quae necessaria esse videbatur eidem Ecclesie."

53. Sforza was *camerarius* from 1537 to his early death in 1564; Farnese was *vicecancellarius* from 1535 to his death in 1589 and probably the most successful benefice-gatherer of the century. Litta, vol. 10, tav. 13, "I Farnesi di Roma."

54. Enea Costantini, *Il Cardinal di Ravenna al governo d'Ancona e il suo processo sotto Paolo III* (Pesaro 1891).

55. Eubel 3.200, 181, 283, 135, 277.

56. Eubel 3.234, 194, 291, 314; AM, vol. 6, fols. 355v–356r; AV, vol. 4, fols. 13v, 31v; AC, vol. 2, fols. 68r, 85v; AC, vol. 6, fol. 64r. Eubel 3.194 says Gonzaga held Fano in 1524; I found no trace of this.

57. Eubel 3.292, 131; AC, vol. 2, fols. 107v, 61r.

58. AM, vol. 6, fol. 251rv: "Providit in titulum Reverendo Domino Joanni Petro Caraphae Episcopo Theatino de Ecclesia Metropoli Brundusina in Regno Neapolitano in Apulia . . . cum retentione Ecclesie sue Theatine ad sex menses tamen et cum decreto quod post sex menses nisi alteram resignaverit vacet, cum retentione beneficiorum suorum." Chieti was raised to an archbishopric in 1526.

59. AV, vol. 3, fol. 45v, 29 July 1524: "Reverendissimus Dominus Cardinalis Egidius rettulit causas quibus movebatur episcopus Theatinus ad cedendum ecclesias suas, videlicet Theatine et Brundusine."

60. AV, vol. 3, fol. 46r.

61. Arm. 40, vol. 8, fol. 217r: "quo piis operibus et contemplationi quibus se totum dedidit." Carafa took Chieti back in 1537.

62. The number of non-Italian bishoprics held by Italian cardinals of this group was as follows: fourteen French, five Spanish, two English, and one Portuguese. Italians continued to enjoy favor in French bishoprics, however. See Frederic J. Baumgarten, "Henry II's Italian Bishops: A Study in the Use and

Abuse of the Concordat of Bologna," *The Sixteenth Century Journal* 11 (1980) 49–58.

63. Eubel 3.255, 283, 136, 177.

64. Eubel 3.321, 163, 155, 337, 181.

65. Eubel 3.305, 306, 105.

66. He was one of the few cardinals among the later promotions of Paul III who were considered unworthy by Ludwig Pastor (n. 48 above), 12.202 n. 1, 579.

67. Eubel 3.311; AV, vol. 7, fols. 32v, 69rv: "Fuit decretum ut idem Reverendissimus Maffeus dictam Ecclesiam Casertanam infra sex menses iuxta tenorem decreti novissime super hoc editi dimittere omnino teneatur."

68. Eubel 3.155.

69. CT 10.410–411.

70. CT 10.324: "Perchè so, che tra le cose, che si possono raggionare tra voi di là familiarmente, potrebbe essere, che si facesse mentione qualche volta in la materia delle pluralità delle chiese delli beneficii del card. Farnese, io vi prego, che a bona occasione voi promettiate per parte mia, ch'io in questo caso so' per dare esempio, non che di ubedire, et che una delle cose, ch'io desidero che stabiliate in concilio è questo, come spero di fargline vedere presto la prova; di questo prometto da parte mia largamente, che da gentil' homo gli ne farò honore."

71. CT 10.305, 341, 372.

72. CT 10.463.

73. Ibid.: "in modo che questi ministri di Francia sono mezzi abottini, recandoselo ad ingiuria et ad affronto, con dir, che la reformatione non si dovaria cominciar da loro."

74. CT 1.621. See Jedin, *Geschichte* 3 (n. 24 above) 120–123, for an account of the reception of this decree in Trent.

75. CT 13.1.166: "Prorogavit terminum ad dimittendum ecclesias per revmos obtentas ad tres menses, et quatenus lapsus esset, terminum trium mensium de novo concessit."

76. Ibid.

77. Ibid.

78. AC, vol. 6, fols. 138v–139r; Eubel 3.289.

79. Eubel 3.269, 196.

80. AV, vol. 7, fol. 45rv; printed in CT 13.1.167. The editors have used the old pagination throughout, which does not coincide with these citations.

81. AV, vol. 7, fols. 44v–45r.

82. Eubel 3.240, 230, 253, 95, 260.

83. He subsequently took back Milan, Lyon, and Narbonne, and held them together from time to time. See Vincenzo Pacifici, *Ippolito II d'Este, Cardinale di Ferrara* (Tivoli 1920).

84. Eubel 3.316.

85. Eubel 3.126, 250, 335. Farnese apparently kept Monreale until 9 December 1573, when he ceded it reserving all fruits and all temporal jurisdictions for himself. AV, vol. 11, fol. 28v.

86. Eubel 3.318, 141.

87. A. Edith Hewett, "An Assessment of Italian Benefices Held by the Car-

dinals for the Turkish War of 1571," *English Historical Review* 30 (1915) 488–501. See also the discussion in A. V. Antonovics, "Counter-Reformation Cardinals: 1534–90," *European Studies Review* 2 (1972) 319–322.

88. AC, vol. 5, fol. 49v; Eubel 3.257 n. 6.

89. AC, vol. 6, fol. 162r.

90. AV, vol. 7, fol. 82v.

91. AV, vol. 7, fols. 44v–45r.

92. AM, vol. 6, fols. 329r, 347v; AV, vol. 3, fol. 58r: "qui si contingerit Ecclesiam ipsam Umbriaticensis cedere, non posset reservare sibi regressum ipsius Ecclesie, ex eo quia Reverendissimus de Valle habet antiquum regressum ad ipsam Ecclesiam."

93. Jedin, *Geschichte* 3 (n. 24 above) 123.

94. AC, vol. 6, fols. 131v–132r; AV, vol. 7, fol. 69r.

95. AV, vol. 7, fols. 72v–73r: "propter qualitatem temporum videlicet et reformationis et concilii animadvertens quantum sint odiosi accessus apud omnes. . . . " Eubel 3.181. This is printed in CT 13.1.168. The editors err on the date of the consistory.

96. AV, vol. 8, fol. 34v: "Fuit decretum quod ab hodierna die non concedentur regressus seu accessus nisi Reverendissimis Cardinalibus quibus ad omnia et quaecunque etc. concedentur." (Printed in CT 13.1.320.)

97. AV, vol. 8, fol. 58rv. (Printed in CT 13.1.320.)

98. AV, vol. 8, fol. 59r. (Printed in CT 13.1.320.)

99. CT 13.1.320–321 n. 4: "et de aliis multis, quos habere credimus, offerrimus nos daturos pleniorem notitiam, data cum competenti dilatione commoditate recensendi scripturas nostras, que sunt in Urbe."

100. Ibid. Cardinals under investigation who appeared in this catalog were A. Farnese, R. Farnese, Crispo, Savelli, Pio, Este, Doria, Capodiferro, Pisani, Gonzaga, Duranti, Sforza, Caetani, Rovere, and Morone. The only two who were alive at the time but not listed were Madruzzo and F. Cesi.

101. AV, vol. 8, fols. 112r–113r: "In Ordinis ecclesiastici confusionem et dicti decreti enervationem, atque Ecclesiarum que interdum personam magis utilem et idoneam requirunt lesionem ac Christifidelium scandalum non modicum." (Printed in CT 13.1.323.)

102. Ibid.

103. Eubel 3.134, 151; AV, vol. 8, fol. 159r; AC, vol. 9, fols. 12v–13r.

104. Eubel 3.178.

105. Eubel 3.134, 151; AC, vol. 9, fols. 81v–82r.

106. Antonovics, "Counter-Reformation Cardinals" (n. 87 above) 320; CT 5.981.

107. AV, vol. 9, fol. 26v; AC, vol. 9, fol. 66r: "Item Sua Sanctitas decrevit et statuit quod de cetero non concederentur sive darentur amplius accessus et regressus etiam Reverendissimis Dominis Cardinalibus, . . . ita tamen quod regressus iam ipsis Cardinalibus reservati in suo robore permaneant."

108. AV, vol. 9, fol. 118r: "nihil tamen fuit conclusum."

109. Those reserving regresses were Alessandro Farnese, Ippolito I d'Este, Guido Ascanio Sforza, Tiberio Crispo, Francesco Pisani, Rodolfo Pio, and Giulio della Rovere. AC, vol. 9, fols. 16r, 12v, 20v, 41v, 53r, 56v, 64r, 65v.

110. Caron (n. 23 above] 341, 368–369.

111. German prelates continued to gather bishoprics. See Antonovics, "Counter-Reformation Cardinals" (n. 87 above) 320; and my "Practical Aspects of Roman Diplomacy in Germany: 1517–1541," *Journal of Medieval and Renaissance Studies* 10 (1980) 193–206.

112. See chapter 4 below, at n. 92.

113. G. Meneghetti, *La vita avventurosa di Pietro Bembo: umanista–poeta–cortigiano* (Venice 1961) 203—205, a list of his benefices; Ferrajoli (n. 28 above) vol. 37 (1914) 315—318 gives a total of thirty-one benefices, including three pensions.

114. Ferrajoli (n. 28 above) vol. 38 (1915) 218–225; Richard M. Douglas, *Jacopo Sadoleto, 1477–1547: Humanist and Reformer* (Cambridge Mass. 1959) 21–22.

115. Douglas (n. 114 above) 215, 294 nn. 60, 61; but Ferrajoli (n. 114 above) 223 declared Sadoleto *not* poor, having an annual income of 2,688 ducats.

116. Hewett (n. 87 above) 489–493.

117. Ibid. 489. Sts. Vincenzo and Anastasia is usually cited as the monastery of the Three Fountains outside Rome.

118. Ibid. 489–493. It is interesting to note that the common services attached to these properties in the fifteenth century seem not to reflect their worth in any meaningful way. If common service taxes were supposed to be roughly one-third of the annual income of a benefice, how can we reconcile the tax of 150 florins on *Tre Fontane* in 1443 with Farnese's 5,000 *scuti* of gold in 1571? The other monasteries on the list brought similarly inflated revenues. See Hermann Hoberg, *Taxae pro communibus servitiis ex libris obligationum ab anno 1295 usque ad annum 1455 confectis,* Studi e Testi 144 (Vatican City 1949) 165, 243, 227, 215, 232, 340.

119. The abbey of Lucedio in Monferrato was one source of ill-will between the Gonzaga and the Farnese cardinals, the subject of litigation for many years from 1535 on. See Giovanni Drei, "La politica di Pio IV e del Cardinale Ercole Gonzaga, 1559–1560," *ASRSP* 40 (1917) 65–115.

120. Arm. 40, vol. 46, fol. 18r; Eubel 3.289.

121. Hewett (n. 87 above) 490, 493. Translated into *scuti di moneta,* Avellana was worth 5,750, Salerno worth 4,250. Fregoso reserved the denomination archbishop of Salerno, the regress, and the collation of benefices.

122. Litta vol. 3 tav. 245. Ottaviano Fregoso, the cardinal's brother, had been doge of Genoa and a French adherent in 1515. The viceroy of Naples charged the cardinal with a felony and sequestered all the incomes of Salerno.

123. But papal control over nonconsistorial benefices expanded from the end of the fifteenth century "with the institution of the Apostolic Reservations of non-consistorial Benefices, through which the Pontiffs, in virtue of the primacy of jurisdiction, began to intervene in the internal government of individual dioceses." Nicola Storti, *La storia e il diritto della Dataria Apostolica dalle origini ai nostri giorni* (Naples 1969) 11.

124. Pier Giovanni Baroni, *La Nunziatura in Francia di Rodolfo Pio (1535–1537),* vol. 13 of *Memorie storiche e documenti sulla Città e sull'antico Principato di Carpi* (Bologna 1962) p. 237: "De la sua vacante, ancor che sia grossa,

pur N.S. ne può disponer di molto poca imperochè Monreale sta a l'Imp., le due abatie di Francia a la Mta Chrma et de la di Monferato [Lucedio] non si è havuto mai la possessione, ne pur la speranza. Non scrivo altro particulare perchè non sono ancor distribuito quelli pezzi che tocca ad dar a N. Sre. Domani sarà Concistorio per far parte a molti di questi cardinali novi che sono tanto poveri et perchè è piaciuto al revmo de Bellay et mons. Macon senza esserne stati recercati da N. Sre, scriver al Chrmo che voglia conferir al revmo et illmo Farnese li sue monasteri che sono in Francia vacanti."

125. Ibid. 245: Pio to Ricalcati, Bar le Duc, 21 August 1535.

126. AC, vol. 2, fol. 38r. Lucedio was also claimed by Ercole Gonzaga, and the struggle over its possession began at this time. Farnese resigned Avignon in 1551, but kept the legation of Avignon until 1565, ceding it only in return for a pension of 4,600 *scuti* from the apostolic camera. MC, vol. 916, fol. 92v.

127. Arm. 41, vol. 9, fol. 296r: "ut decentius sustenari valeas."

128. Arm. 40, vol. 31, fol. 303r: "una cum Sancti Cyriaci in Termis, que titulus sui Cardinalatus existit, ac Perusina, et Suanensi, quibus ex dispositione apostolica preesse dignoscitur, ac quibusvis aliis ecclesiis, monasteriis, prioratibus, praeceptoriis, canonibus et prebendis, dignitatibus, et ceterisque beneficiis ecclesiasticis cum cura et sine cura secularibus et quorumvis ordinum regularibus, que in titulum et commendam vel alias quomodolibet obtinet et in posterum obtinebit, ac pensionibus annuis quas percipit et percipiet in futurum tenendos, regendos, et gubernandos."

129. Arm. 40, vol. 51, fol. 351rv.

130. Arm. 40, vol. 14, fol. 165r.

131. Arm. 40, vol. 20, fol. 29r.

132. Arm. 40, vol. 23, fol. 31r.

133. Arm. 41, vol. 2, fol. 242r; vol. 39, fols. 135r–138r.

134. Arm. 42, vol. 13, fols. 149–150v.

135. G. Mollat, "Les graces expectatives sous le règne de Philippe VI de Valois," *Revue d'histoire ecclésiastique* 32 (1936) 303.

136. Olin 190.

137. ANG 1, *Correspondance des nonces en France Carpi et Ferrerio, 1535–1540*, ed. J. Lestoquoy (Rome 1961) 198: "se chi l'ha morirà, come stava malissimo."

138. Arm. 41, vol. 9, fol. 296r. Also Arm. 41, vol. 9, fol. 298r; vol. 42, fols. 124r–125v; vol. 64, fols. 396r–401v; AV, vol. 3, fol. 16v.

139. See chapter 4 below, at n. 54.

140. Eubel 3.26, 109, 261; Cardella (n. 27 above) 4.224; Ciacconius 3.667.

141. Arm. 41, vol. 9, fol. 296r: "unum duo tria quattuor et tot beneficia ecclesiastica cum cura et sine cura secularia et quorumvis etiam Cisterciensium aut Humiliatorum ordinum regularia quorum in simul fructus redditus et proventus 300 ducatorum auri de camera secundum communem extimationem valoris annui non excedant in Ravenatensi, Regiensi, et Mutinensi Civitatibus et Diocesibus consistentia."

142. Arm. 41, vol. 21, fol. 373r.

143. Arm. 40, vol. 42, fols. 124r–125v: "Et sicut accepimus tu ex illis nullum fructum hactenus reportaveris."

144. Arm. 40, vol. 43, fols. 33r–38v.

145. Arm. 40, vol. 50, fols. 352r–353r; vol. 51, fols. 194r–200v.

146. Arm. 40, vol. 51, fols. 38r–39v: "Pro Cardinale Grimaldo. Sanctitas Noster concessit ei nuper facultatem conferendi beneficia suae Legationis (extra curiam vacatura) dummodo non essent reservata. Nunc concedit ei facultatem illa conferendi etiam si reservata fuerint, dummodo non sint reservata ratione familiaritatis Sanctitatis Nostri et Cardinalium viventium."

147. Arm. 40, vol. 51, fols. 41r–42r: "Reverendissimo Domino Cardinale Grimaldo dixit nolle praeiudicare gratie facte Reverendissimo de Auria."

148. AV, vol. 4, fol. 41r: "Sanctitas Sua concessit Reverendissimis Dominis de Grimano et de Cornelio reservationem beneficiorum ascendentium ad summam quinque millium ducatorum et hoc intelligitur tam de Archiepiscopalibus quam Episcopalibus et de omnibus beneficiis minoribus." Pio Paschini, noting this grant, wrote, "Clemente VII aveva fatto una concessione, per dir poco, assai strano, e che non era molto in uso nemmeno a quei tempi," *Il cardinale Marino Grimani ed i prelati della sua famiglia* (Rome 1960) 43. The device was perhaps more common than Paschini supposed.

149. Arm. 41, vol. 38, fols. 240r–242r; vol. 55, fols. 373r–377r.

150. Arm. 41, vol. 64, fols. 396r–401v: "Et sicut accepimus vos ex gratiis et litteris huiusmodi nullum seu modicum fructum reportaveritis."

151. Arm. 40, vol. 6, fol. 322rv.

152. Arm. 41, vol. 16, fol. 220r.

153. CT 9.978–999; *New Catholic Encyclopedia* 5.750.

154. See below at n. 199.

155. Olin 189.

156. Arm. 40, vol. 43, fols. 33r–38r: "unacum Sancti Thome in Parione que denominatio tui Cardinalatus existit ac omnibus et singulis aliis ecclesiis et monasteriis ceterisque beneficiis ecclesiasticis cum cura et sine cura secularibus et quorumvis ordinum regularibus que ex quibusvis concessionibus vel dispensationibus apostolicis in titulum et commendam ac alias obtines et imposterum obtinebis *ac fructibus ecclesiasticis et pensionibus annuis tibi super similibus fructibus reservatis et assignatis ac reservandis et assignandis quos et quas precipis et precipies in futurum quecunque quotcunque et qualiacunque sint tenendos regendos et gubernandos*" (italics mine).

157. AC, vol. 5, fols. 143v–144v: "500 ducatorum pro Julio Grimano bonae memoriae Marci Patriarchae predicti filio libere et exemptae . . . cum opportuna dispensatione super defectu natalium quem Julius supradictus patitur." Other pensioners who required dispensations for illegitimacy during this period were the son of Emperor Maximilian I, George of Austria, and two sons of cardinals, Paolo de Cupis and Ascanio Cesarini. AC, vol. 6, fols. 58v–59r, 130v–131r, 136v.

158. Ferraris 1.367: "Aliud vocatur interdum *Pensio*, quae est jus percipiendi partem fructuum ex alieno Beneficio; & si conferatur alicui in Titulum perpetuum, est verum Beneficium Ecclesiasticum."

159. See chapter 4 below, at n. 80.

160. D. S. Chambers, "The Economic Predicament of Renaissance Cardinals," *Studies in Medieval and Renaissance History* 3 (1966) 297.

161. The survey summarized by figure 2.6 is confined to Italian benefices.

162. Tommaso de Vio kept 1,300 ducats in annual income from the diocese of Palermo in 1519, for example, and Giovanni Morone kept 1,400 ducats from Modena in 1571. AM, vol. 6, fol. 297v; Eubel 3.252 n. 7.

163. AV, vol. 4, fol. 54v; AC, vol. 3, fols. 39v–40r.

164. AV, vol. 4, fol. 50v; Vat lat 3457, fol. 272rv. Rossi got the abbey, Santa Maria della Colomba, from his uncle, Cardinal Raffaele Riario, 21 August 1517. AM, vol. 6, fol. 178r.

165. Another example is Alessandro Farnese's pension of 2,500 ducats per year from the bishopric of Massa Marittima, money which actually came from the celebrated alum mines at Tolfa. AC, vol. 9, fol. 16r.

166. A few examples from France, Spain, and England are typical: Federico Sanseverino, 3,000 francs from Térouanne in 1498; Raffaele Riario, 2,000 ducats from Cuenca in 1518; Giulio de' Medici (later Clement VII), 2,000 ducats from Worcester in 1522; and Agostino Trivulzio, 1,000 ducats from Lavaur in 1525. AM, vol. 6, fols. 29rv, 238v–239r, 386rv; AV, vol. 3, fol. 92r.

167. AV, vol. 4, fol. 50v: "cum decreto quod quotiens per quattuor menses a Die statute solutionis steterit quominus solverit Reverendissimus Dominus habeat regressum et accessum tam ad ecclesiam quam ad Monasterium. . . . " See also Vat lat 3457, fol. 272rv: "ita tamen quod eveniente casu mortis ipsius Reverendissimi Cardinalis de Monte quod Deus avertat, tunc dictae pensiones cedantur in favorem praefati Domini Archiepiscopi, et sibi debeantur super Mensae Papiensis et Monasterii predictorum fructibus huiusmodi."

168. AV, vol. 4, fol. 54v: "Centum et octuaginta quatuor ducatorum monete Neapolitane super fructibus dicte Ecclesie libera et exempta solvenda in festo Nativitatis Domini Nostri Jesu Christi in Civitate Neapolitana Cum decreto quod reduci non possit ad minorem summam seu aliter invalidari ex quavis causa etiam si medietatem fructuum pensio huiusmodi excederet Ac cum Regressu in eventu non solutionis reductionis aut invaliditatis pro dicto Reverendissimo de Palmieriis."

169. Arm. 40, vol. 18, fol. 262r: "idem F. prope pensionis huiusmodi in terminis et locis non solutionem, penas etiam privationis huiusmodi incurrerit."

170. AC, vol. 6, fols. 138v, 139r; AV, vol. 7, fol. 18r.

171. AM, vol. 6, fols. 215v–216r, 238v–239r, 240rv; Eubel 3.233. Cardinal Riario's activities were not unusual for the early part of the century. In April 1518 he exchanged the Spanish bishopric of Cuenca for Malaga, reserving 2,000 ducats for himself from Cuenca. He then resigned Malaga five months later to his nephew and assigned him the 2,200 ducats as above. The same Cesare simultaneously resigned the archbishopric of Pisa in favor of Riario, who, in turn, resigned it a week later, keeping a pension of 1,500 ducats. By the end of the year 1518, then, Cardinal Riario had divested himself of the cares of office and assured himself an annual income of at least 9,300 ducats of gold. (Malaga's fruits came to at least 8,000 gold florins.)

172. AC, vol. 6, fols. 138v–139r: "ex causa permutationis prefatis Prioratus seu Decanatus, et pensionis et non aliter, nec alio modo, in manibus Suae Sanctitatis sponte cessisset."

173. AC, vol. 6, fol. 155v.

174. AC, vol. 6, fol. 40 rv: "Cum confirmatione Pensionum antiquarum super fructibus mensae episcopalis Carthaginensis Et assignatione novarum item Pensionum annuarum super eisdem fructibus Mille et sexcentorum Ducatorum auri largorum, monete in Hispania nunc et pro tempore currentis, videlicet, pro Juliano d'Alva quondam secretario Serenissime Principissae Hispaniarum una quadringentorum, pro Petro Pacecco, Suae Maiestatis Caesaricae Cappellano alia trecentorum, pro Didaco Lasso de Castella alia trecentorum, pro Doctor N. de Ayala ordinis Sancti Jacobi de Spata professore Suae Maiestatis Cappellano alia ducentorum cum opportuna dispensatione pro eodem, attento Frater professus est, ut illam possit obtinere, pro Michaele de Aguirre, Suae Maiestatis Cappellano, alia centum, et pro Nicolao de Aragonia nepote D. Jo. Ludovici de Aragonia, Advocati consistorialis alia trecentorum ducatorum similium quae transeant ad successores de consensu ipsius Episcopi."

175. AM, vol. 6, fols. 423v–424r.

176. AV, vol. 7, fol. 31v: "necnon michi pensionem annuam Mille ducatorum auri de camera liberam et exemptam super fructibus mensae Archiepiscopalis Neapolitanae quorum medietatem ipsam et alie super illis aliis forsan assignate pensiones annue . . . non excedunt . . . motu proprio dicta auctoritate reservavit."

177. AV, fol. 7, fols. 32r, 32v.

178. AV, vol. 3, fol. 21v; Eubel 3.327; AC, vol. 2, fols. 26rv, 53v. When the bishopric of Vaison went to Salviati in 1535, however, Ridolfi's pension was reduced to 200 ducats per year.

179. AC, vol. 5, fol. 38r; AV, vol. 7, fol. 79r; AV, vol. 8, fols. 90r, 94v; AC, vol. 9, fol. 19r; Eubel 3.35.

180. Jedin, *Geschichte* 3 (n. 24 above) 293; CT 13.1.198: "Quod beneficia Hispaniae non dentur neque in titulum neque in commendam nec alio modo neque etiam in confidentiam *alienigenis*."

181. Eubel 3.308.

182. AM, vol. 6, fols. 339v–340r.

183. AV, vol. 4, fols. 52r, 55rv; AC, vol. 3, fol. 41v; AC, vol. 2, fol. 72r.

184. Two separate briefs: Arm. 40, vol. 28, fol. 45r, fols. 46r–47v.

185. AV, vol. 4, fol. 55v: "Eodem Reverendissimo Domino Cardinali de Cesarinis Referente, quoniam Cesarea Maiestas nominavit Reverendissimum de Cesarinis ad pensiones, unam quingentorum ducatorum super fructibus mensae episcopalis ecclesie Segorbicensis, et aliam etiam quingentorum super fructibus mensae episcopalis Oscensis, D. sua Reverendissima propterea, et ut gratum faceret Cesarei Maiestati cessit in manibus eiusdem Santitatis Sue litti et causae ac omni iuri sibi competenti [*sic*] in regimine et administratione Monasterii Montisaragonum Oscensis diocesis."

186. Federico Odorici, *Il Cardinale Uberto Gambara da Brescia, 1487–1549: Indagini di storia patria* (Brescia 1856) 8.

187. AC, vol. 2, fols. 77v, 92v, 104v; vol. 5, fols. 58v–59r; AV, vol. 7, fols. 63rv, 64v, 70r.

188. AC, vol. 5, fols. 58v–59r; vol. 6, fol. 77r; AV, vol. 7, fols. 70r, 63rv, 64v, 267v–268r.

189. Arturo Segre, "Un registro di lettere del cardinale Ercole Gonzaga (1535–36) con un'appendice di documenti inediti," *Miscellanea di storia*

italiana, R. Deputazione sovra gli studi di storia patria per le antiche provincie e la Lombardia, terza serie 16 (1913) 277–278.

190. AC, vol. 2, fol. 68r: "cum reservatione pensionum, videlicet quingentorum ducatorum pro episcopo solis."

191. AC, vol. 5, fol. 138v; vol. 6, fol. 40r.

192. AC, vol. 5, fol. 182rv; vol. 6, fols. 54v, 58v–59r; AV, vol. 7, fol. 63rv; AC, vol. 9, fols. 25v–26r.

193. Archivio di Stato, Mantua, Archivio Gonzaga, Busta 1945, 1, fol. 1v, 28 April 1550: "Et seben io son quel servitore dell'Imperatore che ogniun sa et che ho mostrato dove è stato bisogno, non voglio però che sua Maiesta mi possa commandar' in cose che non sieno honesti et . . . massimamente dove ne va'l mense della ventura d'un pupillo com'è questo che m'è nipote et sotto la mia tutela."

194. AV, vol. 9, fol. 45v, 26 June 1560, reservation of 4,000 ducats from Salamanca for persons to be named; vol. 11, fol. 33v, 14 January 1587, 3,700 ducats from Cordoba for persons to be named; fol. 91r, 6 December 1589, 3,000 ducats from Granada for persons to be named; vol. 14, fol. 13r, 8 July 1598, Clement VIII reserved 50,000 ducats from Toledo for persons to be named. Examples could be multiplied.

195. AC, vol. 10, fols. 19v–20r: "Sanctitas Sua reservavit super fructibus ecclesiarum Ravenatensis et Bononiensis predictarum pensiones decem millium ducatorum quinque millium super earum qualibet pro Cardinalibus nominandis per Sanctitatem Suam vel Reverendissimos Cardinales Borromeum et de Altemps salvis pensionibus antiquis super dictis ecclesiis iam impositis."

196. AV, vol. 3, fol. 21v; Arm. 40, vol. 7, fol. 67v.

197. AV, vol. 7, fol. 133r: "Necnon eidem Reverendissimo Domino Jacobo Cardinali ne ex cassatione huiusmodi nimium dispendium pateretur aliam pensionem annuam mille ducatorum auri similium super officii Datariatus Sue Sanctitatis." Savelli was reassigned the pension of 1,000 ducats of gold *della camera* from Naples on 11 August 1578, and his pension from the dataria was cancelled. AV, vol. 11, fols. 106v–107r.

198. Amadio Ronchini, ed., *Lettere del Card. Jacopo Sadoleto e di Paolo suo nipote* (Modena 1871) 77–81: "Che certo con meno non mi parrebbe già poter tenere il mio stato con dignita. Io non posso havere a Roma intrata più di 1,700 scudi in tutto; perchè ancor la pensione di Verona . . . ho renunciato a dui miei nipoti virtuosi et costumati."

199. Vat lat 10599–10605, passim. It is surprising to find among the pensioners two members of the reform commission of 1537 appointed to reform the department of the dataria, Gian Pietro Carafa and Gasparo Contarini. Carafa collected 100 *scuti* of gold from 1535 through the pontificate of Julius III; Contarini collected 200 per month from 1535 until April 1541, when he began to receive 500 *scuti* per month for his legation to Germany.

200. Hewett (n. 87 above) 489, 490.

201. Ibid. 491; Vat lat 6203, fols. 124r–149r; Delumeau 1.448.

202. Hewett (n. 87 above) 489.

203. Pio Pecchiai, "La buona morte del cardinale Alessandro Farnese," *Roma: Rivista di studi e di vita romana* (September–December 1943) 1-6: "imposta sotto pena di venir dichiarato in peccato mortale."

204. AV, vol. 3, fol. 21v: "Deinde monasterium Clarrevallis ordinis Cisterciensis mediolanensis diocesis commendatum est Reverendissimo de Cesis cum onere pensionis octo portionum mille ducatorum pro qualibet prout in bulla latius continebitur; salvis etiam remanentibus antiquis pensionibus." The figure of 12,000 ducats of income is Sanuto's, 9.80, 81, 83.

205. AV, vol. 4, fol. 32v: "Dominus Antonius de Bibiena cessit Monasterium Sancte Marie de Alpibus ordinis Cisterciensis Gebenensis diocesis super quo sunt multe pensiones que omnes exprimi possint."

206. AM, vol. 6, fol. 384r; Eubel 3.152; Arm. 40, vol. 7, fol. 67v.

207. Arm. 40, vol. 28, fol. 104r: "propter damna que proximis annis passus fuit."

208. AV, vol. 7, fol. 43rv: "etiam si super illis alie pensiones annue aliis assignate existant et omnes insimul illorum medietate excedant et illos omnes absorbeant et comprehendant."

209. *Dictionnaire de droit canonique* 6 (1957) col. 1347.

210. *New Catholic Encyclopedia* 2.307–308.

211. Ronchini (n. 198 above) 79.

212. Delumeau 1.433–457.

213. CT 10.410-411: "Quanto alla corte di Roma, par' che due cose scandalizino il mondo et gli levino il credito, una l'avaritia, l'altra le pompe ed il luxo."

214. Delumeau 1.446–447; Pio Pecchiai, *Roma nel Cinquecento* (Rome 1948) 380–381.

215. Pecchiai (n. 214 above) ibid., and Partner, "Papal Financial Policy" 55. The Farnese palace cost at least 250,000 gold florins.

216. Antonovics, "Counter-Reformation Cardinals" (n. 87 above) 301–304; Pecchiai (n. 214 above) 370–371.

217. Pecchiai (n. 214 above) 21, and Delumeau 1.453.

218. Arm. 40, vol. 43, fol. 33r: "Cupientes nos tibi ut statum tuum iuxta Cardinalatus sublimitate decentius tenere et expensarum onera que te iugiter de necessitate subire oportet facilius preferre valeas."

219. Olin 191. See Harry G. Hynes, *The Privileges of Cardinals,* Canon Law Studies 217 (Washington D.C. 1945) 7.

220. Hay 16–20.

221. CT 9.978–999.

3.   THE ALIENATION OF INCOMES AND WEALTH

1. Sanuto 1.1.826: "Sichè, la Chiesia di Dio al presente si compra con danari a chi più offerisse."

2. Peter Partner, *The Papal State under Martin V: The Administration and Government of the Temporal Power in the Early Fifteenth Century* (London 1958) 104–122, 167; William E. Lunt, *Papal Revenues in the Middle Ages* (2 vols. New York 1934) 1.135–136; Vat lat 10602, fol. 89r; Vat lat 10604, fol. 160v; Arm. 41, vol. 55, fol. 57rv. This last citation illustrates how alienations had permeated the system. In a brief dated 24 February 1550, Pope Julius III confirmed a rental agreement made between Pope Paul III (d. 1549) and the Genoese merchant Bandinello Sauli. Sauli had paid 33,333 ducats of gold to

the papal *depositario,* Bindo Altoviti, for the privilege of farming the alum mines at Tolfa for the twelve years from 1553 to 1565.

3. AM, vol. 3, fols. 58r–59v; AV, vol. 7, fols. 246v–248r; Melissa M. Bullard, "'Mercatores Florentini Romanam Curiam Sequentes' in the Early Sixteenth Century," *The Journal of Medieval and Renaissance Studies* 6 (1976) 51–71 at 65.

4. Philip Jones, "Medieval Agrarian Society in Its Prime: Italy," *Cambridge Economic History of Europe* 1, ed. M. M. Postan (2d ed. Cambridge 1966) 397, 400, 417.

5. Carlo Cipolla, "Une crise ignorée: comment s'est perdue la propriété ecclésiastique dans l'Italie du nord entre le XIe et le XVIe siècle," *Annales: économies, sociétés, civilisations* 2.3 (1947) 317–327 at 322.

6. Philip Jones, "Le finanze della Badia cistercense di Settino nel XIV secolo," *RSCI* 10 (1956) 90–122.

7. BR 5.183–184: "nihil favor usurpet, nihil timor extorqueat, nulla expectatio praemii iustitiam conscientiamque subvertat."

8. BR 5.194–195: "Praeterquam in casibus a iure permissis, ac de rebus et bonis in emphyteusim ab antiquo concedi solitis, et tunc cum Ecclesiarum evidenti utilitate, ac de fructibus et bonis, quae servando servari non possunt, pro instantis temporis exigentia."

9. *Dictionnaire de droit canonique* 1 (1935) col. 404.

10. Arm. 42, vol. 19, fols. 169r–172v, 5 September 1563: "Non obstantibus felicium recordationum Pauli II, et Pauli IIII ac Bonifacii VIII."

11. Arm. 40, vol. 31, fol. 309r: "ut pro tuo decoro dignitatis te commodius sustenare valeres." Arm. 40, vol. 41, fol. 21r: "ut te pro tuo decoro dignitatis substentare posses."

12. Arm. 40, vol. 23, fol. 167r: "Necessitatibus et commoditatibus tuis, quantum possumus, subvenire volentes, . . . tibi ut omnia et singula, fructus, redditus, proventus, iura, obventiones, et emolumenta, tam mensae Patriarchalis Aquilegiensis, . . . quam omnium et singulorum Monasteriorum et aliorum quorumcunque tam secularium, quam cuiusvis ordinis regularium, quae in titulum aut commendam vel alias quomodolibet obtines, quibusvis personis etiam laicis, cum quibus tuam et ipsius mensae, ac aliorum predictorum conditionem efficere poteris meliorem . . . arrendare . . . facultatem . . . concedimus . . . et indulgemus."

13. Arm. 41, vol. 20, fol. 322r: "Volens certis necessitatibus tuis providere."

14. Arm. 41, vol. 6, fol. 19rv; vol. 9, fol. 307r; vol. 23, fol. 27r.

15. Arm. 41, vol. 9, fol. 307r: "Cum sicut nobis nuper exposuisti, tu pro solvendis nonnullis tuis debitis certa pecuniarum quantitate indigeas." Arm. 41, vol. 23, fol. 27r: "pro satisfaciendo quampluribus creditoribus quam nullo modo reperire posse speras."

16. Arm. 41, vol. 24, fol. 155r; Philip McNair, *Peter Martyr in Italy: An Anatomy of Apostasy* (Oxford 1967) 249.

17. CT 5, p. L.

18. Arm. 40, vol. 18, fol. 4r; vol. 19, fol. 47rv; Ciacconius 3.412; Angelo Martini, "Tentativi di riforma a Padova prima del Concilio di Trento," *RSCI* 3 (1949) 66–79.

19. AC, vol. 2, fol. 39r, 27 August 1535: "Per Reverendissimum Dominum

Tranensem et alios Reverendissimos deputatos fuit lecta confessio Reverendissimi Domini Ravennatensis de suis delictis; et fuit supplicatum Sanctitati suae: quod faceret gratiam eidem Ravennatensi. Sanctitas sua voluit tempus ad respondendum in consistorio proxime futuro." AC, vol. 2, fol. 40r, 30 August 1535: "Sanctissimus Dominus Noster ad preces totius sacri collegii fecit gratiam Reverendissimo Domino Cardinali Ravennatensi secundum cedulam faciendam per Reverendissimos Dominos meos Ghinuccium et Simonettam." Enea Costantini, *Il Cardinal di Ravenna al governo d'Ancona e il suo processo sotto Paolo III* (Pesaro 1891) 366–367, 375, 379.

20. Arm. 41, vol. 2, fol. 23rv. San Bartolomeo, or San Bartolo outside the walls of Ferrara, had an annual income of 12,000 *scuti.*

21. Arm. 41, vol. 2, fol. 30r; vol. 18, fol. 157r; vol. 24, fol. 34r.

22. Arm. 41, vol. 8, fol. 18rv.

23. Arm. 41, vol. 27, fol. 45r. Other examples: Arm. 41, vol. 10, fol. 98r; Arm. 40, vol. 43, fol. 60r.

24. *Dictionnaire de droit canonique* 1 (1935) cols. 403–415.

25. The breakdown is as follows: 11 at two years, 29 at three years, 1 at four years, 2 at five years, 1 at seven years, 1 at eight years, 10 at nine years, 1 at twenty-nine years, and 4 exchanges or sales. Some of the licenses or confirmations did not specify durations.

26. Particularly inclusive were the qualifying clauses attached to the license of 20 July 1550 that Julius III conceded to Federico Cesi, enabling him to rent out the abbey of Chiaravalle. Arm. 41, vol. 57, fols. 181r–182r: "Non obstantibus felicis recordationis Pauli II predecessoris nostri de rebus ecclesie non alienandis et quibusvis aliis apostolicis ac provincialibus et synodalibus constitutionibus et ordinationibus necnon Monasterii et ordinis predictorum iuramento confirmatione apostolica vel quavis alia firmitate roboratis statutis et consuetudinibus privilegiis quoque et indultis eisdem monasterio et ordini sub quibusvis tenoribus et formis ac cum quibusvis clausulis et decretis approbatis et innovatis quibus illorum tenores pro sufficienter expressis habentes illis alias in suo robore per mansuris hac vice dumtaxat specialiter et expresse derogamus Ceterisque contrariis quibuscunque."

27. Arm. 42, vol. 19, fols. 169r–172r: "iuxta lombardia consuetudine in similibus hactenus observari solita."

28. Arm. 40, vol. 32, fol. 49r: "certas et forsan omnes."

29. Arm. 41, vol. 57, fols. 181r–182r. By 1550, the last of the original cardinal-pensioners had died.

30. Arm. 41, vol. 39, fols. 77r–78v, 79r–81r; vol. 68, fols. 125r–126r, 127r–128r, 129r–130v, 131r–132r; Arm. 42, vol. 11, fol. 81r.

31. Arm. 41, vol. 19, fols. 188r–189r; vol. 22, fol. 27rv: "de viginti novem annis in viginti novem annis . . . iuxta morem illarum partium."

32. Arm. 41, vol. 43, fol. 243r.

33. Arm. 40, vol. 7, fol. 205r; vol. 31, fol. 309r; vol. 50, fol. 41rv; Arm. 41, vol. 6, fols. 14r, 19r; vol. 16, fol. 180r; vol. 27, fol. 45r.

34. Arm. 40, vol. 51, fols. 17r–19v; Arm. 41, vol. 18, fols. 314r–316v.

35. Arm. 41, vol. 68, fols. 288r–289r.

36. Pier Giovanni Baroni, ed., *La Nunziatura in Francia di Rodolfo Pio (1535–1537)*, vol. 13 of *Memorie storiche e documenti sulla Città e sull'antico Principato di Carpi* (Bologna 1962) 294.

37. Ibid. 310.

38. Arm. 41, vol. 33, fols. 163r–166r.

39. Arm. 41, vol. 38, fol. 250r.

40. Arm. 42, vol. 11, fol. 81r.

41. Arm. 41, vol. 20, fol. 441r; vol. 36, fol. 500r; Arm. 42, vol. 6, fol. 317r.

42. Arm. 40, vol. 7, fol. 205r; Eubel 3.197.

43. Arm. 41, vol. 6, fol. 14r; Eubel 3.109.

44. Arm. 41, vol. 20, fol. 323r: "Ac dicernentes quod si forsan infra Triennium predictum te cedere vel decedere contingerit nichilominus fructus redditus proventus domus terre decime possessiones bona iura obventiones et emolumenta huiusmodi sint et remanserint eidem Sebastiano pro dicto triennio dumtaxat et non ultra realiter et cum effectu obligata Et successores tui in ecclesia Neocastrensi huiusmodi omnia et singula in dicto instrumento contenta etiam quo ad anticipationem solutionis huiusmodi observare pro dicto triennio dumtaxat teneantur, . . . ac si se ad id personaliter obligassent."

45. Armando Schiavo, "Profilo e testamento di Raffaele Riario," *Studi Romani* 8.4 (July–August 1960) 425.

46. Arm. 41, vol. 22, fol. 278r: "recipere et tenere . . . necnon eosdem fructus redditus et proventus in suos usus et utilitatem convertere libere et licite possint."

47. MC, vol. 907, fols. 214v–215r.

48. Arm. 41, vol. 68, fols. 288r–289r; vol. 18, fol. 157r; vol. 20, fol. 322r; vol. 36, fol. 500rv; vol. 57, fols. 181r–182r.

49. Arm. 41, vol. 39, fols. 79r–81r; vol. 68, fols. 125r–126r, 127r–128r, 129r–130v, 131r–132v.

50. Arm. 40, vol. 43, fol. 162r: "pro affictu annuo duodecim millium ducatorum auri in auro de camera decem Julii pro quolibet ducato computatis."

51. Arm. 42, vol. 15, fols. 277r–280v, 19 June 1561.

52. Arm. 40, vol. 23, fol. 167r: "etiam unico contextu anticipata solutione in pecunia numerata recipere et habere." Another formula: Arm. 41, vol. 24, fol. 155r: "ac precium seu annuum affictum vel responsionem predictam pro dicto Triennio recipiendi."

53. The two prepayments of total sums: Marino Caracciolo rented "certain possessions" of his bishopric of Catania in 1536 for a lump sum, and Alessandro Farnese received a total of 6,000 *scuti* of gold in advance for Avignon in 1542. Arm. 41, vol. 8, fols. 19r–20v; vol. 32, fol. 42r.

54. Arm. 41, vol. 6, fol. 14r; vol. 18, fols. 314r–316v.

55. The single exception involved the monastery of San Lorenzo in Cremona, rented out by Uberto Gambara in 1524 to "dilectis filiis Bartholomeo Fodo et Christoforo Magaitio Laicis Cremonensis redditum eiusdem Monasterii *conductoribus*." Arm. 40, vol. 8, fol. 117r (italics mine).

56. Arm. 41, vol. 68, fols. 129r–130v.

57. Arm. 41, vol. 36, fol. 500r; vol. 68, fols. 125r–126r, 127r–128r, 129r–130v, 131r–132r.

58. Arm. 41, vol. 18, fol. 157r.

59. Arm. 41, vol. 20, fol. 441r: "Antonio Angelo Marcutii, et Bernardino Blanco *eorumque sociis* laicis terrae Caletri Consana diocesis" (italics mine).

60. Arm. 40, vol. 43, fol. 243r; Arm. 41, vol. 22, fol. 126r.

61. Arm. 41, vol. 39, fol. 79r: "Cornelii de Malvagia civis Bononiensis."

62. MC, vol. 884, fol. 124rv; vol. 887, fols. 146r, 163r, 193v. On the importance of the *depositario generale,* see Clemens Bauer, "Studi per la storia delle finanze papale durante il pontificato di Sisto IV," ASRSP 50 (1927) 325; Melissa M. Bullard, *Filippo Strozzi and the Medici: Favor and Finance in Sixteenth-Century Florence and Rome* (Cambridge 1980) 91–118; and Felix Gilbert, *The Pope, His Banker, and Venice* (Cambridge Mass. 1980).

63. Arm. 41, vol. 23, fol. 42r; Bullard, "Mercatores" (n. 3 above) 58–59.

64. MC, vol. 877, fol. 102v; vol. 882, fol. 111v; vol. 889, fol. 15v. On the *dogane,* see Bauer (n. 62 above) 327, 337.

65. MC, vol. 881, fols. 71r–72r, 83r.

66. MC, vol. 904, fol. 26v.

67. Arm. 41, vol. 33, fol. 163r; MC, vol. 862, fol. 6v; Bullard, "Mercatores" (n. 3 above) 55.

68. Luigi was still head of his company in July 1549, but by October 1551 the firm was called the Heirs of Luigi Rucellai. MC, vol. 889, fol. 15v; vol. 893, fol. 12v; vol. 902, fols. 3v, 7v; vol. 904, fol. 1r.

69. Arm. 40, vol. 43, fol. 162r.

70. DBI 2.574; Archivio di Stato, Rome, Archivio Camerale, Camerale Prima, Diversorum del Camerlengo, vol. 369, fol. 16r; MC, vol. 862, fol. 8r; vol. 871, fol. 73r; vol. 872, fol. 80v; vol. 877, fol. 76r; vol. 881, fols. 68v, 84v, 95v; vol. 882, fol. 100v; vol. 884, fol. 85r; vol. 889, fol. 22r; vol. 893, fol. 14r.

71. Sanuto 9.80, 81, 83; AV, vol. 3, fol. 21v; Arm. 41, vol. 57, fols. 181r–182r.

72. AV, vol. 3, fols. 21v, 42v, 43r, 71r, 73v–74r, 100v.

73. MC, vol. 855, fols. 2r, 3r, 7r: "pro expensis magni Turchi."

74. AC, vol. 3, fol. 45r; AV, vol. 5, fol. 60r; Eubel 3.250 n. 6; AC, vol. 2, fols. 53v, 72v, 76r, 78v–79r; Arm. 40, vol. 43, fol. 162r.

75. Arm. 42, vol. 15, fols. 277r–280v.

76. Hay 10.

77. Baroni (n. 36 above) 310: "quali, mi dice l'huomo che è ritornato, sono buone genti, che non è poco, essendo per l'ordinario li Religiosi di queste commende molto disordinati." See also Paolo Prodi, *Il sovrano pontifice: un corpo e due anime: la monarchia papale nella prima età moderna* (Bologna 1982) 274.

78. AM, vol. 6, fol. 139v: "super *moderatione* Bullae Paulinae de rebus ecclesie non alienandis nec ultra triennium locandis" (italics mine).

79. Arm. 41, vol. 39, fols. 77r–79r, 79r–81r: "Cardinalis Crescentius dicens posse concedi ex quo non anticipata solutionis."

80. Arm. 41, vol. 55, fol. 180r. Filippo apparently succeeded Nicolò Ridolfi, the cardinal, who had died in January of the same year.

81. Arm. 41, vol. 57, fol. 181r: "ac iusto et honesto precio." Arm. 42, vol. 6, fol. 317v: "etiam honestis." Arm. 41, vol. 68, fol. 125r: "pariter honestis."

Arm. 42, vol. 11, fol. 81r: "et in evidentem utilitatem," "licita tamen et honestis ac sacris canonibus non contraria."

82. BR 6.496–498.

83. BR 7.58–60: "Cum autem, sicut accepimus, occasione dictarum literarum et motus proprii huiusmodi, diversae lites, quaestiones, et controversiae ortae, ac diversa gravamina, laesiones, perturbationes et incommoda diversis personis generata et illata, ac literae et motus proprii huiusmodi rigorosae executioni demandata fuerint, in eorundem personarum animarum molestiam non modicam."

84. Arm. 42, vol. 16, fols. 97r–98v. Gallio was later promoted to the cardinalate.

85. Arm. 42, vol. 16, fol. 259r. This was the brother of Guido Ascanio Sforza.

86. Arm. 42, vol. 19, fols. 169r–172v. Federico succeeded his uncle Ercole, who had died at the Council of Trent in March 1563.

87. Prodi (n. 77 above) 274–275.

88. Reinhard, *Papstfinanz und Nepotismus* 2.346–362.

89. Archivio di Stato, Milan, Fondo Trivulzio, Cartella 333 (no pagination): "tres locationes triennales de triennio in triennium, et quod una finita alia intelligatur incepta more Ecclesiastico, et in omnibus conforma ad formam Sacr. Concil. Trident. et Sacr. Canon." This was one of four abbeys rented out at this time by Cardinal Marco Gallio and his brother, Tolomeo Gallio, the duke of Alvito, great-great-nephews of the secretary of Pius IV above.

90. *Dictionnaire de droit canonique* 1 (1935) cols. 408–409.

91. See chapter 4 below, however, for the virtual inheritance of benefices by relatives of prelates.

92. On "the dead hand of nepotism," see chapter 4 below, pp. 121 ff.

93. CT 12.143: "Licentia etiam testandi clericis de bonis ecclesiae non esset danda nisi pro causa urgente, ne bona pauperum converterentur in privatas delicias et amplificationes domorum."

94. Sanuto 4.34–36: "Et vene uno messo a Padoa dil legato con uno breve dil papa, excommunicava *etc.*, perchè el papa voleva lui li danari."

95. Ibid. 79–80.

96. Ibid. 50: "dicendo si lamenterà a Maximiano, Franza, Spagna, e tutti reali dil mondo, che la Signoria si fa licito meter man su danari di la Chiesia"; col. 36: "et pocho spendeva, con opinion, con li soi danari, farsi papa." See also Giovanni Soranzo, "Giovanni Battista Zeno, nipote di Paolo II, cardinale di S. Maria in Portico (1468–1501)," RSCI 16.2 (May–August 1962) 249–274.

97. Arturo Segre, "Un registro di lettere del cardinale Ercole Gonzaga (1535–36) con un'appendice di documenti inediti," *Miscellanea di storia italiana, R. Deputazione sovra gli studi di storia patria per le antiche provincie e la Lombardia,* terza serie 16 (1913) 342.

98. Vat lat 6203, fols. 144v–145r: "Questa è la nostra ultima voluntà, et il nostro ultimo Testamento . . . per vigore delle facoltà concesse da sommi Pontifici in generali alli Reverendissimi Cardinali, et in particolare, . . . concesse alla persona nostra da Gregorio XIII santa memoria."

99. Arm. 41, vol. 20, fol. 347r: "De benignitate sedis apostolice provenire dignum est ut ecclesiarum prelatis praesertim S. R. E. Cardinalibus qui pro

eiusdem ecclesie statu salubriter et prospere dirigendo assidue laborare non cessant, disponere de bonis quae viventes possident libera sit . . . in ultima voluntate."

100. Arm. 41, vol. 33, fol. 106rv: "Tibi, de quibuscunque bonis mobilibus etiam preciosis, et si moventibus ac immobilibus et pecuniarum summis, necnon iuribus et actionibus quocunque titulo, iure, modo, via, causa, vel occasione, ad te nunc et pro tempore spectantibus cuiuscunque qualitatis summe valoris et precii seu conditionis fuerint, et in quibuscunque rebus consistant, etiam si illa aut illorum pars ex proventibus ecclesiasticis quarumcunque Ecclesiarum Cathedralium etiam Metropolitanarum ac titulorum Cardinalium, necnon monasteriorum et beneficiorum ecclesiasticorum quorumcunque secularium et regularium que in titulum, commendam, administrationem aut alias obtinuisti et obtines, ac in futurum obtinebis, necnon quorumcunque fructuum similium ecclesiarum monasteriorum et beneficiorum ecclesiasticorum tibi reservatorum et reservandorum, ac quarumcunque pensionum annuarum tibi super quibusvis fructibus redditibus et proventibus ecclesiasticis assignatarum et assignandarum etiam ratione Cardinalatus honoris."

101. Ibid. fol. 106v.

102. Ibid. fol. 107r: "seu in pios vel alios usus etiam forsan contra infideles aut pro fabrica Basilica principis apostolorum de Urbe converti debeant."

103. Ibid.: "quam partem huiusmodi pro laboribus seu recompensa laborum quos hactenus pro dicta Romana Ecclesia pertulisti tibi ac heredibus et quoquo titulo successoribus tuis liberaliter concedimus et donamus."

104. Arm. 40, vol. 43, fols. 145r–147v; Arm. 41, vol. 19, fols. 315r–317v; vol. 22, fols. 21r–26v, 389r–394r; vol. 33, fols. 106r–108v, 304r–306r.

105. Arm. 41, vol. 39, fols. 162r–164v: "ob fidelia et continua servitia que nobis et sedi apostolica hactenus exhibuisti et continue exhibere non cessas."

106. Arm. 41, vol. 21, fol. 361r.

107. Arm. 41, vol. 20, fol. 347r; Arm. 40, vol. 28, fols. 168r–169r; Arm. 41, vol. 8, fols. 372r–373r.

108. Arm. 41, vol. 8, fols. 372r–373r, 7 November 1537: "aut filios etiam spurios etiam ex quovis damnato coitu procreatos . . . aut alias quascunque personas etiam e iure quomodolibet prohibitas et incapaces." This clearly refers to Claudio Aleandro, the cardinal's illegitimate son.

109. Arm. 42, vol. 18, fols. 113r–114v, 177r, 182r–183v.

110. Arm. 41, vol. 33, fol. 106v: "inter quascunque etiam seculares personas sive sint consanguinei, servitores sive alii; . . . ac in quasvis pias et non pias causas et alios quoscunque etiam non pios alias tamen licitos usus."

111. Angelo Maria Bandini, *Il Bibbiena o sia il ministro di stato delineato nella vita del cardinale Bernardo Dovizi da Bibbiena* (Livorno 1758) 50.

112. Federico Odorici, *Il Cardinale Uberto Gambara da Brescia, 1487–1549, Indagini di storia patria* (Brescia 1856) 17.

113. Aluigi Cossio, *Il cardinale Gaetano e la riforma* (Cividale 1902) 458–460.

114. Vat lat 3913, fol. 122v: "Crediamo che fin hora habbiate inteso la morte di quel povero di m. Domenico il quale morse di aepodipsia in manco di tre giorni, Dio hebbe l'anima sua, habbiamo scritto al fratello, che venga qua, et vedremo per ordine quello, che si troverà."

115. Ibid. fol. 128v: "che per commune fama se intende haver havuto M. Domenico."

116. Ibid.: "non trovandose soi denari noi staressemo sotto de molto perchè non ci ha saldato li conti de cinque anni del manegio delle nostre Chiese." See Hubert Jedin, *A History of the Council of Trent,* trans. Dom Ernest Graf (2 vols. London 1957) 1.439 n. 4 for the minor scandal created by this incident.

117. Giuseppe Spezi, ed., *Lettere inedite del Card. Pietro Bembo e di altri scrittori del secolo XVI* (Rome 1862) 58–59: "Oltre che ho deliberato nel mio animo, che se Torquato non mi farà contento di quel solo piacere, che tanto ho desiderato da lui, dico di farsi dotto, al che egli mi par molto poco inclinato, io non gli lascerò valuta d'un solo picciolo oltra quelli beneficii che io già dati gli ho, e lascerò tutto alla mia Elena."

118. Ibid. 60–61: "Sopra le quali cose ti dico, che se tu in due anni non farai bello et honorevole progresso e profitto nelle lettere, sii certo che non haverai parte alcuna della mia heredità; non la casa da Padova, non il mio studio, nè cosa alcuna, che sia in lui, nè in detta casa; non le cose che ho qui, che sono per lo valore di qualche migliaio di ducati, et in fine non una strenga nè uno stoviglio. E quando io non avesse la Elena, nè i figliuoli di mess. Giovan Matteo Bembo, nè di mess. Bernardin Belegno miei nipoti, sì lascerò io tutto il mio più tosto ad alcun mio amico o servitore, che m'ama e ubbidisce, che a te; il quale non m'ubbidisci, e perciò non m'ami. . . . E per aventura che anco di Villa Nova e di Coniolo penserò di far miglior profitto, che di lasciargli a te; e basterammi lasciarti esser arciprete di Cortarolo con la pension Bressana, e fieno eziandio questi due sostenamenti della tua vita maggiori di quello che haverai da me meritato."

119. Bembo's wills of 1535 and 1544 are printed in Vittorio Cian, *Un decennio della vita di M. Pietro Bembo (1521–1531)* (Turin 1885) 201–203.

120. Arm. 41, vol. 39, fol. 251r.

121. The term *spoils* means "loot" or "booty" in Latin, Italian, and English. This is clearly not the meaning attached to the term by the church.

122. Cristoforo Jacobazzi had earlier inherited, by means of resignation in his favor, the bishopric of Cassano and other church property from his uncle, Cardinal Domenico Jacobazzi. On the occasion of Cristoforo's death, however, there was no prelate in the family to be so favored.

123. Arm. 41, vol. 19, fol. 121r: "Moti singularibus meritis bonae memoriae Christophori Cardinalis de Jacobaciis fratris tui, et pro nostra erga te paterna benevolentia, tuaque erga nos observantia, Tibi omnia et singula spolia res et bona ad dictum Christophorum Cardinalem ratione ecclesie Cassanensis cui vivens praeerat tempore sui obitus spectantia ubicunque reperiantur et cuiusvis valoris sint ac in quibusvis rebus consistant . . . quae ad nos et Cameram apostolicam spectent gratiose donamus et liberaliter elargimur per presentes."

124. Arm. 42, vol. 11, fol. 264r: "bonam memoriam Joannem Antonium olim episcopum seu electum venafranensis tuum ut accepimus patruum."

125. Arm. 40, vol. 23, fol. 257r: "de illis libere et licito ad libitum vostrum disponere."

126. Arm. 40, vol. 32, fol. 25r: "non solum fructus redditus et proventus huiusmodi sed etiam masseritia et utensilia ac lectos fulcetos in domo Episcopali pro usu Episcopi Cortonensis."

127. Arm. 40, vol. 33, fol. 188r; vol. 42, fol. 285r.
128. AV, vol. 3, fol. 53r.
129. Arm. 40, vol. 20, fols. 26r–27v. Three separate papal briefs. Cardinal Antonio Sanseverino had originally been nominated as guardian and tutor, but he had asked to be excused from the task. Briefs to Sanseverino, Count Orsini, and Ansaldo Grimaldi. Guardianship to the count "exceptis dumtaxat pensionibus ecclesiasticis ipsis pupillis per modernum Archiepiscopum Nicosiensis debitis et seu debendis, quecunque alia bona iura dictorum pupillorum durante pupillari etate."
130. Arm. 42, vol. 18, fols. 365r–366v, 390r–391v: "Pro Anna moniali filia olim Cardinalis Mantuanae."
131. Arm. 40, vol. 41, fol. 156rv.
132. Arm. 40, vol. 50, fol. 231rv: "Cardinalis Colonna cum esset verus debitor Dominorum Martini Bonvizi Andree Sbarse et sociorum de Neapoli lucensium mercatorum in notabili quantitate excedente summam XVII milium ducatorum."
133. Arm. 41, vol. 55, fols. 178r–180r: "et presertim summa viginti milium ducatorum moneta illarum partium vel circa."
134. Josephus Cominus, *Gregorii Cortesii Monachi Cassinatis, S. R. E. Cardinalis, omnia quae huc usque colligi potuerunt, sive ad illum spectantia* (2 vols. Padua 1774) 1.43.
135. Bandini (n. 111 above) 50.
136. Schiavo (n. 45 above) 429.
137. Ciacconius 3.353.
138. MC, vol. 881, fol. 3r.
139. Ciacconius 3.621.
140. Archivio di Stato, Modena, Archivio Segreto Estensi, Sezione "Casa e Stato," Serie: Documenti spettanti ai principi Estensi (1204–1810), Busta 387, fasc. 2037–VIII, fol. 1: "In omnibus . . . aliis suis bonis mobilibus et immobilibus terribus et actionibus ubicunque consistentes . . . etiam fructibus ac reditibus bonorum suorum quorumcunque et etiam ecclesiasticorum Dictus Dominus Testator instituit ellegit nominavit et esse voluit suum heredem universalem Illustrissimum Excellentissimum principem et Dominum nostrum Dominum Alfonsum Estensem Ducem ferrariae eius fratrem."
141. Ibid. Busta 389, fasc. 2038–III, vol. 1.
142. Ippolito II had quarreled bitterly with his nephew Luigi throughout most of his life, according to his biographer, and had steadfastly refused to leave him any of his wealth. At the last hour, however, either his mind changed or his hand was forced by a corrupt servant. See Vincenzo Pacifici, *Ippolito II d'Este, Cardinale di Ferrara* (Tivoli 1920) 354–355. We have seen, however, that Ippolito II did, in fact, resign ecclesiastical benefices in favor of the same nephew.
143. Litta vol. 8, supp. 2, tav. 534.
144. Vat lat 6203, fols. 145v–146r: "Et perchè Mariano Vescovo e Bernardino sopradetti . . . sopra a trent'anni in qua diedero, sapendo certo il contrario falsa voce che noi havessimo figlioli che studiavano a Padova, et che volevamo

le nostre entrate per loro pensando per levare questa mala fama indurre a spender le nostre entrate secondo la volontà loro dechiaramo si come havemo detto sempre di non haver havuti, ne haver figlioli, ne maschi, ne femine, et questa esser stata mera calumnia datali sopradetti nostri fratelli."

145. Castelgandolfo and Rocca Priora. Bernardino Savelli married a relative of Pope Sixtus V in 1589 or 1590, and Castelgandolfo was raised to a duchy for him by the pontiff. Delumeau 2.810. Pope Clement VIII bought Rocca Priora, Castelgandolfo, and other Savelli property in 1604. AV, vol. 14, fol. 96rv.

146. Reinhard, *Papstfinanz und Nepotismus* 2.258.

147. Vat lat 6203, fols. 125v–126r. See Delumeau 1.448, who has the funeral costing some 3,000 *scuti*.

148. Vat lat 6203, fol. 126v: "et di qualunque altro loco dove si trovarranno frutti alla morte nostra, et facciano riscuotere l'entrate et dinari, di tutti li sopradetti luoghi se si trovassero affittati, et tutti i dinari, che havemo sopra le chiese di Conca, Coria, Napoli, Capua, et Catanzaro, et facciano riscuotere li frutti delli denari posti nella gabella della seta del Prencipe di Bisignano, et tutte l'entrate poste in qualsivoglia luogho, et modo, et per qualsivoglia causa, et tutti i denari, et crediti in qualunque luogho, et modo et per qualsivoglia causa, et tutti li danari, et crediti in qualunque luogo se ci doveranno."

149. Vat lat 6203, fols. 126v–127r: "Volemo ancora che di tutti li danari, che seranno cavati da gl'ori, argenti, e mobili, et di grani, biade, et vini come di sopra, et anco delli danari, che seranno riscossi di tutte l'entrate, et affitti, et di tutti li crediti suoi doverranno, et di tutte le quantità di danari, che avanzassi, che da noi non ne fusse disposto per testamento per codicelli per legati, per donatione, . . . ne faccino comprare tanti censi, o monti non vaca-bili, . . . "

150. Delumeau 2.783–824. See AV, vol. 3, fol. 126rv for the institution of the funded papal debt, the *monte fidei*, by Clement VII, 10, 12 October 1526. See chapter 5 below, at n. 39.

151. Vat lat 6203, fol. 127r.

152. Vat lat 6203, fol. 127v: "Et ogni volta che seranno ricomprati li censi, o resi li dinari o restituiti li dinari posi nella gabella della seta del Prencipe di Bisignano, o prese l'entrate, et denari delli legatarii, et donatarii, che seranno passati a meglior vita, volemo che facciano havere sempre curati reinvestire li sopradetti dinari in tanti altri censi, o monti non vacabili, et quante volte seranno ricomprati, et pagati li legatarii, et donatarii, et esseguito tutto quello si contiene nel presente testamento, et in ogni altra scrittura, che se toccarà fatta da noi quello che avanzerà lo facciano mettere in tanti altri censi, o monti in accres-cimento dell'heredità."

153. Vat lat 6203, fols. 127v–138r.

154. Vat lat 6203, fols. 138r–148v.

155. Vat lat 6203, fols. 139r–143v, and passim.

156. Vat lat 6203, fols. 143r–144r: "et vedranno esse bisogno per aiuto, et protettione, a tutti li Signori Cardinali della Congregatione del Santo Uffitio, al Signor Cardinal Farnese, Signore et parente, al Cardinal d'Aragona, al Car-dinal Sforza, al Cardinal Ascanio Colonna, al Serenissimo Cardinal de Medici

Gran Duca di Toscana, alli Serenissimi Signori Duchi di Parma et Piacenza et d'Urbino, et a tutti li altri Signori Cardinali et Serenissimi Prencipi, che loro sanno esser noi stati amati."

157. Vat lat 6203, fol. 124v.

158. Arm. 42, vol. 16, fols. 301r–302v; vol. 17, fols. 117r–118v, 124r–126v, 440rv.

159. Harry G. Hynes, *The Privileges of Cardinals,* Canon Law Studies 217 (Washington D.C. 1945) 153.

160. See Delumeau 2.820–824.

161. Reinhard, "Nepotismus" 145–185, 173.

4. THE DISTRIBUTION OF CHURCH PROPERTY: SACRED OFFICE

1. Reinhard, "Nepotismus"; Hay 34.

2. Hay 34–35.

3. Hay 35–37; Reinhard, "Nepotismus" and "Papa Pius: Prolegomena zu einer Sozialgeschichte des Papsttums," *Von Konstanz nach Trient: Festgabe für August Franzen,* ed. Remigius Bäumer (Paderborn 1972) 261–299.

4. Hay 34–41.

5. Hay 37.

6. Hay 44–45, 104–105.

7. Reinhard, "Nepotismus" 176–177, "Papa Pius" (n. 3 above) 296–297, and *Papstfinanz und Nepotismus* 1.156–160.

8. Reinhard, "Nepotismus" 161–162. Reinhard asserts that this was an attempt to weaken the power of the papacy, not antipathy to nepotism.

9. Hay 34.

10. Hay 86; BR 5.608 (translated in Olin 54–64).

11. Reinhard, "Papa Pius" (n. 3 above).

12. Sanuto 5.148.

13. Litta vol. 5 tav. 560–561.

14. Sanuto 5.180: "dicendoli habi questo almeno nel picol papato dil fratello."

15. Sanuto 5.191: "dicendo non voleva romper la fede data."

16. Sanuto 5.204: "pregando li cardinali lo volesseno acceptar etc. Quali li deteno bone parole."

17. Marcellus II was the only other Italian pope of the sixteenth century who failed to create a family member cardinal (1555). He refused to allow his family to come to the eternal city, but his feeling might have changed had he lived. His pontificate lasted but three weeks (9–30 April).

18. BR 5.608.

19. Ibid.; translation from Olin 59–60.

20. Archivio di Stato, Modena, Archivio Segreto Estensi, Sezione "Casa e Stato," Serie: Documenti spettanti ai principi Estensi (1204–1810), Busta 386, 2037–III, fol. 7rv.

21. D. S. Chambers, "The Economic Predicament of Renaissance Cardinals,"

Studies in Medieval and Renaissance History 3 (1966) 293; Delumeau 1.434–435.

22. Vat lat 6407, fol. 47r.

23. Vat lat 6407, fols. 88r, 90r.

24. Vat lat 6407, fol. 86r: "Et così anche per debito della servitù mia, et del desiderio di tanto effetto, in tutto ciò che per mè si possa, offerisco à Vostra Signoria Illustrissima lo stato, che se 'l venda, se 'l impegni, et ne faccia ogni suo servitio, et ne disponga come li piace, che n'è vera Padrona; Et di mè stesso, et de' figli miei, et di quant'altro ho al mondo, sà bene, che n'è liberamente, et parimente Padrona; et che hora et sempre, siamo stati, siamo, et saremo per servirla, et per metterci la vita continuamente, Et à Vostra Signoria Illustrissima bacio le mani, pregando Nostro Signor Iddio per lei."

25. Vat lat 6407, fols. 118r, 120r, 128r, 136r: "il qual essendo nobile, ricco, et di buon spirito, desidera sotto l'ombra, et con l'essempio di nobili, et santi costume di Vostra Signoria Illustrissima seguitar per alcuni anni cotesta corte."

26. Vat lat 6407, fol. 158r; Vat lat 6408, fol. 73r; Vat lat 6407, fols. 220r, 245r, 247r.

27. AV, vol. 8, fol. 86v.

28. AC, vol. 9, fols. 2r, 9r, 15v. For more on the trial and on those implicated as heretics with Morone, see C. Corvisieri, "Compendio dei processi del Santo Uffizio di Roma (da Paolo III a Paolo IV)," ASRSP 3 (1880) 261–290, 449–472. Cardinals on our list who were included were Tommaso Badia, Pietro Bembo, Gasparo Contarini, Gregorio Cortese, Federigo Fregoso, Jacopo Sadoleto, Francesco Sfondrato, and Cristoforo Madruzzo, all of them deceased by then except Madruzzo. Reginald Pole of England was also cited. Paul IV, then, was deeply suspicious of the orthodoxy of the very men who had served with him on the reform commission of 1537: Contarini, Sadoleto, Pole, Fregoso, Cortese, and Badia. Another reformer, Ercole Gonzaga, had suspicious books seized by the Inquisitors of Mantua on the order of Paul IV. The right to keep and read such materials was restored to Gonzaga by Pius IV on 8 May 1560. See Arm. 42, vol. 13, fol. 187rv.

29. Vat lat 6409, fols. 6rv, 12r, 38r, 41r, 76r, 98r, 113r, 125r, 135r, 145r; AC, vol. 9, fol. 15v.

30. AC, vol. 9, fol. 11r.

31. Ibid.

32. Ibid. fols. 10r, 11r.

33. Vat lat 6409, fols. 94r, 113rv, 90r, 100r; Vat lat 6408, fols. 27r–30r; Vat lat 6409, fol. 10r. Listed chronologically.

34. Vat lat 6409, fol. 6r: "Lodato sia Dio, che le cose del lungo et confuso conclave ha fatto finalmente risolvere in bene, con elettione bona et santa, et grata come s'intende all'universo. Per quella cognitione ch'io ho delle bone et dignissime qualità di questo nostro signore et maxime per la molto mansuetudine et benignità sua, di che quella vostra corte havea piu bisogno che d'altro per ristorarla et consolarla delle rigidità et immuità [?] passate; Io me ne sono molto allegrato."

35. BR 5.203–204.

36. BR 6.185–186: "in posterum veros et indubitatos Sanctitatis Suae et Romanorum pro tempore Pontificium, et non privilegium nec ficte familiares et continuos commensales censeri, reputari, et esse."

37. Arm. 41, vol. 3, fols. 122r–124r. Among them were Girolamo Verallo, Girolamo Aleandro, Uberto Gambara, and Durante Duranti, none of whom had as yet acquired the red hat.

38. Arm. 41, vol. 36, fols. 478r, 479r–480r.

39. Arm. 42, vol. 13, fols. 224rv, 225r, 226r. Among them appear a Pietro Bembo, Claudio Aleandro (the cardinal's son), and an Antonio Giberti.

40. *Nuntiaturberichte aus Deutschland nebst ergänzenden Aktenstücken: Abtheil I, 1533–1559* 1 supp. 1 (Tübingen 1963) 129: "che non hebbi mai grazia di metter huomo alcuno in quella Rota, il che è stato per aventura a quasi tutti li Reverendissimi cardinali concesso."

41. MC, vol. 902, fol. 12r: "Perchè la mente di signori padroni è che li familiarii dell'Illustrissimo et Reverendissimo camerlengo restino sospesi intorno al pagamento delle decime di loro benefitii."

42. AM, vol. 6, fol. 405r; AV, vol. 4, fols. 32v, 34r; AC, vol. 2, fols. 59v, 88v; vol. 5, fols. 32r, 56r; vol. 6, fols. 63r, 139r, 140v–141r; AV, vol. 7, fol. 111r; AC, vol. 9, fols. 12v–13r, 56v, 64r.

43. AM, vol. 6, fol. 405r; AC, vol. 2, fol. 59v; vol. 5, fol. 32r.

44. AV, vol. 7, fol. 22r; AC, vol. 9, fol. 81rv.

45. Walter Friedensburg, "Der Briefwechsel Gasparo Contarinis mit Ercole Gonzaga nebst einem Briefe Giovanni Pietro Carafas," QFIAB 2 (1899) 173–174.

46. Ibid. 176–177: "Non fu mai fatta resignatione più libera di questa et più santa. Perchè nè io mi sono mosso per alcun rispetto humano a farla, nè lui ne ha mai saputo cosa alcuna, onde o con parole o con cenne habbi potuto mostrare ambitione di simil cosa."

47. Ibid. 175.

48. Ibid. 178: "et havendo già fatta questa deliberatione secondo la conscienza mia et quello che m'è spirato da Dio, non posso mutare nè voglio manco."

49. Ibid. 179–180.

50. Ibid. 180–181: "poichè da Sua Beatitudine mi fosse impedito di darlo a quella persona che sola per la bontà et scienza m'è paruta degna d'haverlo."

51. Eubel 3.194.

52. Eubel 3.282.

53. Richard M. Douglas, *Jacopo Sadoleto, 1477–1547: Humanist and Reformer* (Cambridge Mass. 1959) 10, 245.

54. Sanuto 5.913: "Vene l'orator di Ferara, e presentò una lettera dil cardinal di Ferara fiol dil ducha, di credenza et fo introducto uno so' nontio. Par esso cardinal voy il possesso di do beneficiati a Ruigo. El principe disse non era da cardinal di tuor beneficii sì picoli, et si vedrà."

55. BR 6.606.

56. Arm. 40, vol. 14, fol. 217rv; vol. 15, fols. 76r, 89r; vol. 19, fols. 293r–294r.

57. Harry G. Hynes, *The Privileges of Cardinals,* Canon Law Studies 217 (Washington D.C. 1945) 150.

58. Ferraris 4.35.

59. Fifteen minutes of papal briefs awarding goods of dead familiars to cardinal-patrons between 1516 and 1545: Arm. 40, vol. 4, fol. 74r; vol. 15, fol. 84r; vol. 26, fol. 227rv; vol. 20, fol. 64r; vol. 23, fol. 5r; vol. 26, fol. 66r; vol. 41, fol. 139r; vol. 46, fols. 114r, 122r; Arm. 41, vol. 2, fol. 252rv; vol. 4, fol. 23r; vol. 9, fol. 257r; vol. 21, fols. 45r, 223r.

60. For example, the benefices that reverted to Nicolò Gaddi at the death of a familiar in 1536 consisted of three *commende* in the diocese of Novara "and also each and every other ecclesiastical benefice with and without care, which was possessed by the late Gaudenzio Abondio, . . . and which value together or separately 60 ducats." Arm. 41, vol. 4, fol. 23r: "necnon omnia et singula alia beneficia ecclesiastica cum cura et sine cura que quondam Gaudentius Abundius obtinebat . . . quorum insimul seu cuiuslibet LX ducatorum." The formula for grants of expectancies to familiars was the same as that for cardinals, but the sums were tiny by comparison. See Arm. 41, vol. 18, fols. 344r–349r, a grant for expectancies in the diocese of Liège to the amount of 30 ducats for a familiar of Alessandro Cesarini. One of Dionisio Lorerio's familiars received a similar grant—expectancies worth 24 ducats from the diocese of Pesaro: Arm. 41, vol. 22, fols. 28r–31v.

61. Arm. 40, vol. 19, fols. 293r–294r: "quecunque beneficia ecclesiastica tam secularia quam regularia ad tuam collationem provisionem presentationem institutionem seu quamvis aliam dispositionem communiter vel divisim ratione quarumcunque cathedralium etiam metropolitanarum et aliarum ecclesiarum et monasteriorum prioratuum et beneficiorum per te tunc quomodolibet obtentorum et obtinendorum pertinentia etiam si dispositioni apostolice specialiter vel generaliter reservata vel affecta forent quocunque tempore extra Romanam Curiam vacantia."

62. Arm. 41, vol. 8, fols. 186r–188r: "Cum dudum nos ut pauperes et alii clerici gratias expectativas per nos eis pro tempore concessas prosequentes ex gratiis expectativis huiusmodi fructum reportare possent."

63. Ibid.; Arm. 41, vol. 16, fols. 216r–219r.

64. Arm. 41, vol. 8, fols. 186r–188r: "perinde ac si electionem huiusmodi infra tempus per dictas Constitutiones statutum fecisses."

65. Arm. 41, vol. 10, fol. 52rv.

66. Arm. 42, vol. 6, fols. 281r–286r.

67. Arm. 41, vol. 16, fols. 216r–219r: "ac quorumvis aliorum monasteriorum etiam consistorialium prioratuum et beneficiorum ecclesiasticorum per te tunc quomodolibet obtentorum et obtinendorum pertinentia."

68. Ibid.

69. Recipients included Girolamo Ghinucci (1538), Durante Duranti (1538), Marino Grimani (1540), Cristoforo Madruzzo (1541), Durante Duranti again (1552), and Giulio della Rovere (1552). Arm. 41, vol. 10, fols. 344r, 409r–410r; vol. 18, fols. 220r–222r; vol. 20, fols. 402r–404r; vol. 64, fols. 89r, 140r–141r.

70. Arm. 41, vol. 2, fols. 58r–59r: "ac si tu Nannetensis ecclesie preesses."

71. Arm. 41, vol. 33, fol. 89rv: "per que de beneficiis ecclesiasticis personis benemeritis et tibi obsequentibus ac alias gratis et acceptis providere ac erga illos gratiosum te reddere possis."

bishop of Grosseto; Alessandro Campeggio, bishop of Bologna; Giovanni Battista Campeggio, bishop of Majorca; Giovanni Campeggio, bishop of Parenzo; Filippo Maria Campeggio, abbot of the monastery in Martorano.

115. AC, vol. 6, fol. 41r; AV, vol. 8, fol. 170rv; vol. 7, fol. 172r; Eubel 3.233, 206.

116. AV, vol. 4, fols. 26v–27r; AC, vol. 2, fol. 43r.

117. Arm. 40, vol. 33, fols. 244r–245r; Eubel 3.272, nn. 8, 10; AV, vol. 7, fol. 41r.

118. AC, vol. 5, fols. 143r–144r; Eubel 3.174, nn. 7, 8, 9.

119. AC, vol. 9, fols. 55r, 63rv: "cum decreto quod ipse Julius esset perpetuo inhabilis ad quacunque beneficia Ecclesiastica." This decree may be connected to Giulio's illegitimacy. It may also reflect repercussions of the commentary that Cardinal Marino Grimani wrote on *Romans* and *Galatians* in 1542. See P. J. Laven, "The *Causa Grimani* and Its Political Overtones," *Journal of Religious History* 4 (1967) 184–205, and Marvin W. Anderson, "Luther's Sola Fide in Italy: 1542–1551," *Church History* 38 (1969) 25–42.

120. Girolamo Garimberti, *La prima parte delle vite overo fatti memorabili d'alcuni papi, et di tutti i cardinali passati* (Venice 1567) 227: "nel quale in poco spatio di tempo havemo veduti tre Cardinali suoi successori, uno fratello, e doi nipoti, con Vescovi, Arcivescovi, Abbati, e altri posti in dignità dall' amorevolezza del Cardinal Marco."

121. Ibid.

122. Eubel 3.168.

123. AM, vol. 6, fol. 264v; Eubel 3.274.

124. Douglas (n. 53 above) 68–69.

125. AC, vol. 5, fol. 64r; vol. 6, fol. 159rv. Alessandro Guidiccioni presided over Lucca until 1600, when he resigned in favor of another Alessandro Guidiccioni. Eubel 3.229 n. 7.

126. AC, vol. 5, fol. 64r.

127. AV, vol. 8, fol. 88r, 14 June 1557.

128. Eubel 3.140 nn. 5, 6, 7, 8.

129. Ibid.

130. Ibid.

131. AM, vol. 6, fols. 144r, 177r; Eubel 3.279 nn. 4, 5, 6; AV, vol. 4, fol. 51r; AC, vol. 3, fol. 37v; vol. 2, fols. 32v, 34v; Eubel 3.175; AC, vol. 2, fol. 53r; Eubel 3.149 n. 5; AC, vol. 2, fols. 34r, 69v, 90v, 97r; Eubel 3.134; AC, vol. 2, fol. 102r; Eubel 3.181 n. 4; AC, vol. 2, fol. 45r.

132. AC, vol. 2, fol. 53r: "Pensione annua 160 ducatorum super dictis duabus partibus fructuum LXXX videlicet, pro Alexandro Geraldino . . . et reliquos LXXX pro Ascanio etiam Geraldino solvenda post obitum dicti Angeli et non alias."

133. AC, vol. 2, fol. 58r.

134. Eubel 3.181 nn. 4, 5.

135. AC, vol. 2, fol. 45r; Arm. 41, vol. 4, fols. 115rv, 117r.

136. Friedensburg (n. 45 above) 179: "sii prima satisfacto a l'honor de Dio et al bisogno de quella cità; dopo che quanto si puole, si satisfaci etiam alla

famiglia dello episcopo morto et di quel primo, il quale lo commise a la fede di V.S. solamente per rispecto della sua famiglia."

137. Archivio di Stato, Mantua, Archivio Gonzaga, Busta 1945, 1, fols. 24v–25r; "Quanto all'Abbadia di Lamoli vacata per morte di quel figlio di M Guidobaldo nostro, potete esser' certo che quando io non havessi obligata la fide mia non sarei mancato di tener memoria di voi per tutte le ragioni che havete tocco nella vostra et per molte altre appresso, ma come sapete io fui grandissimo et domestichissimo amico di M Guidobaldo, & egli hebbe tanta fide in me che volle che io havessi il regresso alla detta Abbadia sapendo che in ogni evento io la tornerei sempre in casa sua, et io che voglio che il mondo conosca che chi ha da far' meco ha da far' con gentilhuomo et con persona sincera et fidele, non mancherei di darla ad un altro de suoi figliuoli non solo questa volta ma sempre che tornasse in persona mia."

138. Arm. 40, vol. 8, fols. 150r, 151rv, 152r, 153r–154v.

139. AV, vol. 8, fol. 137v; AC, vol. 9, fol. 16r. "Spoils" and pensions also went to relatives in holy orders, just as they did to laymen. See Eubel 3.12 n. 7; Arm. 40, vol. 18, fol. 159r; vol. 49, fols. 379r, 380r, 430r, 432r; vol. 23, fol. 60r; vol. 42, fol. 311r.

140. Archivio di Stato, Florence, Carte Strozziani, serie I, filza 338, fol. 40r: "della quale certamente haviamo sentito non piccolo dispiacere per l'affettione che portiamo à casa vostra; alle honore et commodo della quale non mancheremo mai in tutto quelche potremo: Et se il subdiaconato di Santa Maria del Fiore, o altri benefitii, che egli teneva saranno del Padronato di casa vostra lasseremo che à vostro piacere ne disponiate et che vi ne accordiate fra di voi. Et quando ancora stieno alla nostra dispositione non mancheremo di mostrarvi che ve amiamo, et state sano."

141. Ibid. fol. 41r.

142. Ibid. fol. 42r: "Et per quanto si aspetterà à noi non mancheremo di admettere tal provisione, si come l'approviamo pensando che habbia à venire in honor' et utile di vostro figliolo, et in consequentia vostro, et di vostra casa."

143. AC, vol. 9, fol. 36v: "Providit ecclesie Agathensis de persona Americi de Sancto Severino clerici Neapolitani bonae memoriae Cardinalis Sancti Severini ex fratre germano nepotis."

144. Garimberti (n. 120 above) 215–216: "Sebene l'imperfettioni di Papa Alessandro Sesto, o per dir piu propriamente, la brutta vita sua, sia stata di un pessimo esempio all'età nostra; nondimeno per non defraudarlo di quell'honore, per il quale merita di esser annomerato tra i Principi grati, che sono stati in questi nostri tempi ingratissimi, dirò qualche cosa della sua gratitudine."

145. Ibid. 216.

146. AC, vol. 2, fol. 65r: "et Ludovicum Borgiam Alexander VI Sanctitatis Suae Promotoris Nepotem."

147. Vat lat 10600, fols. 116v, 131v, and passim through Vat lat 10604.

148. Vat lat 3457, fol. 271r; AC, vol. 3, fol. 36r; AV, vol. 4, fol. 50v; BR 6.143–144. "Lecta fuit per Reverendissimum Dominum meum de Cesis minuta Bulle per quam providetur ne de cetero filii ex fornicatione geniti prelatorum et presbiterorum possint obtinere ullo undique temporis ecclesias cathedrales

monasteria seu quevis alia beneficia parentum suarum etiam per interpositas personas nec etiam pensiones super ecclesiis et beneficiis obtentis per parentes suos." 30 May 1530, AC, vol. 3, fol. 36r.

149. AV, vol. 7, fol. 267v; BR 7.93–95.

150. AV, vol. 7, fol. 148v: "Quod huiusmodi cessiones et dimissiones non in favorem alicuius sed pure et libere in manibus Sanctitatis Sue fieri deberent."

151. AV, vol. 8, fol. 104r.

152. AC, vol. 9, fols. 66r, 71r.

153. AV, vol. 9, fols. 118r, 121v, 122v, 182r.

154. Lucilio's indulgence, Arm. 40, vol. 31, fols. 3r–4v: "te ad honores dignitates ac officia publica et privata ecclesiastica et secularia, necnon ad successiones paternas et maternas ac agnatorum et cognatorum et aliorum consanguineorum acsi de legitimo matrimonio procreatus esses, auctoritate apostolica legitimum declaramus." Torquato's indulgence is identical, Arm. 40, vol. 41, fols. 3r–4v.

155. G. Meneghetti, *La vita avventurosa di Pietro Bembo: umanista–poeta–cortigiano* (Venice 1961) 154–169.

156. Arm. 41, vol. 10, fol. 37rv.

157. AC, vol. 2, fol. 90r.

158. AC, vol. 6, fols. 29v, 30r.

159. AC, vol. 6, fols. 130v–131r: "Absolvens etc. etiam super defectu natalium dictum Paulum electum, quem ex Episcopo genitus et soluta vel coniugata patitur."

160. Eubel 3.281.

161. AV, vol. 7, fol. 110r; Eubel 3.125 nn. 5, 6, 7.

162. Arm. 42, vol. 11, fols. 87r, 97r, 236r; Eubel 3.36 n. 4, 255.

163. AC, vol. 9, fol. 23v.

164. AC, vol. 9, fol. 53r.

165. AC, vol. 9, fol. 54r.

166. Litta vol. 8 supp. I, tav. 316–317.

167. Hay 104–105 remarks that "culturally royal secretaries in England and France were no different from their opposite numbers in Rome. But when they were laymen they were freer agents and had a greater incentive to exercise power and influence since they could transmit their gains to their direct heirs. This was more difficult, it seems, with the wealthiest cardinals, . . . " But through the *licentia testandi* and the other practices we have outlined it was not really very difficult.

168. Quoted in Reinhard, "Nepotismus" 176.

169. Ibid.

170. Ibid.

171. Reinhard, "Papa Pius" (n. 3 above) 296–297, and "Nepotismus" 176–177.

172. Reinhard, "Papa Pius" (n. 3 above) 297.

173. New formulae appear in the records under Pius V (1566–1572) and Gregory XIII (1572–1585). For example, reservations of pensions from benefices now carry blanket dispensations for defect of birth, "if they are required." See AV, vol. 10, fol. 104r (17 December 1571); vol. 11, fol. 10r (24 October 1572,

"cum dispensatione pro pensionariis super defectu natalium, si indigent"); fol. 167v (8 November 1582).

174. Reinhard, *Papstfinanz und Nepotismus* and "Ämterlaufbahn und Familienstatus: Der Aufstieg des Hauses Borghese, 1537–1621," QFIAB 54 (1974) 328–427.

175. See AV, vols. 10, 11, 12, passim.

5. THE DISTRIBUTION OF CHURCH PROPERTY: SECULAR OFFICE AND FAMILIES

1. See Peter Partner, *The Papal State under Martin V: The Administration and Government of the Temporal Power in the Early Fifteenth Century* (London 1958) for the beginning of the process.

2. See Partner, "Papal Financial Policy" 61.

3. See chapter 1 above, at n. 25.

4. See Reinhard, "Nepotismus" 167–185.

5. For example, the number of volumes of the Register of Supplications grew from an average of thirteen per year under Sixtus IV to an average of almost thirty per year under Paul IV. See Bruno Katterbach, *Inventario dei Registri delle Suppliche*, vol. 1 of *Inventari dell'Archivio Segreto Vaticano* (Vatican City 1932) 44–149. The supplications dealt with matters spiritual. For temporal offices, see Walter von Hofmann, *Forschungen zur Geschichte der kurialen Behörden vom Schisma bis zur Reformation* (2 vols. Rome 1914) 2.187–196. For the curia, see Niccolò del Re, *La curia romana: lineamenti storico-giuridici* (3d ed. Rome 1970).

6. William E. Lunt, *Papal Revenues in the Middle Ages* (2 vols. New York 1934) 2.135–136; Felice Litva, "L'attività finanziaria della Dataria durante il periodo tridentino," *Archivum Historiae Pontificiae* 5 (1967) 79–174; Delumeau 2.772; Peter Partner, "The 'Budget' of the Roman Church in the Renaissance Period," *Italian Renaissance Studies: A Tribute to the Late Cecilia M. Ady*, ed. E. F. Jacob (London 1960) 256–278; Clemens Bauer, "Studi per la storia delle finanze papale durante il pontificato di Sisto IV," ASRSP 50 (1927) 319–400.

7. Litva (n. 6 above) 134; von Hofmann (n. 5 above) 1.288.

8. Litva (n. 6 above) 135, 147 n. 92. Peter Partner's estimate is similar: 2,000 offices for sale by 1520 and an invested capital of 2,500,000 gold florins, "The 'Budget'" (n. 6 above) 257–258.

9. Partner, "Papal Financial Policy" 23.

10. Litva (n. 6 above) 82–95, 138–153; Delumeau 2.774–782; Michele Monaco, "Il primo debito pubblico pontificio: il Monte della Fede (1526)," *Studi Romani* 8.5 (1960) 553–569; Partner, "Papal Financial Policy" 21.

11. Léonce Celier, *Les Dataires du XVe siècle et les origines de la Datérie Apostolique* (Paris 1910) 116–122.

12. Del Re (n. 5 above) 443–452; Nicola Storti, *La storia e il diritto della Dataria Apostolica dalle origine ai nostri giorni* (Naples 1969). The department was abolished in the reforms of Vatican II in 1967.

13. Litva (n. 6 above) 147, 156.

14. Partner, "Papal Financial Policy" 47.

15. Ibid.

16. Delumeau 2.774.

17. Vat lat 10600, fols. 78r, 79v, 80r, 82r, 137v. Litva (n. 6 above) 138 states that the Knights of Loreto were founded in 1546; Delumeau 2.776 states that the Knights of Loreto were founded by Sixtus V in 1586. The records of the camera apostolica, however, show that knighthoods of Loreto were being sold from at least November 1545: MC, vol. 881, fols. 84v, 95v.

18. Litva (n. 6 above) 143.

19. Delumeau 2.774, 776.

20. AV, vol. 4, fol. 49v; vol. 8, fol. 58v; MC, vol. 902, fols. 12v, 21v, 27v, 75r, 79r; Litva (n. 6 above) 138–153.

21. Litva (n. 6 above) 166.

22. Ibid. 166–168.

23. Melissa M. Bullard, *Filippo Strozzi and the Medici: Favor and Finance in Sixteenth-Century Florence and Rome* (Cambridge 1980) 125. The DBI (4.235) says that Armellini paid 15,000 ducats for the office of *camerlengo;* Luigi Staffetti, *Il cardinale Innocenzo Cybo* (Florence 1894) 40 says he paid 70,000 ducats. There is no doubt about Vitelli, AV, vol. 9, fols. 184v–185r: "accepto ab eo pretio septuaginta millium ducatorum auri in auro," 17 November 1564.

24. Archivio di Stato, Rome, Archivio Camerale, Camerale Prima, Ufficiali Camerali, vol. 1718, fol. 15r.

25. Ibid. fols. 19rv, 23v, 27v, 28r, 36r.

26. Ibid. fol. 26r: "in perpetuum seu ad beneplacitum partium." There were 140 *scutiferi,* and each office cost 800 to 820 *scuti* of gold. Litva (n. 6 above) 166.

27. Ufficiali Camerali (n. 24 above) vol. 1718, fol. 27v; von Hofmann (n. 5 above) 2.187–196.

28. Von Hofmann (n. 5 above) 2.121, 90.

29. Vat lat 10604, fol. 127r: "A Madonna Bernardina Capo di ferro . . . per ordine di Sua Santità per la integra valuta de la meta de li officii vacati per morte di Julio Mignanello suo nipote donateli."

30. Wolfgang Reinhard, "Ämterlaufbahn und Familienstatus: Der Aufstieg des Hauses Borghese, 1537–1621," QFIAB 54 (1974) 328–427.

31. Edoardo Martinori, *Genealogia e cronostoria di una grande famiglia Umbro-romana: I Cesi* (Rome 1931) 7–9.

32. Ibid. 43–47.

33. Ibid. 47–49.

34. Ibid. 53, 56, 21; Litta vol. 2, tav. 150, 155.

35. Martinori (n. 31 above) 10, 21, 53–86. Cardinal Federico Cesi bought the *feudo* of Monticelli for his nephew.

36. Ibid. x, 10. Acquasparta became a duchy in 1586, and the last Cesi, the thirteenth duke of Acquasparta, died in 1888.

37. Partner, "Papal Financial Policy"; Delumeau 2.768–824.

38. Delumeau 2.845–937; Melissa M. Bullard, "'Mercatores Florentini Romanam Curiam Sequentes' in the Early Sixteenth Century," *The Journal of Medieval and Renaissance Studies* 6 (1976) 51–71 and *Filippo Strozzi* (n. 23

above); Felix Gilbert, *The Pope, His Banker, and Venice* (Cambridge Mass. 1980); Vat lat 10600, fols. 78r, 79v, 80r, 82r, 137v; MC, vol. 877, fol. 99rv; vol. 881, fols. 99v–100r; vol. 884, fol. 99v.

39. Delumeau 2.783–824 has explored this system in detail. *Monti* were bought in blocks by bankers and then resold to individual investors. After the "erection" of the *Monte Giulio* in 1550, the number of such bond issues proliferated. Forty-five new *monti* were created between 1550 and 1605.

40. Bullard, *Filippo Strozzi* (n. 23 above) 93.

41. Francesco Cristofori, *Storia dei Cardinali di Santa Romana Chiesa* (Rome 1888) 301–356; William E. Lunt, *Financial Relations of the Papacy with England: 1327–1534*, vol. 2 of *Studies in Anglo-Papal Relations during the Middle Ages* (Cambridge Mass. 1962) 724–823.

42. Lunt (n. 41 above) 729.

43. Cristofori (n. 41 above) 301, 356. I did not see the Soderini, Pandolfini, or Ridolfi banks in the records, but Melissa Bullard did, "Mercatores" (n. 38 above).

44. Archivio di Stato, Rome, Archivio Camerale, Camerale Prima, Diversorum del Camerlengo, vol. 369, fol. 46r; Bullard, *Filippo Strozzi* (n. 23 above) 117.

45. MC, vol. 880, fol. 7r; Vat lat 10604, fols. 178v–180r; MC, vol. 893, fol. 34r.

46. MC, vol. 877, fol. 99rv; Vat lat 10604, fol. 106r; AC, vol. 9, fols. 61r, 81r; Eubel 3.88; Delumeau 2.845–937, especially 857, 861, and 877–893.

47. MC, vol. 889, fol. 2v; vol. 904, fol. 98v; DBI 4.27–33.

48. Bullard, "Mercatores" (n. 38 above) 55–56.

49. Diversorum del Camerlengo (n. 44 above) vol. 369, fol. 22v; Eubel 3.19; Bullard, "Mercatores" (n. 38 above) 69 and *Filippo Strozzi* (n. 23 above) 125, 128.

50. AV, vol. 4, fol. 10v; Arm. 40, vol. 19, fol. 26r; MC, vol. 871, fol. 117v.

51. Litta vol. 2 (1st ed.), "Gaddi di Firenze," no pagination.

52. AM, vol. 3, fols. 13v–14r: A description of the sale of some real property in July 1503 to satisfy a debt of 3,124 ducats and 18 *solidi* which the Medici bank owed the college of cardinals.

53. MC, vol. 862, fols. 5v–6r, 17r; vol. 866, fols. 158rv, 167rv; Bullard, "Mercatores" (n. 38 above) 58.

54. Bullard, "Mercatores" (n. 38 above) 59; Delumeau 2.849, 858, 861.

55. Litta vol. 8 supp. 2, tav. 268–269, 284–285.

56. Ibid.

57. MC, vol. 855, fols. 32r, 37v.

58. Litta vol. 8 supp. 2, tav. 268–269, 284–285. This is the same Puccio Pucci who practiced law. See Lauro Martines, *Lawyers and Statecraft in Renaissance Florence* (Princeton 1968) 485.

59. Bullard, "Mercatores" (n. 38 above) 59.

60. Litta vol. 5 tav. 289.

61. Delumeau 2.877–937.

62. MC, vol. 877, fols. 55r, 77r; vol. 880, fols. 4r, 141r; Vat lat 10602, fol. 58r; Vat lat 10604, fol. 106r.

63. Arm. 40, vol. 19, fol. 346r; MC, vol. 882, fol. 112v; vol. 884, fol. 88v.

64. MC, vol. 867, fol. 9r; vol. 871, fols. 3r, 16r, 40v, 60r, 68r, 162r, 169r, 171r; vol. 884, fols. 12v, 24r, 33v, 34r, 63rv; Arm. 41, vol. 55, fol. 466rv.

65. MC, vol. 866, fols. 178r, 180r, 182r; vol. 884, fols. 12v, 24r, 33v, 34r, 63rv; Arm. 40, vol. 41, fol. 111r; Vat lat 10600, fols. 78r, 79v, 80r, 137v.

66. MC, vol. 857, fols. 53v–60r, 98v–100v, 102r–104r, 104v, 105v, 106r; AM, vol. 3, fol. 49v; MC, vol. 859A, fols. 38r, 46r, 46v; vol. 862, fol. 11r; vol. 871, fols. 1v, 34r, 48r; Arm. 40, vol. 51, fol. 238r; MC, vol. 877, fols. 54v, 77v, 78v, 82v–83r, 100v; vol. 880, fol. 151v; vol. 881, fol. 97v; vol. 882, fol. 104r; vol. 884, fol. 95r; vol. 902, fol. 35v.

67. Bullard, "Mercatores" (n. 38 above) 69 and *Filippo Strozzi* (n. 23 above) 171–172.

68. Delumeau 2.873.

69. Arm. 40, vol. 28, fol. 269r, 4 December 1530: Reconfirmation of the governorship of Gualdi for Cardinal Antonio Maria del Monte, originally conferred upon him during the conclave that elected Leo X. For confirmations of governorships distributed to the cardinals during the conclave that elected Julius III, see the following: Arm. 41, vol. 55, fols. 7r, 8r, 13r, 14r, 23r, 33r, 35r, 41r, 44r, 46r, 48r, 62r, 66r, 88r, 89r, 110r, 176r.

70. The castellans of Ostia and Civitavecchia were separate jurisdictions, for example.

71. See the powers granted to Giovanni Guidiccioni as governor of Rome, 25 October 1534: Arm. 40, vol. 49, fol. 63rv.

72. MC, vol. 871, fol. 73r.

73. Arm. 40, vol. 42, fol. 231r; Enea Costantini, *Il Cardinal di Ravenna al governo d'Ancona e il suo processo sotto Paolo III* (Pesaro 1891) 36–38.

74. Arm. 40, vol. 33, fol. 249rv; Arm. 41, vol. 16, fols. 206r–207r; vol. 55, fol. 65r.

75. Arm. 40, vol. 49, fols. 57rv, 169rv.

76. Pier Giovanni Baroni, *La Nunziatura in Francia di Rodolfo Pio (1535–1537)*, vol. 13 of *Memorie storiche e documenti sulla Città e sull'antico Principato di Carpi* (Bologna 1962) 259–260: "S'è peccato amar li suoi et desiderar ei non patiscono, in questo mi conosco et confesso al par d'ogni altro grandissimo peccator et tanto maggior quanto ch'io ben veggo ho sempre ad esser così."

77. Ibid. 268: "Ho compreso che N. Sre nel levare di ditta rocca al sig. vostro padre l'ha fatto con grandissimo dispiacere dubitando de non vi dar causa de starne malcontento, et si risolve trovar modo di ricompensarli in altro." The pope had replaced Pio at Rimini because it had recently all but succumbed to a *colpo di stato* by its erstwhile *signori,* the Malatesta family.

78. Ibid. xxviii–xxxv; Arm. 41, vol. 55, fol. 262r; Arm. 41, vol. 57, fols. 204r, 217r; Arm. 42, vol. 6, fols. 237r–238r. Both Baroni and Litta say that Leonello's brother, Alberto Pio, was the last count of Carpi, deprived by the emperor in 1522. Briefs of both Julius III and Paul IV, however, address Leonello Pio as count of Carpi. Litta vol. 5 tav. 572–573.

79. MC, vol. 855, fols. 38v, 48r, 55r, 57v, 59v, 70v, 71v, 72v, 88v, 90r.

80. MC, vol. 877, fol. 29r. Ranuccio had a lieutenant to do the actual supervision in 1539, one Bartolomeo Peretti, perhaps a relative of Felice Peretti, the future Sixtus V.

81. MC, vol. 855, fols. 38v, 55r, 59v.

82. MC, vol. 866, fols. 33v, 48v, 49v, 52r, 55r, 62v; vol. 871, fols. 118r, 162r, 171r; vol. 872, fol. 49v; vol. 877, fols. 29r, 54r; vol. 887, fols. 104v, 111r, 129v, 163r, 173r, 184r; Arm. 41, vol. 55, fol. 274r.

83. MC, vol. 871, fols. 13v, 54v, 74r, 79v, 88v, 110r, 136r, 140r; vol. 880, fols. 151v, 155r, 156r, 164v.

84. A number of women of noble family appear in the fiscal records throughout the period, receiving moneys from the apostolic camera or the dataria. For example: 15 ducats of gold per month to Catharine Colonna, 1497–1501 (MC, vol. 856, fols. 56r–76v; vol. 857, fols. 5r, 10v); 8 ducats per month to Lucrezia Farnese, 1497–1500 (MC, vol. 857, fol. 2rv); 4 *scuti* per month to Franceschina Paleologina, 1531–1534 (Vat lat 10599, fols. 97r–159r); 423 ducats from "the fruits of her dowry" from the Tolfa alum mines to Lucrezia della Rovere Colonna, 1537–1545 (MC, vol. 877, fols. 82v–83r; vol. 881, fols. 10v, 28r); 354 ducats, also from the fruits of her dowry, to Hortensia Colonna Pallavicino, 1545 (MC, vol. 881, fol. 28v); 40 ducats for the ordinary provision of Giulia Malatesta, 1557–1558 (MC, vol. 904, fols. 45r, 145v); 400 ducats to Vittoria Leonissa, 1558–1559 (MC, vol. 904, fols. 72r, 169v); pensions to Catherine Sauli, 1559 (MC, vol. 904, fol. 187rv).

85. Vat lat 10603, fols. 107v, 118r; Vat lat 10604, fols. 81v–106v; MC, vol. 881, fol. 97v; Vat lat 10604, fol. 179r.

86. AC, vol. 2, fols. 68v, 74r–75v, 87rv.

87. Eubel 3.27; MC, vol. 872, fols. 102v, 129r; vol. 880, fol. 4r; AC, vol. 6, fol. 131v.

88. Vat lat 10599, fols. 97r–140r. For Catherine's dowry, see Bullard, *Filippo Strozzi* (n. 23 above) 158ff.

89. Vat lat 10599, fols. 97r–159r.

90. Ibid. Alessandro and Ippolito also received 1,000 ducats of gold each from the camera to go to welcome Charles V on his arrival in Italy on 26 July 1529: MC, vol. 862, fol. 8r.

91. Vat lat 10599, fols. 137r–155v.

92. Vat lat 10600, fol. 101v: "per pagar mancie a Nipoti & parenti de Sua Santità"; Vat lat 10601, fols. 109r, 110v: "per resto d'argento & robe facte per Illustrissimo Signore Ranutio Farnesio priore di venetia nepote di Sua Santità"; Vat lat 10601, fol. 85r; Vat lat 10602, fols. 49v, 50v: "per dare ala Signora Victoria Farnese per andar ala caccia con Madamma"; Vat lat 10603, fol. 72r: "quale Nostro Signore la dona per uno cochio Sua Excellentissima fa fare"; Vat lat 10601, fol. 53v: "per spendere in suo piacere questo Carnevale"; Vat lat 10602, fol. 84r: "una cinta di lapis lazoli et altre cose comparate et portate a Madamma Duchessa de Camerino per Mancia di capo d'anno presente"; Vat lat 10604, fol. 94r: "per pagare uno Diamante in tavola legato in anello comprato da Messer Bartholomeo Vettori in Roma per donarlo ad una dele Sorelle dil Reverendissimo et Illustrissimo Camerlengo."

93. MC, vol. 867, fol. 20v; Vat lat 10601, fols. 53r–112v; Vat lat 10602, fols. 46r–105r; Vat lat 10603, fols. 55r–107v; MC, vol. 881, fol. 15r.

94. MC, vol. 871, fol. 32v; vol. 872, fol. 112r: "pro non nullis eius antiquis debitis satisfaciendis et multis expensis extraordinariis."

95. MC, vol. 882, fols. 100v–101r.

96. Vat lat 10601, fol. 86r: "alo Illustrissimo Sforza Conte di Santa Fiore quali Nostro Signore li dona per spendere in le noze di sua consorte"; fol. 87r: "per conto di drappi che Illustrissimo Conte di Santa Fiore ha pigliati per donare a la sua consorte per ordine di Nostro Signore."

97. Vat lat 10601, fols. 104v, 105r, 106v.

98. Vat lat 10601, fol. 111v; Vat lat 10602, fol. 48r.

99. ANG 3, *Correspondance des nonces en France Capodiferro, Dandino et Guidiccione: 1541–1546*, ed. J. Lestoquoy (Rome 1963) 114, 118, 244; Vat lat 10602, fols. 60v–99v; Vat lat 10603, fols. 54v, 61r–93r.

100. Vat lat 10603, fols. 95r–118r; Vat lat 10604, fols. 100v–174r.

101. Vat lat 10600, fols. 110r–136v.

102. Vat lat 10600, fols. 143r–144v, 116r–121v. (The pagination of this volume is irregular.)

103. Vat lat 10600, fols. 122v–148r; Vat lat 10601, fols. 47v–111v; Vat lat 10602, fols. 47r–49v.

104. MC, vol. 872, fol. 122v.

105. Vat lat 10603, fols. 54r, 60v.

106. 25,581 *scuti* in 1542; 25,633 in 1543; 33,060 in 1544; 33,588 in 1545; 29,500 in 1546; 26,000 in 1547; 12,500 in 1548; and 8,000 in 1549. The last 8,000 was the "ordinary provision" of Margaret of Austria. Vat lat 10602, fols. 50v–80r, 82v, 104r; Vat lat 10603, fols. 54r–59r, 61r–91v, 94r–116r; Vat lat 10604, fols. 81r–110r, 111v, 136v–159r, 160r, 177v.

107. AC, vol. 6, fol. 131v.

108. Margaret of Austria, duchess of Parma and Piacenza, received a much smaller pension during the pontificates of Paul IV and Pius IV—155 *scuti* per year from the apostolic camera. MC, vol. 904, fol. 110r; vol. 907, fol. 78rv.

109. Vat lat 10605, fol. 42r.

110. Vat lat 10605, fols. 26r, 29v, 33r, 36v, 40r, 44r, 47v, 51v, 54v, 57r, 60r, 62v, 65r, 67v.

111. For example, Vat lat 10605, fol. 26r: "per la sua provisione del presente mese."

112. Vat lat 10605, fols. 27v, 38r, 42v, 46r, 50r, 53v, 56v, 67r.

113. CT 10.441.

114. MC, vol. 902, fols. 1v, 70r, 2r, 57r, for "ordinary" pensions; fols. 19r, 23r, 39r, 41r, 44r, 45v, 50v, 51r, 52v, 54rv, 55r, 63rv, 67r, 68r, 70r for particular subsidies.

115. MC, vol. 902, fol. 37v: "non ha potuto godere l'entrate del stato per la malignità dei tempi."

116. Nephew Antonio Carafa, *marchese* of Montebello, was governor general of the church at 1,000 *scuti* per month; Diomede Carafa, a great-nephew, was castellan of Sant'Angelo and later a cardinal; Alfonso Carafa, also a great-nephew, was the cardinal of Naples with regular subsidies from the apostolic camera and especially a grant of 4,000 *scuti* of gold from the pope in April 1559. MC, vol. 902, fols. 18v, 19v, 34v, 55r, 59v, 63r, 70v; vol. 904, fols. 25r, 43v, 67v–68r, 75v, 77rv, 110v–111r, 139v, 151v, 184–185r; Arm. 42, vol. 10, fol. 94r.

117. See n. 90 above.

118. See above at n. 104.

119. MC, vol. 902, fols. 20r, 35v, 37r, 73v–74r; vol. 904, fols. 52rv, 53r; vol. 902, fols. 42rv, 43rv.

120. Florido Zamponi, ed., *Avvertimento del cardinal di Mantova al nipote Cesare per l'andata sua in corte di Roma* (Florence 1872) 20: "queste tante e così honorate parentele che in poco tempo il papa ha fatto con li Signori d'Italia; e non è dubbio, che in certo modo sua Maestà havera presa qualche ombra di questo."

121. MC, vol. 907, fol. 100v.

122. MC, vol. 907, fol. 139r.

123. MC, vol. 907, fols. 139v, 141r: "que idem Sanctissimus Dominus Noster illi dono dat, ex dignis causis."

124. MC, vol. 907, fol. 18r; vol. 908, fols. 2v, 3v; vol. 910, fols. 1r, 5v, 11v, 20r, 24v, 68v, 75v, 82r.

125. MC, vol. 907, fol. 165r. This was an order to the collector in the kingdom of Spain to pay Annibale 400 ducats a month. It was cameral money nevertheless.

126. AC, vol. 10, fol. 204v.

127. MC, vol. 916, fols. 4r, 13r.

128. MC, vol. 916, fol. 21v.

129. MC, vol. 916, fol. 4r: 2,200 *scuti* to Gabriele d'Altemps and his wife.

130. MC, vol. 907, fol. 216r; vol. 908, fol. 129v; vol. 916, fol. 35v: "que Sanctitas Sua ei dono dedit ut partem suorum debitorum commodius persolvere possit." Carlo Borromeo had a reputed annual income of 52,000 *scuti*.

131. MC, vol. 916, fols. 47r–48r. These were *scuti* of silver.

132. AV, vol. 10, fols. 19v–20v: "ut commodius nubere possit."

133. Ibid.: "et Reverendissimus Dominus Morenus dixit quod hoc non erat necesse quia Sanctitas Sua erat Dominus consanguineorum suorum et poterat de illis disponere ad sui libitum."

134. Reinhard, *Papstfinanz und Nepotismus*.

135. Arm. 40, vol. 41, fol. 109r; vol. 49, fol. 72r: "Accedit etiam quod ipsa Cecilia duplici affinitatis vinculo nos pertingit, eoque novissimo quod alteram ex filiabus nato dilecti filii nobilis viri Camilli Caietani Sermonetae Domini affinis nostri copulavit."

136. Table 5.13 is derived from Cristofori (n. 41 above) 301– 356.

137. Pio Paschini, *Domenico Grimani, cardinale di San Marco († 1523)* (Rome 1943) 3.

138. Ibid. 27–29; Pio Paschini, *Il cardinale Marino Grimani ed i prelati della sua famiglia* (Rome 1960) 50.

139. Litta vol. 4 tav. 468–469.

140. Ibid.

141. Angelo Maria Bandini, *Il Bibbiena o sia il ministro di stato delineato nella vita del cardinale Bernardo Dovizi da Bibbiena* (Livorno 1758) 14.

142. Staffetti (n. 23 above) 127–130. The ten-year-old Giulia was married at this very time to Guidobaldo della Rovere, with the connivance of her mother,

Caterina Cibo, and his father, Francesco Maria della Rovere. The marriage set off a conflict between the Rovereschi and the new pope, Paul III, which lasted until the death of Francesco Maria. The Rovereschi then capitulated and gave up their duchy of Camerino (Giulia's inheritance) to the Farnesi. Giulia died at age twenty-three.

143. ANG 1, *Correspondance des nonces en France Carpi et Ferrerio, 1535–1540,* ed. J. Lestoquoy (Rome 1961) 249, 309, 387, 396, 403, 405, 417, 421, 456, 471, 570–620; ANG 3 (n. 99 above) 5, 8, 9, 118, 130–131, 135, 136, 139, 201.

144. Carlo Capasso, "Pasquinate contro i Farnesi nei Codd. Ottobon. 2811–2812," *Studi dedicati a Francesco Torraca nel XXXVI anniversario della sua laurea* (Naples 1912) 399–410; CT 10.824.

145. CT 10.824.

146. Ibid.: "la quale per ogni ragione non doverà esser recusato da loro et maxime dalla matre del duca d'Urbino, la quale havendo un altro figlio, come ha, et per consequente desiderando di honorarlo forse in grado ecclesiastico ci concorrà tanto più volentieri."

147. AC, vol. 6, fol. 105v.

148. AC, vol. 6, fol. 134r.

149. Archivio di Stato, Bologna, Archivio Malvezzi-Campeggi, Seconda Serie, 32/269.

150. See chapter 1 above, at n. 25.

151. Partner, "Papal Financial Policy" 61.

152. Reinhard, "Nepotismus."

153. Walter Friedensburg, "Der Briefwechsel Gasparo Contarinis mit Ercole Gonzaga nebst einem Briefe Giovanni Pietro Carafas," QFIAB 2 (1899) 295: "perchè mentre i privilegi ecclesiastici nelle famiglie si perdono facilmente alla morte del Papa che li a concessi, i possessi temporali restano."

154. Zamponi (n. 120 above) 25–27: "L'altra cosa è che V.S. deve procurare appresso Nostro Signore e li Signori Cognati suoi, che quello che s'ha da fare per comodo e grandezza loro, se faccia presto, perchè posto che il papa possa vivere molti anni, il che è però incerto et posta nella voluntà de Dio, innanzi ch'un casa di Gentil'homini privati sia stabilita nel luogo di prencipe con Stato e giurisditione di qualche importanza et nuova, vi vuole del tempo assai. Però non è da perderlo, et a me non soccore cosa che mi paia più riuscibile che quello di Camerino, dandolo Nostro Signore al conte Federico. . . .

Vi è anco Salerno, ch'è bella pezza et honorata, e porta seco titolo de Prencipe conveniente ad un Nepote di Papa, et è facile di poterlo havere per gratia e cortesia di Sua Maestà et anco per non essere venduto ma impegnato al Signor Marchese di Pescara, il quale se satisfarebbe molto bene ogni volta che se gli restituisse il suo denaro, e se gli facesse il fratello Cardinale."

155. Partner, "Papal Financial Policy" 61.

156. Ibid.

157. Delumeau 2.819.

Bibliography

MANUSCRIPT SOURCES

Archivio di Stato, Bologna
  Archivio Malvezzi-Campeggi, seconda serie.
Archivio di Stato, Florence
  Carte Strozziani, serie I.
Archivio di Stato, Milan
  Fondo Trivulzio.
Archivio di Stato, Modena
  Archivio Segreto Estensi, sezione "Casa e Stato," serie: Documenti spettanti ai
  principi Estensi (1204–1810).
Archivio di Stato, Rome
  Archivio Camerale, Camerale Prima, Mandati Camerali.
  Archivio Camerale, Camerale Prima, Diversorum del Camerlengo.
  Archivio Camerale, Camerale, Prima, Ufficiali Camerali.
Archivio Segreto Vaticano, Vatican City
  Acta Cameraii.
  Acta Miscellanea.
  Acta Vicecancellarii.
  Armarium 40.
  Armarium 41.
  Armarium 42.
Biblioteca Apostolica Vaticana
  Codices Vaticani latini.

SOURCES IN PRINT

Acta Nuntiaturae Gallicae: Correspondance des nonces en France . . . 14 vols.
  to date. Rome 1961–.

Baroni, Pier Giovanni. *La Nunziatura in Francia di Rodolfo Pio (1535–1537)*. Vol. 13 of *Memorie storiche e documenti sulla Città e sull'antico Principato di Carpi*. Bologna 1962.

Bullarium Romanum. 25 vols. Turin 1857–1885.

Concilium Tridentinum: Diariorum, actorum, epistularum, tractatuum nova collectio. 13 vols. to date. Freiburg im Breisgau 1961–.

Dillenberger, John, ed. *Martin Luther: Selections from His Writings*. Garden City N.Y. 1961.

Ferraris, Lucius. *Prompta biblioteca canonica, juridica, moralis, theologica, necnon ascetica, polemica, rubricitica, historica*. 9 vols. Rome 1770–1784.

Friedensburg, Walter. "Der Briefwechsel Gasparo Contarinis mit Ercole Gonzaga nebst einem Briefe Giovanni Pietro Carafas," *Quellen und Forschungen aus italienischen Archiven und Bibliotheken* 2 (1899) 161—222.

Garimberti, Girolamo. *La prima parte delle vite, overo fatti memorabili d'alcuni papi, et di tutti i cardinali passati*. Venice 1567.

Giovio, Paolo. *La vita del Cardinale Pompeo Colonna scritta per Monsignor Paolo Giovio vescovo di Nocera e tradotta per M. Lodovico Domenichi*. Florence 1544, 1549.

Hewett, A. Edith. "An Assessment of Italian Benefices Held by the Cardinals for the Turkish War of 1571," *English Historical Review* 30 (1915) 488-501.

Nuntiaturberichte aus Deutschland nebst ergänzenden Aktenstücken: Abtheil I, 1533–1559. 12 vols. Augsburg, Gotha, Berlin 1892–1953. Vol. 1, Supp. 1, Tübingen 1963.

Olin, John C., ed. *The Catholic Reformation: Savonarola to Ignatius Loyola, Reform in the Church, 1495–1540*. New York 1969.

Oratio Prima Synodi Lateranensi habita per Egidium Viterbiensem Augustiniani ordinis Generalem. Rome 1512.

Paquier, Jules. *Lettres familières de Jérome Aléandre (1510–1540)*. Paris 1909.

Ronchini, Amadio, ed. *Lettere del Card. Jacopo Sadoleto e di Paolo suo nipote*. Modena 1871.

Sanuto, Marino. *I diarii*. 59 vols. Venice 1879–1903.

Segre, Arturo. "Un registro di lettere del cardinale Ercole Gonzaga (1535–1536) con un'appendice di documenti inediti (1520–1548)," *Miscellanea di storia italiana, R. Deputazione sovra gli studi di storia patria per le antiche provincie e la Lombardia*, terza serie 16 (1913) 275–458.

Spezi, Giuseppe, ed. *Lettere inedite del Card. Pietro Bembo e di altri scrittori del secolo XVI*. Rome 1862.

Strauss, Gerald, trans. and ed. *Manifestations of Discontent in Germany on the Eve of the Reformation*. Bloomington Ind. 1971.

Zamponi, Florido, ed. *Avvertimento del cardinal di Mantova al nipote Cesare per l'andata sua in corte di Roma*. Florence 1872.

SECONDARY WORKS

Alberigo, Giuseppe. *Cardinalato e collegialità: Studi sull' ecclesiologia tra l'XI e il XVI secolo*. Florence 1969.

————. *I vescovi italiani al Concilio di Trento (1545–1547)*. Florence 1959.

Anderson, Marvin W. "Luther's Sola Fide in Italy: 1542–1551," *Church History* 38 (1969) 25–42.

Antonovics, A. V. "Counter-Reformation Cardinals: 1534–1590." *European Studies Review* 2 (1972) 301–328.

————. "A Late Fifteenth-Century Division Register of the College of Cardinals," *Papers of the British School at Rome* 35 (n.s. 22) (1967) 87–101.

Bandini, Angelo Maria. *Il Bibbiena o sia il ministro di stato delineato nella vita del cardinale Bernardo Dovizi da Bibbiena*. Livorno 1758.

Baraldi, Giuseppe. *Elogio del cardinale Tommaso Badia di Modena*. Modena 1830.

Barraclough, Geoffrey. *The Medieval Papacy*. London 1968.

————. *Papal Provisions*. Oxford 1935.

Bauer, Clemens. "Die Epochen der Papstfinanz: ein Versuch," *Historische Zeitschrift* 138 (1927) 457–503.

————. "Studi per la storia delle finanze papale durante il pontificato di Sisto IV," *Archivio della R. Società Romana di Storia Patria* 50 (1927) 319–400.

Baumgarten, Frederic J. "Henry II's Italian Bishops: A Study in the Use and Abuse of the Concordat of Bologna," *The Sixteenth Century Journal* 11 (1980) 49–58.

Belloni, C. *Un banchiere del Rinascimento, Bindo Altoviti*. Rome 1935.

Bernabei, Nicola. *Vita del Cardinale Giovanni Morone Vescovo di Modena . . .* Modena 1885.

Bouwsma, William J. *Venice and the Defense of Republican Liberty: Renaissance Values in the Age of the Counter-Reformation*. Berkeley and Los Angeles 1968.

Brown, G. K. *Italy and the Reformation to 1550*. Oxford 1933.

Bullard, Melissa M. *Filippo Strozzi and the Medici: Favor and Finance in Sixteenth-Century Florence and Rome*. Cambridge 1980.

————. "'Mercatores Florentini Romanam Curiam Sequentes' in the Early Sixteenth Century," *The Journal of Medieval and Renaissance Studies* 6 (1976) 51–71.

Capasso, Carlo. "Pasquinate contro i Farnesi nei Codd. Ottobon. 2811–2812." In *Studi dedicati a Francesco Torraca nel XXXVI anniversario della sua laurea*, 399–410. Naples 1912.

Cardella, Lorenzo. *Memorie storiche de' Cardinali della Santa Romana Chiesa*. 10 vols. Rome 1792–1797.

Caron, Pier Giovanni. *La Rinuncia all'Ufficio Ecclesiastico nella storia del diritto canonico dalla Età Apostolica alla Riforma Cattolica*. Milan 1946.

Celier, Léonce. "Alexandre VI et la réforme de l'église," *Mélanges d'archéologie et d'histoire* 27 (1907) 65–124.

————. *Les Dataires du XVe siècle et les origines de la Datérie Apostolique*. Paris 1910.

Chambers, D. S. "The Economic Predicament of Renaissance Cardinals," *Studies in Medieval and Renaissance History* 3 (1966) 289–313.

Church, Frederic C. *The Italian Reformers, 1534–1564*. New York 1932.

Ciacconius, Alphonsus. *Vitae et res gestae Pontificum Romanorum et S. R. E.*

Cardinalium ab initio nascentis Ecclesiae usque ad Clementem IX . . . 4 vols. Rome 1630–1677.

Cian, Vittorio. *Un decennio della vita di M. Pietro Bembo (1521–1531).* Turin 1885.

Cipolla, Carlo M. "Une crise ignorée: comment s'est perdue la propriété ecclésiastique dans l'Italie du nord entre le XIe et le XVIe siècle," *Annales: économies, sociétés, civilisations* 2.3 (1947) 317–327.

———. *Moneta e civiltà mediterranea.* Venice 1957.

———. *Mouvements Monétaires dans l'Etat de Milan (1580–1700).* Paris 1952.

Cochrane, Eric, ed. *The Late Italian Renaissance: 1525–1630.* New York 1970.

———. "New Light on Post-Tridentine Italy: A Note on Recent Counter-Reformation Scholarship," *Catholic Historical Review* 56 (1970) 291–319.

———. "What Is Catholic Historiography?," *Catholic Historical Review* 61 (1975) 169–190.

Cominus, Josephus. *Gregorii Cortesii Monachi Cassinatis, S. R. E. Cardinalis, omnia quae huc usque colligi potuerunt, sive ad illum spectantia.* 2 vols. Padua 1774.

Consorti, Aida. *Il cardinale Pompeo Colonna, su documenti editi e inediti.* Rome 1902.

Corvisieri, C. "Compendio dei processi del Santo Uffizio di Roma (da Paolo III a Paolo IV)," *Archivio della R. Società Romana di Storia Patria* 3 (1880) 261–290, 449–472.

Cossio, Aluigi. *Il cardinale Gaetano e la riforma.* Cividale 1902.

Costantini, Enea. *Il Cardinal di Ravenna al governo d'Ancona e il suo processo sotto Paolo III.* Pesaro 1891.

Cristofori, Francesco. *Storia dei Cardinali di Santa Romana Chiesa.* Rome 1888.

Daniel-Rops, Henri. *The Catholic Reformation.* Translated by John Warrington. 2 vols. Garden City N.Y. 1964.

Delaruelle, E., E. R. Labande, and Paul Ourliac. *L'Église au temps du Grand Schisme et de la crise conciliaire (1378–1449).* Vol. 14 of *Histoire de l'église depuis les origines jusqu'à nos jours.* 2 vols. Paris 1962–1964.

Delumeau, Jean. *Vie économique et sociale de Rome dans la seconde moitié du XVIe siècle.* 2 vols. Paris 1957–1959.

Dictionnaire de droit canonique. Paris, 1935–.

Dictionnaire d'histoire et de géographie ecclésiastiques. 17 vols. to date. Paris, 1912–.

Dittrich, Franz. *Gasparo Contarini, 1483–1542: eine Monographie.* Braunsberg 1885.

Dizionario biografico degli Italiani. 15 vols. to date. Rome, 1960–.

Douglas, Richard M. *Jacopo Sadoleto, 1477–1547: Humanist and Reformer.* Cambridge Mass. 1959.

Drei, Giovanni. *I Farnesi: grandezza e decadenza di una dinastia italiana.* Rome 1954.

———. "La politica di Pio IV e del Cardinale Ercole Gonzaga, 1559–1560," *Archivio della R. Società Romana di Storia Patria* 40 (1917) 65–115.

Elton, G. R. *Reformation Europe: 1517–1559.* New York 1963.

Eubel, Conrad. *Hierarchia Catholica Medii et Recentioris Aevi.* 6 vols. Regensburg 1913.

Evennett, H. Outram. *The Spirit of the Counter-Reformation.* Edited by John Bossy. Cambridge 1968.

Fanfani, Amintore. *Indagini sulla "Rivoluzione dei Prezzi".* Milan 1940.

——. *Storia del lavoro in Italia dalla fine del secolo XV agli inizi del XVIII.* Vol. 3 of *Storia del lavoro in Italia.* Milan 1959.

Ferrajoli, Alessandro. "Il ruolo della Corte di Leone X (1514–1516)," *Archivio della R. Società Romana di Storia Patria* 34 (1911) 363–391; 35 (1912) 483–539; 36 (1913) 519–584; 37 (1914) 307–360, 453–484; 38 (1915) 215–281, 425–452; 39 (1916) 53–77, 537–576; 40 (1917) 245–277; 41 (1918) 87–110.

Galante, Andrea. *La Corrispondenza del Card. Cristoforo Madruzzo nell' Archivio di Stato di Innsbruck.* Innsbruck 1911.

Garampi, G. *Saggi di Osservazioni sul valore delle antiche monete pontificie.* Rome 1766.

Gilbert, Felix. *The Pope, His Banker, and Venice.* Cambridge Mass. 1980.

Gillmann, F. "Die Resignation der Benefizien," *Archiv für katholisches Kirchenrecht* 80 (1900) 50–79, 346–378, 523–569, 665–788; 81 (1901) 223–242, 433–460.

Göller, Emil. *Die päpstliche Pönitentiarie von ihrem Ursprung bis zu ihrer Umgestaltung unter Pius V.* 2 vols. Rome 1907, 1911.

Gottlob, Adolf. *Aus der Camera Apostolica des 15. Jahrhunderts: ein Beitrag zur Geschichte des päpstlichen Finanzwesens und das endenden Mittelalters.* Innsbruck 1889.

Guelfi, F., and C. Baldi. *Ricerche storico-biografiche di Monte San Savino.* Siena 1892.

Guerrini, Paolo. "L'ingresso episcopale a Brescia dei due cardinali veneti Francesco e Andrea Cornaro," *Brixia Sacra* 8 (January–April 1917) 5–23.

Guicciardini, Francesco. *Selected Writings.* Edited by Cecil Grayson. Translated by Margaret Grayson. London 1965.

Hay, Denys. *The Church in Italy in the Fifteenth Century.* Cambridge 1977.

Hoberg, Hermann. *Taxae pro communibus servitiis ex libris obligationum ab anno 1295 usque ad annum 1455 confectis.* Studi e testi 144. Vatican City 1949.

Hofmann, Walter von. *Forschungen zur Geschichte der kurialen Behörden vom Schisma bis zur Reformation.* 2 vols. Rome 1914.

Hynes, Harry G. *The Privileges of Cardinals.* Canon Law Studies 217. Washington D.C. 1945.

Jedin, Hubert. "Concilio e riforma nel pensiero del Cardinale Bartolomeo Guidiccioni," *Rivista di storia della Chiesa in Italia* 2 (1948) 33–60.

——. *Geschichte des Konzils von Trient.* 3 vols. Vol. 2, Freiburg 1957; vol. 3, Freiburg, Basel, Vienna 1970.

——. *A History of the Council of Trent.* Translated by Dom Ernest Graf. 2 vols. London 1957.

Jones, Philip. "Le finanze della Badia cistercense di Settino nel XIV secolo," *Rivista di storia della Chiesa in Italia* 10 (1956) 90–122.

——. "Medieval Agrarian Society in Its Prime: Italy." In *Cambridge Eco-*

nomic History of Europe 1 (2d ed.), edited by M. M. Postan, 340–431. Cambridge 1966.

Kalkoff, Paul. *Aleander gegen Luther: Studien zu Ungedrückten Aktenstücken aus Aleanders Nachlass.* Leipzig 1908.

Katterbach, Bruno. *Inventario dei Registri delle Suppliche.* Vol. 1 of *Inventari del'Archivio Segreto Vaticano.* Vatican City 1932.

———. *Referendarii utriusque Signaturae a Martino V ad Clementem IX et Prelati Signaturae Supplicationum a Martino V ad Leonem XIII.* Studi e testi 55. Vatican City 1931.

Klotzner, Josef. *Kardinal Domenikus Jacobazzi und sein Konzilswerk: ein Beitrag zur Geschichte der Konziliaren Idee.* Rome 1948.

Laven, P. J. "The *Causa Grimani* and Its Political Overtones," *Journal of Religious History* 4 (1967) 184–205.

Litta, Pompeo. *Famiglie celebri italiane.* 10 vols. Milan 1819–1883.

Litva, Felice. "L'attività finanziaria della Dataria durante il periodo tridentino," *Archivum Historiae Pontificiae* 5 (1967) 79–174.

Lunt, William E. *Financial Relations of the Papacy with England: 1327–1534.* Vol. 2 of *Studies in Anglo-Papal Relations during the Middle Ages.* Cambridge, Mass. 1962.

———. *Papal Revenues in the Middle Ages.* 2 vols. New York 1934.

Lutz, Heinrich. "Kardinal Morone: Reform, Konzil und Europäische Staatenwelt." In *Il Concilio di Trento e la Riforma Tridentina, Atti del Convegno storico internazionale,* 363–381. Trent 1965.

Marcora, Carlo. "Il Cardinal Ippolito I d'Este, Arcivescovo di Milano (1497–1519)," *Memorie storiche delle diocesi di Milano* 5 (1958) 325–520.

Martines, Lauro. *Lawyers and Statecraft in Renaissance Florence.* Princeton 1968.

———. *The Social World of the Florentine Humanists: 1390–1460.* Princeton 1963.

Martini, Angelo. "Tentativi di riforma a Padova prima del Concilio di Trento," *Rivista di storia della Chiesa in Italia* 3 (1949) 66–79.

Martinori, Edoardo. *Genealogia e cronostoria di una grande famiglia Umbro-romana: I Cesi.* Rome 1931.

McNair, Philip. *Peter Martyr in Italy: An Anatomy of Apostasy.* Oxford 1967.

Meneghetti, G. *La vita avventurosa di Pietro Bembo: umanista–poeta–cortigiano.* Venice 1961.

Merzbacher, Friedrich. "Das Testamentsrecht des Corpus Juris Canonici," *Österreichisches Archiv für Kirchenrecht* 19 (1968) 289–307.

Mollat, G. "Les graces expectatives du XIIe au XIVe siècle," *Revue d'histoire ecclésiastique* 42 (1947) 81–102.

———. "Les graces expectatives sous le règne de Philippe VI de Valois," *Revue d'histoire ecclésiastique* 32 (1936) 303–312.

Monaco, Michele. "Le finanze pontificie al tempo di Clemente VII (1523–1534)," *Studi Romani* 6.3 (1958) 278–296.

———. "Il primo debito pubblico pontificio: il Monte della Fede (1526)," *Studi Romani* 8.5 (1960) 553-569.

Moroni, Gaetano. *Dizionario di erudizione storico-ecclesiastica da S. Pietro sino ai nostri giorni.* 103 vols. Venice 1840–1861.

Odorici, Federico. *Il Cardinale Uberto Gambara da Brescia, 1487–1549: Indagini di Storia Patria*. Brescia 1856.

O'Malley, John W. *Giles of Viterbo on Church and Reform: A Study in Renaissance Thought*. Leiden 1968.

Pacifici, Vincenzo. *Ippolito II d'Este, Cardinale di Ferrara*. Tivoli 1920.

Partner, Peter. "The 'Budget' of the Roman Church in the Renaissance Period." In *Italian Renaissance Studies: A Tribute to the Late Cecilia M. Ady*, edited by E. F. Jacob, 256–278. London 1960.

————. "Papal Financial Policy in the Renaissance and Counter-Reformation," *Past and Present* 88 (1980) 17–62.

————. *The Papal State under Martin V: The Administration and Government of the Temporal Power in the Early Fifteenth Century*. London 1958.

————. *Renaissance Rome: 1500–1559*. Berkeley and Los Angeles 1976.

Paschini, Pio. *Il cardinale Marino Grimani ed i prelati della sua famiglia*. Rome 1960.

————. *Domenico Grimani, cardinale di San Marco († 1523)*. Rome 1943.

————. "La nomina del patriarca di Aquileia e la Repubblica di Venezia nel secolo XVI," *Rivista di storia della Chiesa in Italia* 2 (1948) 61–76.

Pastor, Ludwig. *The History of the Popes from the Close of the Middle Ages*. Translated by Ralph Francis Kerr. 2d ed. 40 vols. St. Louis and London 1923–1928.

Pecchiai, Pio. "La buona morte del cardinale Alessandro Farnese," *Roma: Rivista di studi e di vita romana* (September–December 1943) 1–6.

————. *Roma nel Cinquecento*. Rome 1948.

Prodi, Paolo. *Il sovrano pontifice: un corpo e due anime: la monarchia papale nella prima età moderna*. Bologna 1982.

Ratti, Nicola. *Della famiglia Sforza*. 2 vols. Rome 1794–1795.

Re, Niccolò del. *La curia romana: lineamenti storico-giuridici*. 3d ed. Rome 1970.

Reinhard, Wolfgang. "Ämterlaufbahn und Familienstatus: der Aufstieg des Hauses Borghese, 1537–1621," *Quellen und Forschungen aus italienischen Archiven und Bibliotheken* 54 (1974) 328–427.

————. "Nepotismus: der Funktionswandel einer papstgeschichtlichen Konstanten," *Zeitschrift für Kirchengeschichte* 86.2 (1975) 145–185.

————. "Papa Pius: Prolegomena zu einer Sozialgeschichte des Papsttums." In *Von Konstanz nach Trient: Festgabe für August Franzen*, edited by Remigius Bäumer, 261–299. Paderborn 1972.

————. *Papstfinanz und Nepotismus unter Paul V. (1605–1621): Studien und Quellen zur Struktur und zu quantitativen Aspekten des päpstlichen Herrschaftssystems*. Vol. 6 of *Päpste und Papsttum*. 2 vols. Stuttgart 1974.

Roover, Raymond de. *The Rise and Decline of the Medici Bank: 1397–1494*. Cambridge Mass. 1963.

Schiavo, Armando. "Profilo e testamento di Raffaele Riario," *Studi Romani* 8.4 (July–August 1960) 414–429.

Soranzo, Giovanni. "Giovanni Battista Zeno, nipote di Paolo II, cardinale di S. Maria in Portico (1468–1501)," *Rivista di storia della Chiesa in Italia* 16.2 (May–August 1962) 249–274.

Staffetti, Luigi. *Il cardinale Innocenzo Cybo*. Florence 1894.

Storti, Nicola. *La storia e il diritto della Dataria Apostolica dalle origini ai nostri giorni.* Naples 1969.

Vincentini, Fr. Antonio. *Il card. Dionisio Laurerio di Benevento nelle memorie raccolte dal suo concittadino e correligioso P. Giuseppe Romano.* Benevento 1925.

Walz, P. Angelo. *I cardinali domenicani: note bio-bibliografiche.* Rome 1940.

Index

NOTE: Since the subject of this book is the cardinalate, those cardinals who later became pope are indexed under the cardinal name. Cross-references are provided.